Mexican Miracles

Virgins, Saints and Shrines of Mexico

Robert Bitto

Copyright © 2023 by Robert Bitto
All rights reserved. This book or any portion thereof may not be reproduced or used in any manner whatsoever without the express written permission of the publisher except for the use of brief quotations in a book review.
Printed in the United States of America
First Printing, 2023
ISBN 979-8371386547

www.mexicounexplained.com

This book is dedicated to "all who believe."

Ask, and it shall be given you; seek, and ye shall find; knock, and it shall be opened unto you: For every one that asketh receiveth; and he that seeketh findeth; and to him that knocketh it shall be opened.

---Matthew 7:7-8

Neither shall they say, Lo here! or, lo there! for, behold, the Kingdom of God is within you.

---Luke 17:21

Verily, verily, I say unto you, He that believeth in me, the works that I do shall he do also; and greater works than these shall he do; because I go unto my Father.

---John 14:12

AUTHOR'S NOTE

One can't separate Mexico from religion. Modern Mexican religious beliefs and practices, while for the most part seem outwardly Catholic, have solid foundations that go back thousands of years. Often the early Spanish clergy in the New World built churches and shrines at temples and pilgrimage sites that had been in use by untold generations of the faithful. This made conversion to Christianity easy and convenient for the church fathers. What developed in many instances was a sort of syncretism, a blend of old and new belief systems, still visible today in Mexico. With these deep roots, a profoundly faithful people has continued to thrive in this country well into the 21st Century. Along with the deep faith so evident in Mexico, there comes apparitions, stories of miracles, and other wonderful encounters with the divine. This book covers some of the famous and little-talked-about shrines, miraculous occurrences and inexplicable religious events that Mexico is known for. Some of these stories might even give the staunchest and most pragmatic non-believer cause to stop and think. Sometimes, though, it's fine not to be so scientifically inclined. After all, what's wrong with allowing a sense of wonder to come back into our lives? As this is my third book in the Mexico Unexplained series, I'd like to thank you for walking alongside me on this journey as I continue to explore the magic, the mysteries and the miracles of Mexico. All I ask from you is that you open your mind, and your heart.

TABLE OF CONTENTS

VIRGINS ... 1
- THE VIRGIN OF GUADALUPE: MOTHER TO US ALL ... 3
- THE VIRGIN OF SAN JUAN DE LOS LAGOS ... 7
- THE VIRGIN OF ZAPOPAN ... 13
- THE WEEPING VIRGIN OF MONTERREY ... 19
- OUR LADY OF TALPA, VIRGIN OF MANY MIRACLES ... 25
- THE MIRACLE OF THE VIRGIN OF FORGIVENESS ... 31
- LA VIRGEN DEL BUEN SUCESO, SANTIAGO TIANGUISTENCO ... 37
- LA VIRGEN GIGANTE DE XICOTEPEC ... 39
- NUESTRA SEÑORA DE TONATICO ... 41
- NUESTRA SEÑORA DE LA SOLEDAD DE ACAPULCO ... 43
- NUESTRA SEÑORA DE TZOCUILAC ... 45
- LA SANTISIMA MADRE DE LA LUZ ... 47
- LA VIRGEN DE LA IMACULADA CONCEPCIÓN DE CHIGNAHUAPAN ... 49

CRISTOS ... 51
- JESUS IN THE SKY AND THE FLOWERING CROWN OF THORNS ... 53
- THE BLACK CHRIST OF OTATITLÁN ... 59
- THE LUCKY BABY JESUS OF TLALPAN ... 65
- THE GIGANTIC BABY JESUS OF ZÓQUITE ... 71
- BABY JESUS OF THE LITTLE PEANUT ... 75
- THE BLACK CHRIST OF CHALMA ... 81
- EL CRISTO ROTO THE BROKEN JESUS OF AGUASCALIENTES ... 87
- THE BLACK CHRIST OF SAN ROMÁN ... 93
- THE SANTO NIÑO AND THE MIRACLES OF PLATEROS ... 99
- OUR LORD OF WONDERS A TALE OF TWO JESUS SHRINES ... 105
- THE STUBBORN JESUS OF GIL DE LEYVA ... 111
- EL SEÑOR DE LA SANTA ESCUELITA ... 113
- OUR LORD OF POISON ... 115

MEXICAN CATHOLIC SAINTS AND HOLY ONES ... 117
- FELIPE DE JESÚS MEXICAN MARTYR IN JAPAN ... 119
- TORIBIO ROMO MEXICAN MARTYR AND ANGEL TO MIGRANTS ... 125
- JOSÉ SÁNCHEZ DEL RIO MEXICO'S BOY SAINT ... 131
- MADRE LUPITA ANGEL TO THE POOR ... 135
- GUADALUPE'S MESSENGER JUAN DIEGO CUAUHTLATOATZIN ... 141
- THE CHILD MARTYRS OF TLAXCALA ... 147
- JUNIPERO SERRA SAINT OR VILLAIN? ... 153
- THE MIRACULOUS LIFE OF RAFAEL GUÍZAR Y VALENCIA ... 159
- JOSÉ MARÍA DE YERMO Y PARRES FROM PRIVILEGE TO SAINTHOOD ... 165
- MARÍA NATIVIDAD VENEGAS DE LA TORRE PATRONESS OF MEXICAN NURSES ... 169
- DON VASCO DE QUIROGA BISHOP OF UTOPIA ... 171

SOR JUANA INÉZ DE LA CRUZ A MAGNIFICENT LIFE 177
THE CASE OF THE BI-LOCATING NUN 183

MEXICAN FOLK SAINTS, HEALERS AND MYSTICS 189

THE SANTA MUERTE: DEATH RESPECTED 191
JESUS MALVERDE: ROGUE OR SAINT? 195
TERESA URREA: MYSTIC, HEALER, REVOLUTIONARY 199
EL NIÑO FIDENCIO: MIRACULOUS HEALER OR FAKE? 205
PACHITA: PSYCHIC SURGEON, MEDIUM AND MYSTIC 211
JUAN SOLDADO: FOLK SAINT OF MIGRANTS AND THE WRONGLY ACCUSED 217
MARÍA LIONZA: MEXICO'S IMPORTED INDIGENOUS SAINT 223
DON PEDRITO JARAMILLO: HEALER, CLAIRVOYANT, FOLK SAINT 229

OTHER RELIGIOUS CURIOSITIES 235

THE MAGIC OF MILAGROS 237
ARCHANGEL MICHAEL AND THE WELL OF MIRACLES...............................241
THE MIRACULOUS HEALING WATERS OF TLACOTE....................................247
THE SORCERERS OF CATEMACO 253
A FEMALE PRISONER MEETS THE BABY JESUS...259
SAINT ANTHONY AND THE HANDICAPPED BOY 261
THE RISE IN EXORCISMS IN MEXICO...263
BIBLIOGRAPHY..269

VIRGINS

Considered to be the holiest of saints, the earthly mother of Jesus, the Virgin Mary, is revered throughout Mexico. Many Marian apparitions and miracles attributed to the Virgin have been occurring throughout Mexico for over five centuries. Sometimes referred to as the Mother of God or Queen of Heaven, among other names, in Mexico the Virgin Mary takes on many forms and has many shrines devoted to her. One of the most frequented pilgrimage sites on the planet is in the heart of Mexico City and is devoted to the "Queen of Mexico" who appeared on a hill to an Aztec peasant in the early years of the Spanish Conquest. There are many other smaller and lesser-known devotions throughout the country, too, and some are so localized that many fellow Mexicans have never heard of them. Nevertheless, they are still important to the local communities which they serve and deserve recognition.

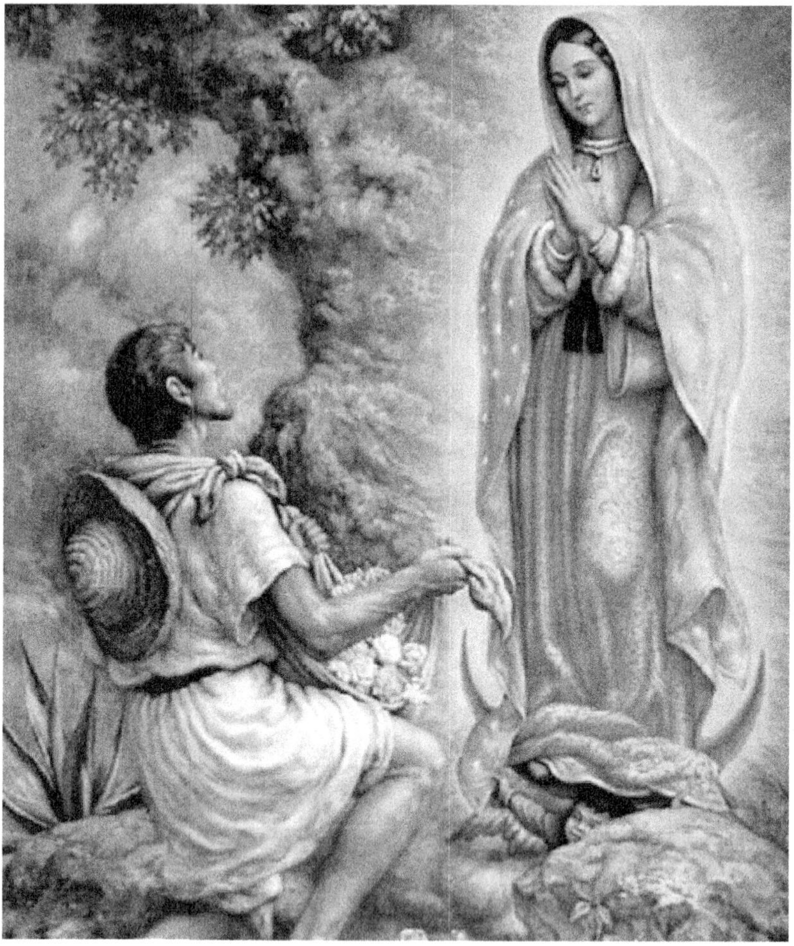

THE VIRGIN OF GUADALUPE: MOTHER TO US ALL

She has many names: Queen of Mexico, Empress of the Americas, Protectoress of the Unborn, *La Virgen Morena* and Mother to us All. She is known formally as the Virgin of Guadalupe, a uniquely Mexican apparition of the Virgin Mary.

Just twelve years after the Spanish arrived in Mexico, on December 9, 1531, a recently baptized Indian man named Juan Diego was walking near Tepeyac Hill right outside Mexico City when he heard beautiful music that sounded like the singing of birds. A cloud appeared and then an image of the sun formed around what appeared to be a young woman dressed like an Aztec princess wearing a cloak full of stars. The woman spoke to Juan Diego in his own language, Nahuatl, and told him not to be afraid. She also requested that a chapel in her honor be built on the top of the hill. Juan Diego went down into Mexico City to tell the Bishop of Mexico, Juan de Zumárraga, of what he saw and heard, which would be later referred to as the First Apparition.

The Second Apparition occurred later that day when Juan Diego returned to the hill. He told Virgin that he had failed with the bishop but she told him to persist. The Virgin was emphatic that a temple devoted to her must be built on that hill and that he could not fail again. Juan Diego promised to try again and then retired to his home.

The next day Juan Diego returned to the bishop's residence to plead with him again to do as the Lady on the hill requested. Zumárraga told Juan Diego that he needed a sign from this mysterious woman, something that would prove to him that this was Mary, the mother of Jesus Christ. When Juan Diego left, the bishop had him followed but the people following him lost track of him when he crossed a ravine and returned to the bishop with no information about the hill or the mysterious woman. When Juan Diego returned to Tepeyac, the Virgin was waiting for him there. This is known as the Third Apparition. Juan Diego expressed his regret in not being able to convince the bishop for the second time and told the shimmering woman that the bishop requested some sort of sign to prove that what he was saying was true. The Virgin then told Juan Diego to return in the morning and she would provide him with what was needed.

    Juan Diego did not return in the morning. His uncle, Juan Bernardino, was very sick and Juan Diego tended to him and even arranged for a doctor's visit. The visit to the lady on the hill was on his mind, but he couldn't tear himself away from his family responsibilities. The following morning, Juan Bernardino was not feeling better and asked Juan Diego to go into town and get a priest to make his last confession and to absolve him of all of his sins before he died. Juan Diego did as his uncle wished, but in order to go into town, he had to pass by the hill at Tepeyac. He was a little reluctant to do so because he missed his meeting time with the lady on the hill the previous morning. When Juan Diego skirted the hill the woman appeared again, behind the rays of the sun and in a cloudburst as she had done the other times. This encounter is known as the Fourth Apparition. The Virgin consoled Juan Diego and told him that there was no need for him to get a priest or any more doctors because his uncle had already been healed. On to the matter of the sign to present to the bishop, the lady told Juan Diego to climb to the top of the hill and to gather the flowers at its crest. Juan Diego ascended Tepeyac Hill and was surprised to see vibrantly colored Castilian roses in full bloom at the top of the hill. This was strange because it was December and the frosts had already come and the area was desolate and devoid of flowers. Juan Diego gathered some of the beautiful dew-covered roses in his cactus-fiber cloak, known as a *tilma*, and went down to the heart of Mexico City to deliver this celestial sign to Bishop Zumárraga. When he got to the bishop's palace to request an audience, the people there knew him as "the pestering Indian," and refused to acknowledge him. When one of the guards saw that Juan Diego was carrying something bunched up in his cloak, he went towards him and saw the beautiful flowers. The guard reached in to take one but couldn't. The rose he tried to grab looked more like an illustration than a real flower. Convinced that Juan Diego had something of importance, the guard granted him access to the bishop. When Zumárraga asked Juan Diego what he had for him, the humble Indian unfurled his cloak and a variety of beautiful roses cascaded to the ground. The bishop and those present dropped to their knees, not just because of the flowers but because of the image that appeared on the front of Juan Diego's cloak: the image of Our Lady of Guadalupe, the one known to reverent Catholics to this day. The church authorities removed Juan Diego's cloak, and that same piece of cactus cloth, which should have lasted no more than 20 years, hangs now in the Basilica of the Virgin of Guadalupe which now stands on the top of that hill at Tepeyac where the apparitions appeared.

    Soon after a small church was built on Tepeyac in 1532, masses of Indians converted to Christianity and word spread throughout New Spain of the miraculous apparitions, the curing of Juan Diego's uncle, and the beautiful roses that served as the sign from Heaven. Critics claim that the whole story was made up and that the image is a fake. The fact that the "lady on the hill" appeared in a place that been connected to a former Aztec goddess, that the woman supposedly spoke the Indian language and looked like a Native has some people wondering if this wasn't an elaborate trick to make the process of conquest easier. To the world's billion or so Catholics, there is no doubt that the Mother of God, the "mother of us all" appeared to a humble servant that day on a hill in Mexico.

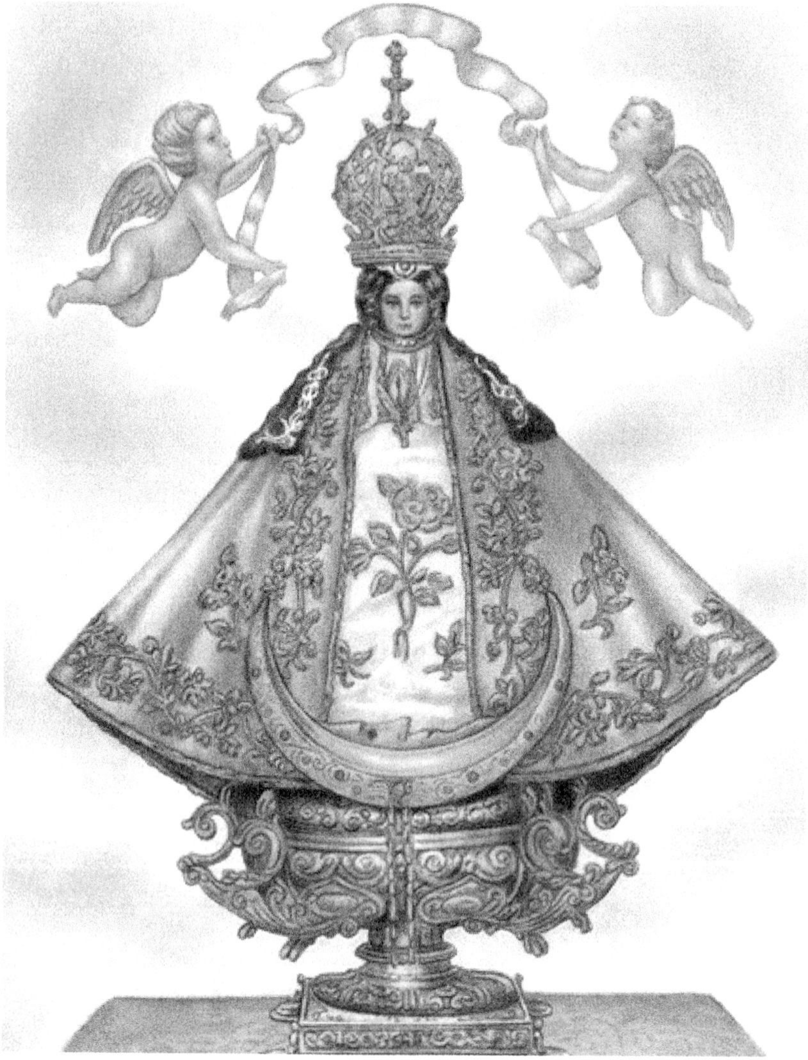

THE VIRGIN OF SAN JUAN DE LOS LAGOS

The year was 1623. A family of aerial acrobats was traveling through the towns and villages of rural New Spain. One of their stops was San Juan Bautista Mezquititlán, a small town in what is now the northeastern part of the Mexican state of Jalisco. Soon after they arrived the acrobats set up their poles and ropes and were eager to perform to the delight of the villagers that evening. To heighten the suspense of their show, the father of the acrobatic family instructed that daggers facing upward should be inserted into the dirt beneath their performance space, which was routine for them to do. Audiences were always thrilled at the element of danger that the daggers introduced. That afternoon, while practicing, one of the girls of the family, who was about 7 at the time, was swinging on the ropes, lost her grip, then slipped and fell into the field of daggers. Her panicked parents, horrified at the sight, rushed to her aid, but she was already dead.

The parents later took the girl's body to the local chapel to be anointed by the parish priest and to be prepared for burial. The caretaker of the chapel, an elderly native woman named Ana Lucía Antes who was very close to her 80th year, had heard of the tragic accident before the parents arrived with the little girl's body. Ana Lucía had fetched a tattered statue of the Virgin of the Immaculate Conception to present it to the parents. This statue had been brought to the village in 1542 by a Spanish priest and at the time of the accident it was nearly 90 years old. It had been made in the traditional Purépecha Indian way of plastering a mixture of corn meal and orchid juice to a wooden frame to mold the figure, a folk-art method that is still in use today. Because of how it was made, the figure had not stood the test of time very well. The Virgin statue had always been special to Ana Lucía and when it was retired from the main church, she kept it in her own quarters. She claimed that she was able to talk directly to the Virgin Mary through the statue, and that the statue talked back. Many villagers thought her to be eccentric, but the deeply devoted Ana Lucía was so convinced of the statue's power that she told the parents of the deceased girl to have faith in God and the Virgin Mary and to pray for their little girl who was then lifeless and wrapped in a burial shroud before them. Ana Lucía placed her beloved statue on the girl's lifeless body and a small group of people who had gathered there began to pray. Within the hour, they detected movement within the shroud and then they all heard the muffled soft voice of the little girl calling for her mother. The father unwrapped the shroud and the little girl emerged, unscathed. News of the miracle traveled fast and even caught the faraway attention of the King of Spain who, by royal decree, granted the town the right to incorporate as a city to henceforth be known as San Juan de Los Lagos.

The story of the traveling aerialists does not end with the resurrection of their little girl. The father of the acrobat family wanted to show his devotion to the Virgin and to give thanks to the small chapel of the town. He asked if he could borrow the Virgin statue to have it refurbished in Guadalajara. The parish priest gave him permission to take the statue to the regional capital. There, the acrobat met an unnamed artist who completely redid the statue, even giving it elegant clothing and an elaborate golden Byzantine-type crown. Her face is smooth, and her hands are folded delicately in prayer. She stands less than 2 feet tall on a crescent moon, as is typical of many representations of the Virgin Mary throughout Mexico, as an unconscious tribute to the memory of the pre-Columbian moon goddess Coyolxauhqui. The statue now is pretty much the same as it was after its refurbishment almost 400 years ago. It remains today in a building on the same site of the original miracle, incased in glass and with two silver angels flying above it holding a banner boldly proclaiming in Latin, *Mater Immaculata ora pro nobis*. This translates in English to "Immaculate Mother pray for us."

Since the story of the acrobat's daughter in 1643 there have been tens of thousands of reports of miracles, intercessions and favors granted that have been attributed to the Virgin of San Juan de Los Lagos. In the mid-17th Century news of the miracles of the Virgin spread like wildfire through colonial New Spain and the small chapel devoted to the statue could not handle the increasing influx of pilgrims, some of whom traveled from hundreds of miles away. To accommodate the growing number of visitors, in 1732 construction began on a much larger church made mostly of pink sandstone, with work on the main building completed by 1779. It would take 11 more years to finish the impressively towering baroque spires that would cap off the new church. The shrine is accented in Tuscan columns and cornices with the main altar fashioned of sandstone and cypress wood, done in neoclassical style. Behind the altar are 6 original oil paintings by the Flemish artist Peter Paul Rubens. The various construction and renovation projects occurring at the Virgin of San Juan de Los Lagos complex have been completely funded by a steady flow of gifts to the shrine. In the 1970s, two hundred years after the completion of the new church, the Vatican declared the church to be a basilica. The Basilica of the Virgin of San Juan de Los Lagos currently attracts 7 million visitors annually from all over the world with one million of them coming for the *fiestas* devoted to the Virgin in late January and early February. Another important devotional date is August 15th. It was on that date in 1904 when then Pope Pius X granted the statue a canonical coronation thus further sanctifying it and solidifying it as one of the major Catholic pilgrimage sites in all Latin America.

To the right of the main entrance to the basilica is a room meant for devotions. A faithful person will make a promise to the Virgin and if the person's prayers are answered the person will undertake a pilgrimage to the shrine and may leave something there. Sociologists call this exchange "petitionary devotion" where there is a reciprocity attached to holy sites or objects. In the words of Frank Graziano, author of the book *Miraculous Images and Votive Offerings in Mexico*, the writer states:

"Devotion to miraculous images is concerned almost exclusively with petitioning sacred power for purposes that range from banal desires to resolution of life-threatening crises. It is a practical, goal-directed, utilitarian devotion; a survival strategy; a way of interpreting reality; and a resource enhancement realized through collaboration with a sacred patron. Miracles are petitioned above all for health-related matters, but also for matters concerning employment, family, pregnancy and childbirth, romantic love, education, migration, and agriculture, among others. Petitionary devotion consists primarily of making miracle requests together with promises to offer something in exchange. In written petitions the promises, or vows, are sometimes explicit, like a signed agreement instead of a handshake, but usually the reciprocation remains unspecified. Promises may be made in prayer, before or after the miracle, but votaries also petition miraculous images without explicitly obligating themselves. Reciprocation is nevertheless always required and when no terms are stated it is likely to take the form of a shrine visit to give thanks in person. Votaries have little to lose in these arrangements, known as votive contracts, because they themselves establish the terms and are under no obligation unless the miracle is granted."

In this votive exchange the person will leave behind at the shrine a physical representation of the favor or miracle granted. For example, a devotee may pray to the Virgin of San Juan de Los Lagos to intercede in the serious illness of a child. If the child recovers, the faithful person may create or have commissioned an ex voto painting of the event and leave it in the shrine's room of devotions. Paintings are usually done on tin but can be found on wood or cardboard and sometimes illustrated in simple pencil or crayons. The result of this phenomenon of offering physical objects as thanks is a room from floor to ceiling of devotional folk art, from the crude to the ornate. In all of Mexico, this room at the Basilica of the Virgin of San Juan de Los Lagos probably houses the biggest concentration of religious folk art outside of the Museo de Arte Popular in Mexico City. Gifts to the Virgin may not take the form of the devotional paintings, however. The room, with its high ceilings and steep stone staircase is full of hundreds of mementos of miracles, from crutches and braces to articles of clothing and dirty teddy bears to pieces from car wrecks. Flowers, both real and those made of corn husks, are also abundant. In addition to being very visual, this large devotions room is probably the most emotional part of the whole Basilica. Highly devoted people go there to leave their offerings while praying with tears pouring down their faces. It is often hard to tell whether the tears are those of sadness from a horrible life event or those of joy for having successfully connected with the divine.

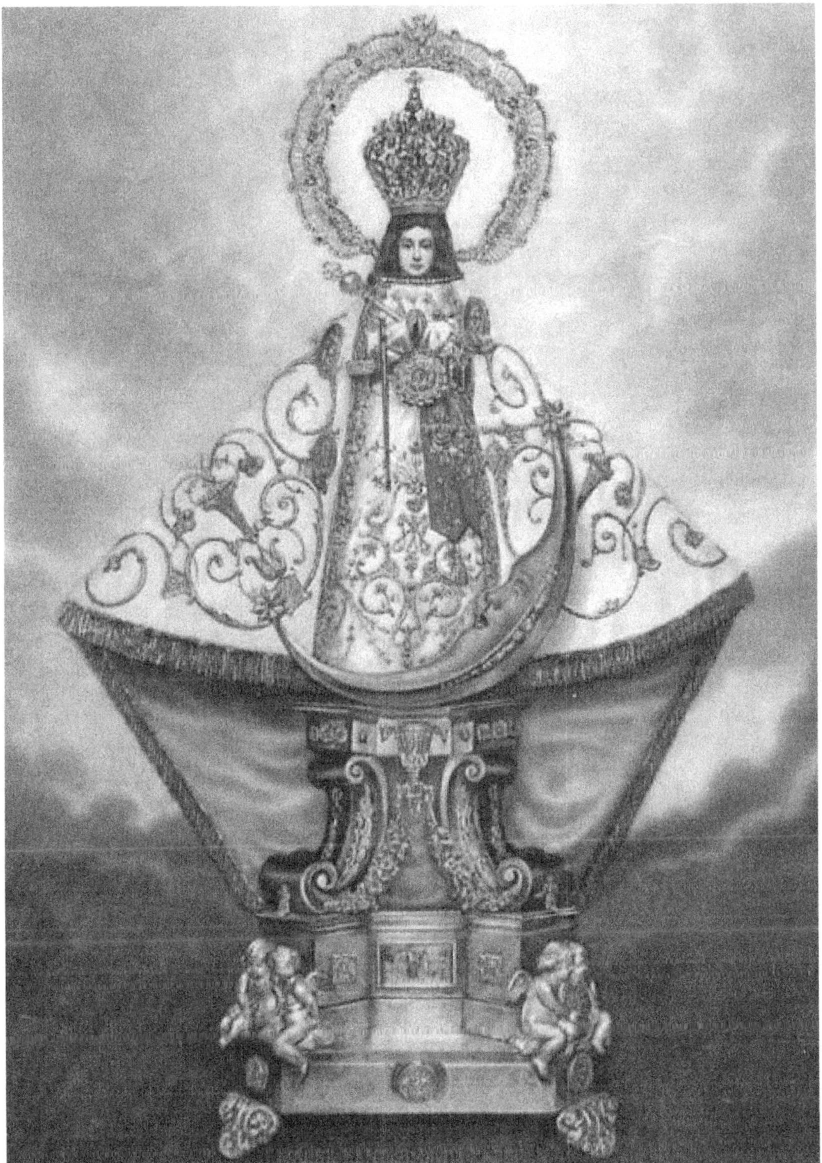

THE VIRGIN OF ZAPOPAN

The year was 1531. A young Franciscan friar named Antonio de Segovia arrived in the area just west of the modern Mexican city of Guadalajara. The country was recently christened Nueva Galicia by the Spanish who had formally conquered it the year before under the leadership of Nuño de Guzmán. At the time of the Spanish arrival, the region was called *Tonallan tlahtocayotl*, in English, "The Kingdom of the East," and was ruled by the powerful indigenous queen called Cihualpilli Tzapotzinco, whose name loosely translates to "the sweet fruit of the zapote tree," in English. Queen Cihualpilli lorded over 12 tributary states and because of the recent conquest of the Aztec Empire to their immediate east, the nobles of her dominions looked to the queen for help in staving off a similar catastrophe that had befallen their stronger and more sophisticated Aztec enemies. Cihualpilli ordered her vassal states to submit to the Spanish and then after their surrender they would work out a peaceable solution of coexistence. Half the leaders of the queen's tributary states did not agree with her plan and vowed to fight the European invaders. Those who agreed with the queen's plans of peace sent delegates to meet the Spanish attack force just outside the Tonallan Kingdom. It took only a matter of months for the conquistadors to subjugate the vassal states of Tonallan that were part of the resistance. To further along the peace process, the great queen herself was one of the first indigenous people in the area to convert to Christianity to serve as an example to her subjects. Her name at baptism was Juana Bautista and after things settled down she remained the figurehead ruler of Tonallan.The 40-year-old Fransciscan Antonio de Segovia did not arrive to the lands of Queen Cihualpilli unprepared. He started his journey in the New World in the Yucatán arriving with the "second wave" of Spanish conquerors in 1525. In the 5 years between his landing in Mexico and his arrival in the Guadalajara area, Segovia learned several indigenous languages and absorbed everything he could about the native cultures of Mexico so as to be a more effective evangelizer. He made his way to central Mexico in 1529 and ended up in Pátzcuaro in the modern Mexican state of Michoacán at the time of the Nuño de Guzmán invasion of Cihualpilli's kingdom. As he was ordered to end up in this kingdom, he thought it best to arrive with a small statue of the Virgin Mary as the Immaculate Conception. The Franciscan had heard that the indigenous people of this new area had worshipped the child goddess Teopintzintl and that a shrine existed in the town of Zapopan in the Tonallan Kingdom's vassal state of Atemajac where pilgrims came to give offerings of partridges and rabbits. With this small statue of the Virgin worn around his neck, Segovia thought he would best introduce Christianity to the natives by using an image that was somewhat like the goddess they had been worshipping for centuries.

The modern-day statue of the Virgin of Zapopan enshrined and crowned in the Basilica of Zapopan looks nothing like the statue that once hung around the neck of the Franciscan Friar, although the body we can barely see through all the subsequent embellishments is the same Virgin Segovia brought to the area in 1531. The original doll-like image has survived remarkably well over the centuries due to the materials used in its crafting. The statue was made by Purépecha Indians in Pátzcuaro using traditional methods. First, a skeleton was constructed out of sugar canes and cornstalks. Then, a special paste or dough called *tatzingueni* was applied to flesh out the figure. This *tatzingueni* was made of corn stalk pulp and the juice of a local orchid which gave the paste a latex quality and would prevent the finished product from rotting or spoiling. The indigenous craftsmanship, which has since been studied by scientists, has lasted almost 5 centuries.

Segovia arrived in Nueva Galicia as a simple minister, traveling without shoes – discalced, in Roman Catholic Terms – and with the Virgin Mary statue around his neck. Many indigenous people who encountered Segovia claimed to see rays of light emanating from the small statue and word spread throughout Nueva Galicia of the Virgin's mysterious powers. The Franciscan converted thousands of Indians as a result. Things seemed to be going well for the Spanish throughout most of the 1530s until many of the Tonallan nobles started to complain about colonial abuses of power. The peace brokered by Queen Cihualpilli ended in a full out rebellion of several coordinated indigenous groups called the Mixton War in 1541. By the end of the year the Spanish gained complete control over the area again and this time held on to it. The area around Zapopan had been depopulated because of the fighting and on December 8 of 1541 the new town of Zapopan was founded by the Spanish who settled it mostly by bringing in natives from other regions. As a gift for accepting the Spanish peace agreements, Antonio de Segovia gave his statue of the Virgin to the people of Zapopan who took care of it and built a small adobe shrine to it, much like the one they used to have to honor the child-goddess Teopintzintl. It was at this time when the statue got its first title, La Pacificadora, or "she who makes peace." The story doesn't end here; the statue's importance grew with time and the Virgin of Zapopan is now one of the main pilgrimage sites in all of Mexico. Many events and miracles have led up to this.

Since the late 1600s the city of Guadalajara had suffered more than its share of calamities. Great lightning storms and epidemics of smallpox and measles swept through the city regularly. In 1721, the city was attacked by a mysterious and deadly plague that decimate the population and it was at this time that the bishop of Guadalajara ordered the Virgin of Zapopan to leave its shrine and visit each neighborhood of the city to try to help end the plague. In 1655 a previous Bishop of Guadalajara had given the Virgin the title of "La Milagrosa", or "The Miracle-Worker" because of the many miracles attributed to the devotion to the statue and by the early 1700s the Virgin of Zapopan had been considered a powerful intercessor. So, in 1721 on order of the church leaders the statue was carried throughout the various *colonias* of Guadalajara and the plague miraculously ended. That was not to be the last tour of the statue. After the caretaker of the church of San Juan de Dios was struck by lightning and the priest administering his last rites was also killed by a lightning bolt, the ecclesiastical authorities agreed that it would be best to make the Virgin of Zapopan a traveling statue. In 1734 the bishop of Guadalajara Nicolás Carlos Gómez de Cervantes met with local governmental officials to have the Virgin of Zapopan declared "The Patroness and Advocate of the City." By November 14th of 1734, she was given formal title of "Patroness and Protector of Lightning, Storms and Epidemics of this Most Noble City and its Inhabitants." The next year, the Virgin was tasked with traveling throughout the neighborhoods of Guadalajara and the towns of Nueva Galicia from June until October, a ritual that has continued to the modern day. You can even go online to track the Virgin and follow her various stops and events connected with her visits. It has only been in recent times that a special exact replica statue called "La Virgen Peregrina," or, in English, "The Pilgrim Virgin," has taken the place of the real statue and has traveled the familiar summer route throughout the country. The real statue is safe and sound under glass in the main niche in the Basilica. The annual return of the traveling Virgin to Zapopan attracts an estimated one million people along the route home.

During the Mexican War of Independence in the early part of the 19th Century, the Virgin of Zapopan was given military rank and yet another title, "La Generala," or "The General." It was then when the statue was given a sword and a general's staff to signify its role in protecting the members of the military. The accoutrements and the clothing added to the Virgin increased with time and its importance continued to grow. For quite some time the statue was completely veiled as there was fear that exposure to light would somehow decompose the figure. Because the caretakers realized the durability of the craftsmanship of the piece, she has since spent her time unveiled and clothed in a gold-embroidered dress. In 1919 with the visit of the Pope, she was given a gold crown adorned with rubies and pearls, and a small platform of solid silver, weighing 55 kilos. Under her hands is a reliquary of gold and precious stones, with a gold image of the Baby Jesus in the center. Because the Virgin of Zapopan was given the title of "Queen of Jalisco" in 1921, she holds a gold scepter adorned with pearls, diamonds and rubies and a golden staff. She was also given the keys to Guadalajara at this time. Somewhere along the line, the statue was given a small suitcase of gold, which remains beside her in the niche at the basilica. Because of this suitcase, she has also been declared "Patron Saint of Travel Agents." The simple crescent moon at her feet that was originally made of the *tatzingueni* paste has been since covered in gold. Over the years, the statue has also acquired curly brown hair. As the statue became more embellished and more important to the Mexicans over time, the structure housing it expanded in area and complexity. What was essentially once a small adobe hut catering to locals has turned into an impressive basilica that is a major destination for the faithful throughout the Catholic World. Construction of the larger abbey and basilica began in 1689, and as a result, the building is a prime example of Spanish colonial baroque architecture. As the Virgin garnered more titles and more accessories, the basilica became more ornate and complex as well. The current basilica has meditation gardens, an Italian marble altar, statues carved of cypress wood and many interesting architectural features of various orders and styles. For believers and non-believers alike, the Basilica of Our Lady of Zapopan is a definite feast for the eyes.

    In October of 2015 massive flooding hit the city of Guadalajara because of Hurricane Patricia. As believers are quick to note, this natural disaster happened immediately after the Virgin's processional period ended and there were no deaths from the storm. The population had ample time to pray for celestial help as they were told a week before to expect the worst storm in the history of Mexico. Perhaps the powers of the many-titled Virgin who has gained the reverence of millions over the centuries played an important role in mitigating a catastrophe, or perhaps the people of central Mexico just got lucky. We may never know for sure.

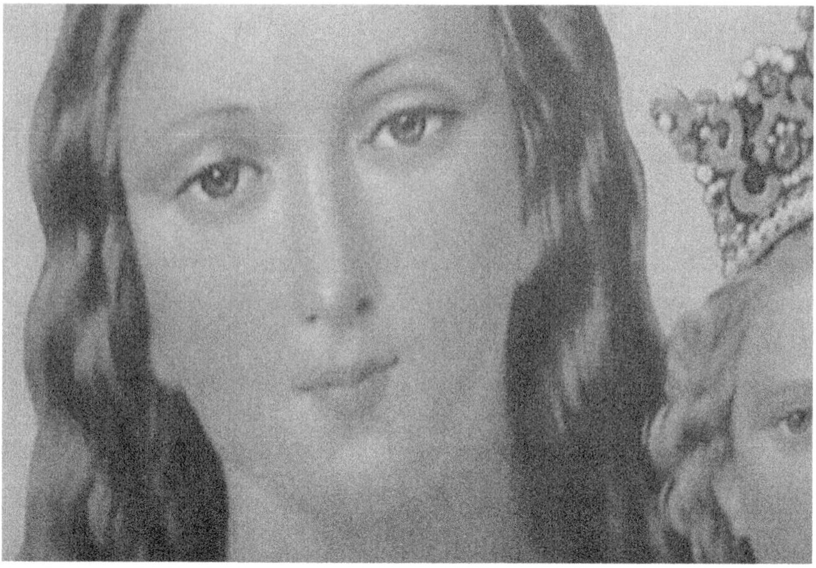

THE WEEPING VIRGIN OF MONTERREY

Ermilia Carrasco – known to her friends as "Mila" - considers herself to be an average Mexican grandma. She lives in a modest home in the Nuevas Colonias district in the city of Monterrey, the capital of the Mexican state of Nuevo Leon and the third largest city in Mexico. Ermilia has maintained her humble composure in the face of perhaps hundreds of interviews since the late 1990s. For nearly twenty years the señora's home has been visited by tens of thousands of people, including documentary filmmakers from as far away as Australia and Japan, who have hoped to catch glimpse of the various miracles said to take place on her humble premises. The focal point in Mila's home is a curious image familiar to Catholics around the world. It's a standard depiction of the Madonna and Child known to English speakers as Our Lady Help of Christians or to Spanish speakers as Nuestra Señora María Auxiliadora. In Mexico she is also sometimes called La Virgen de Noche, or the Virgin of the Night. The image, measuring about eighteen inches across, is a print on sturdy cardboard and is sandwiched between two pieces of glass. While many Mexicans have similar mass-produced icons in their homes, this one is notorious because the Virgin cries. Not only does she cry, she cries on a daily basis. She cries in front of people and on camera. Those who have witnessed this phenomenon leave the Carrasco home incredibly moved with no worldly explanation to describe what they have witnessed. Many visitors have also told of other small miracles occurring in the modest house in Monterrey.

Ermilia Carrasco received the image now known as the Weeping Virgin, or *La Virgen que Llora*, from a man named Father Renzo, a member of the Catholic order of Salesians based in Cochabamba, Bolivia. Father Renzo was in Monterrey in the late 1990s for a conference and while there he gave away dozens of images of Mary Help of Christians to parishioners after a visit to the local church. The Virgin is the protector and patroness of the Salesian Order and her veneration goes back to the Middle Ages. In the popular image, the Virgin is holding the Christ Child who has outstretched arms. Both mother and child are topped with bejeweled golden crowns and their facial features are very soft and northern European. In fact, the Baby Jesus of this image, with his chubby cheeks and mid-length curly blond hair, looks very similar to the American child actress Shirley Temple. This depiction of the Virgin has been historically venerated and called upon to ward off non-Christians who would cause harm, specifically Muslim invaders of Europe, and to protect against evil forces that would harm the Church or true Christian believers. This Marian devotion was particularly important to Father Don Bosco, who was later made a saint by the Catholic Church, who used this Virgin as the cornerstone of the founding of his Salesian Congregation. The main shrine to María Auxiliadora is thus found in the northern Italian city of Turin, in the basilica there. The statue in Turin was even given a special canonical coronation by Pope Leo XIII in 1903. This Virgin is also venerated in the Eastern Orthodox Church. The earliest record of devotion in the East dates to 1030 in Ukraine where she was given credit for helping fend off a barbarian invasion. In spite of the deep history of this Virgin in Europe and unlike Mexico's more home-grown Marian apparitions – the Virgin of Guadalupe, the Virgin of Zapopan and the Virgin of San Juan de los Lagos – Mary Help of Christians has very little connection to Mexico. Although this may be the case, believers affirm that God is speaking through this particular image for a certain very important reason and people should pay attention to what message this European Virgin may have to give to Mexicans.

 When Carrasco brought home the image from church on that day in 1998, she placed it on the small table set up as a devotional altar in her living room. Many homes in Mexico, however modest they may be, have a similar set-up: a small sacred space such as a simple, cloth-covered table up against the wall or in the corner, for family saints, candles and other objects of religious devotion. Within days Mila noticed tears coming out of the eyes of the Virgin. The tears rolled right down the image without causing any buckling or other harm to the paper surface. She showed her family and then word spread throughout the neighborhood of what people had immediately branded a miracle. To protect the image from excessive handling, Mila encased the icon in glass, which seemed to have no effect on the crying phenomenon. The Virgin continued to weep, every single day. Within weeks the story spread beyond her family, friends and neighborhood and people started to show up at the Carrasco's doorstep from other parts of Mexico hoping to be able to ask the Virgin for assistance or intercession. As this was still her family home, with all the regular family activities going on inside of it, Mila had created a handwritten sign to post on her front door to announce hours that her living room would be open to the curious. This is the system she uses to this day, with a rosary prayed on the premises every day at 3:00 in the afternoon. Since the late 1990s, though, the living room which was the destination of a few pilgrims per day has been transformed into a full-fledged shrine with statues, candles and makeshift pews in which the devout and the curious can sit in quiet contemplation.

Not only has the scope of the shrine increased over time, so have the miracles associated with the Carrasco's former living room. Alongside the main table on which the crying image sits, there stands a nearly life-size plaster statue of Our Lady Help of Christians which was given to the Carrasco family, like so many of the other objects in the shrine, by a devout person who was helped by his visit to the home. Within weeks of the statue's installation, it also began to cry, but the tears were not a salty liquid, as are the tears coming out of the original image. The statue's tears are an oily substance, and they only appear infrequently, not daily like the icon. Also, Mila received a wooden rosary from a pilgrim as a token of thanks which also seems to be exhibiting unusual properties. The rosary was brought back from Rome in 2005 and was said to have been blessed by Pope John Paul II. During one of her 3:00 rosary prayer sessions, the rosary became sticky and then oily and began to give off a fragrant smell of roses. Since then, when handled, the rosary has also been seen to "cry", even in front of cameras. The smell associated with the rosary has also been said to fill the shrine even when no flowers are present. Many visitors do bring flowers to the shrine which is part of another curious Phenomenon in the Carrasco home. One day, while cleaning up the flower petals on the floor, a woman noticed what appeared to be an image of the Virgin of Guadalupe on one of the petals. Over the course of the next few weeks more images appeared on other flowers, too, notably the face of Christ and other likenesses of the Virgin of Guadalupe. A face of Christ even appeared on a tissue used to wipe away the tears of the main icon. Mila has saved all of these items and has displayed them for the camera crews and the curious. Another unusual religious manifestation that happened in the Carrasco home occurred on the cement floor of the shrine itself. When cleaning the floor with a mop one day, sometime in the mid-2000s, Mila noticed a faint outline image of the Virgin of Guadalupe appearing when the floor was wet. This, too, has been demonstrated repeatedly and has been recorded on film.

    The various phenomena present in the Carrasco home has not only attracted pilgrims but has drawn the attention of paranormal researchers and debunkers. The image of the crying Virgin between the glass can be picked up and turned around and examined. No pipes or ducts for water are present to induce the tears. The other things happening in the home also seem to defy explanation. A paranormal research team from Australia speculated that there was something different about the location, that a paranormal phenomenon specific to the Carrasco's living room was causing all of the religious manifestations. The film crew making a documentary for Australian television even recorded noises and movement inside the shrine while there were no people present. Could all of the happenings in the Carrasco living room be the product of a spirit of some sort? What of the original icon? Have other people who have received similar icons from the Bolivian priest in the late 1990s been experiencing similar things happening in their homes? The answer to this is, "No." It is curious to note that the town of Cochabamba, Bolivia – where the icon hails from - is known for its own similar curious religious phenomena. Cochabamba is not only famous for having the tallest statue of Christ in the world – called Cristo del la Concordia, or The Christ of Peace – it is home to a weeping statue of Jesus in its main cathedral which also is said to emit blood. Cochabamba has also been home to a rash of stigmatists, those who suffer from the stigmata, or bleed from locations on the body corresponding to the wounds of Christ. Has the Cochabamba connection been overlooked by investigators in this case in Monterrey?

What does the Catholic Church think of what is going on in Ermilia Carrasco's former living room? The Church is taking this all very seriously. There are around 400 cases around the world of images of Mary in various forms – icons, statues, etc. – shedding tears or bleeding. Many cases are swiftly debunked as hoaxes or explained away as the result of natural phenomena, such as accumulations of atmospheric moisture on statues. The Vatican has assigned a local priest to follow the case, Father Luis Eugenio Espinoza. Espinoza, who holds a doctorate in theology from the University of Louvain in Belgium and who is a professor at the University of Monterrey, urges caution when investigating alleged miraculous phenomenon. In an April 2016 interview with the Mexican publication *La Crónica*, Father Espinoza explained that the Church will wait several decades, usually 2 full generations, before it declares something like what is happening in Monterrey a miracle. In the article Espinoza explained, "It is the potential failure that we have when we speak of a miracle and then we see that other factors intervene. We must know how to separate the supernatural, the inexplicable from the miraculous. The true miracle always has as its purpose to bring the faithful to the Church and to preach with good."

For Monterrey resident Ivonne Navarro there is no doubt that the Virgin present in the Carrasco home has heard her prayers. On her visit to the shrine she asked for her sister to hear from her nephew again. Her sister hadn't seen her son in 20 years and knew no news about him. While in Ivonne's presence, the Virgin icon shed tears. When Ivonne returned home later that day, her daughter greeted her at the door to tell her the news that her sister finally had contacted her son, who appeared at her home earlier that day.

Whether a paranormal phenomenon, the product of restless spirits or a real dose of the divine, the Weeping Virgin of Monterrey has filled untold thousands with hope and continues to inspire a sense of wonder.

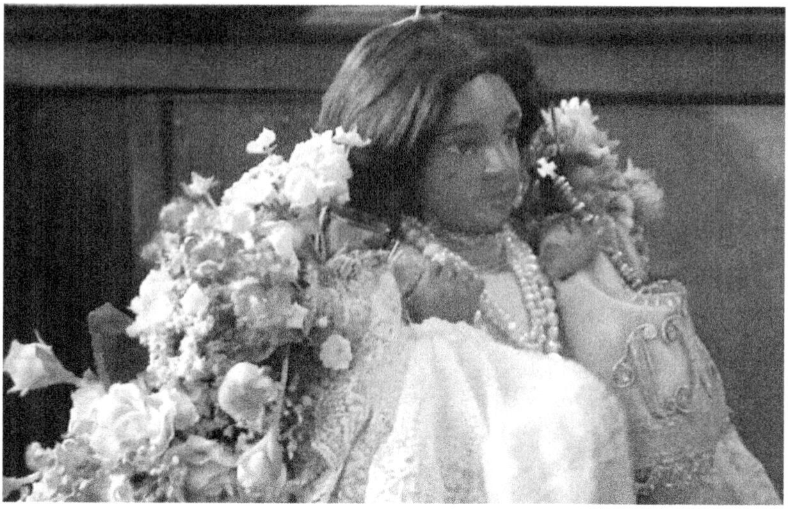

OUR LADY OF TALPA, VIRGIN OF MANY MIRACLES

    The year 1660 saw a great plague hit the western region of the province of Nueva Galicia in the Viceroyalty of New Spain. In the remote mountainous area of what is now the Mexican state of Jalisco, thousands of people died over the course of a few months. Desperate for an end to the sickness, groups of people banned together to make a pilgrimage to the small mining town of Talpa. For many decades the church there had been the home of a statue of a very powerful Virgin and many who had put their faith in her and made offerings before her had received unbelievable miracles. Groups of pilgrims arrived petitioning the Virgin for relief from the plague and within three days they received what the asked for: no more people died and there was no more sickness in the land. Little known outside the immediate area, after the cessation of the plague the Virgin of Talpa became known throughout New Spain and began receiving pilgrims from hundreds of miles away. The miracle of the ending of the 1660 plague was not the first unbelievable event connected with this statue, which is of the Madonna and Child done in the manner of the Virgin of the Rosary. Her history of miracles begins several decades earlier.

    Spanish conquistador Nuño de Guzmán first came to the region in the 1530s. His conquest of the various indigenous groups of Nueva Galicia was so violent that the region remained in a state of unrest for many years. The area around modern-day Talpa was part of a chiefdom ruled by Nahua people who were loosely related to the Aztecs but were not controlled by the Aztec Empire. Nestled high in the mountains, among forests of pine, walnut and maple, the original name of Talpa was Tlalpan, a Nahuatl name combining the words *tlalli*, meaning "land" and *pan*, "above" or "atop." Captains of Nuño de Guzmán, Juan and Cristóbal de Oñate and Juan Fernández de Híjar came to the region of Tlalpan in 1540 and subjugated it peacefully. Spanish settlers began arriving almost immediately, attracted to local mineral resources, and by 1585 a small Spanish town grew up near the original indigenous settlement. By 1599, the royal authorities in Guadalajara formally recognized the town and christened it Santiago de Talpa. The town fell under the administration of the nearby municipality of Guachinango. Father Manuel de San Martín arrived at Talpa sometime in the 1570s or 1580s and he brought with him a statue of the Virgin of the Rosary. An anonymous native artist from the Lake Pátzcuaro region fashioned the statue out of corn paste as was customary at the time. The Virgin had a beautiful face and intricate details, and the townsfolk built a small chapel for her and two other religious items: a statue of Santiago and wooden carving of Christ on the cross. In the early 1600s the Spanish miners abandoned the town and many of the buildings fell into disrepair. In one version of the Virgin of Talpa story, an indigenous family took the three religious pieces from the small chapel and kept them among family members in different places. In another version of the story before the chapel was abandoned the pieces were buried under some floorboards. In September of 1644 with more people moving into the area the Church assigned Pedro Rubio Félix to minister to the small town of Talpa and stationed him in the nearby town of Guachinango. One of Father Félix's first tasks in Talpa was to reverse some four decades of neglect and restore the chapel. He started renovations immediately and ordered the return or the exhumation of the three religious artifacts previously used in the chapel. When the Spanish priest examined the items, he assigned local artisans to refurbish the pieces. The wooden Christ and the wooden statue of Santiago only needed minor repairs. The Virgin, however, made of the more delicate corn paste, needed a major overhaul. The statue had been nearly destroyed by worms and her clothing eaten by moths. Some considered her a total loss.

    The stories of what happened next diverge once again. In one version of the Our Lady of Talpa story, the damage to the statue was so extensive that she needed to be taken to a faraway village to be repaired by an elderly master indigenous artisan who was familiar with the old ways of making figures from corn paste. It took days to deliver the Virgin to the old artisan but on the day after he completed work on the statue, she was miraculously back in the chapel at Talpa, occupying her former space on a small altar table but now in flawless condition. Believers in this history claim that the Virgin was either transported back to her home in a flash of divine light or that she ran to Talpa herself. The second version of the story has actual written documentation attached to it, with witness testimonies taken down by representatives of the royal authorities in Guadalajara who came to Talpa after hearing what happened. In this version, an indigenous woman named María Tenache was charged with taking the deteriorated figure of the Virgin to another village to have it worked on. When María tried to pick up the statue, it emitted a flash of light so powerful that it knocked her over. A half dozen witnesses in the chapel at the time described what happened next: the small room filled with a warm, bright light and near the ceiling appeared swirling clouds and small flying angels. It was as if the witnesses were looking straight up to heaven itself. María regained consciousness after the intense light subsided and in the place of the worm-eaten corn paste figure of the Virgin of the Rosary stood a colorfully painted duplicate made from a hard cedarwood. Many in the town heard thunderous noises during this event and many people ran to the chapel to see what happened. Word of the statue's transformation soon left the town and the next day Father Félix visited Talpa from his permanent residence at Guachinango. The priest came with three other men to examine the Virgin. A member of the party remarked that the face and hands of the Virgin felt like human flesh and to test whether what he was feeling was actual living material, he took a candle and burned the Virgin's right cheek. A burn mark in the same place exists on Our Lady of Talpa to this day. The priest lit candles and led the faithful present in hours of prayer. The two candles on the small altar remained intact for three days, burning but never going down. The anomalies associated with what happened in this small chapel eventually got the attention of the royal Audencia in Guadalajara and the visit of officials produced the formal documentation of the event. The transformation of the statue is known formally as *El Milagro de la Renovación*, or the Miracle of the Renewal.In 1649 Father Félix began supervising the building of a new church to replace the small and often crowded chapel. The larger structure, called La Nueva Iglesia de Nuestra Señora del Rosario, opened on September 19, 1651. Nine years after the building of the new church and after the ending of the plague, church officials ordered a replica of the miraculous statue to be built. Because of the popularity of the Virgin in the region the replica was called "La Peregrina," or "The Pilgrim," in English, and she traveled from village to village going to those people who could not make the journey to see the original Virgin in the town of Talpa. Even with the traveling duplicate version of the statue alleviating some of the numbers of visitors to the small town, the popularity of the Virgin grew, and pilgrims began arriving from all parts of New Spain, even from as far away as the modern-day American Southwest, to ask the Virgin for assistance with a variety of life's woes. By 1670, the archbishop ordered an even larger structure to be built at Talpa to accommodate the faithful and by 1672 the new grander church was completed just in time for the Virgin's feast day.

    The Basilica of Our Lady of the Rosary, also known as the Basilica of Our Lady of Talpa, today dominates the town of 15,000 and receives millions of visitors per year, mostly from the state of Jalisco and the states surrounding it. Although popular in Mexico, many outside the country have never heard of the Virgin of Talpa, known colloquially as "La Chaparrita." Typical of similar Mexican religious destinations, the town caters to pilgrims with curio sellers and a general carnival atmosphere surrounding the basilica. The faithful honor Our Lady of Talpa several times per year. The first day is February 2, for the Catholic holiday of Candlemas, known as *La Candelaria* in Spanish, the day commemorating the presentation of Jesus at the Temple. The second time the Virgin is honored is during the Novena of El Señor San José from March 11th to March 19. The faithful honor the Virgin for the third time during the year on May 12th in a ceremony called La Coronación de la Señora del Rosario, during which the statue is cleaned, re-dressed, ceremonially "re-crowned" and returned to her sacred niche in front of hundreds of pilgrims. Depending on the calendar, the main fiesta of the Virgin of Talpa starts sometime at the end of September and ends on the first Sunday of October. This "main event" begins with a large fireworks display to remind the faithful of how the Virgin transformed herself in front of the humble Maria Tenache and the other onlookers on that day in 1644. As is typical in Mexican fiestas, there is a large procession through the town, followed by special masses and celebrations throughout the week. In recent years the town of Talpa has sponsored an arts and crafts show to coincide with the main fiesta week. While the feast days are important, the basilica receives pilgrims throughout the year. Many people who ask for help or give thanks to the Virgin for prayers answered will leave votive offerings of flowers, devotional paintings called *retablos*, or metal milagro charms. The Virgin has seen many millions of people in over three and a half centuries and many of these people claim their lives have been completely transformed by prayers to her or just by making the trip to see her. The Virgin of Talpa remains one of the most fascinating, enduring and lesser-known miracles of Mexico.

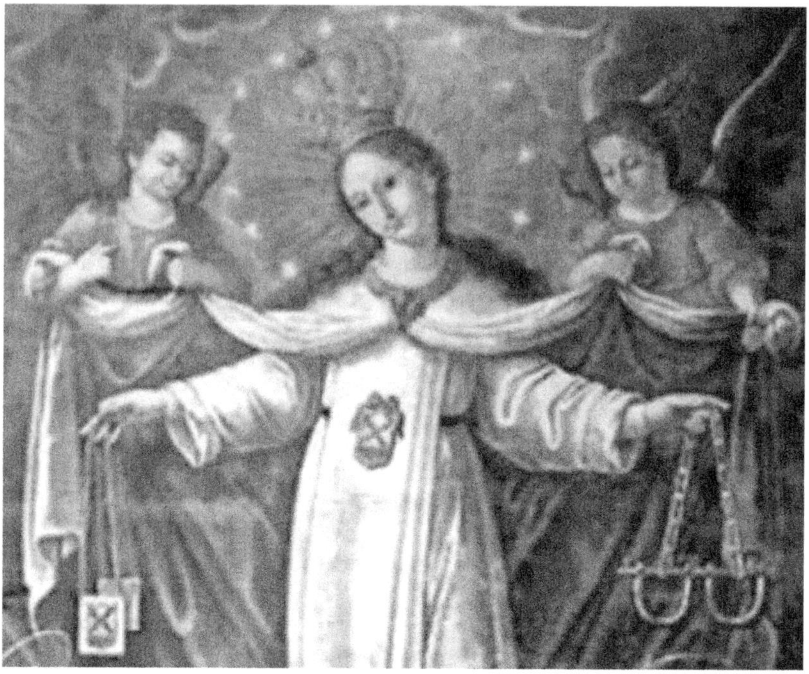

THE MIRACLE OF THE VIRGIN OF FORGIVENESS

The date was October 16, 1566, and the place was Mexico City, the colonial capital of New Spain. The Third Marquis of Falces, a man named Gastón de Peralta, had just arrived with his entourage and assumed the position of Viceroy, or the king's official representative in the country which had been under Aztec control only 47 years earlier. King Phillip II of Spain sent the marquis to bring stability to his overseas possession after the death of the previous Viceroy Luis de Velasco and the interim rule of the Audencia. There had been unrest among newly conquered native peoples and among some of the first generation of Spaniards born in the New World who had demanded more autonomy from Spain. Among Viceroy Peralta's entourage was a strongly built man in his mid-thirties with reddish-blond hair and very pale skin. The man was Simon Pereyns, a portrait artist who originally hailed from Antwerp in the lowland country of Flanders which was then part of the Spanish Netherlands and is now part of modern-day Belgium. At the age of 28 Pereyns had moved from Flanders to the Iberian Peninsula and settled in Lisbon where he lived a year and then moved to Toledo before moving on to Madrid. Inspired by both the style of 16th Century Roman painters and the Flemish masters of his homeland, Pereyns became a celebrated portrait painter at the Spanish Court and was said to have created 2 paintings of King Phillip II which do not survive to this day. Many of his works are lost, but Pereyn's artistic career is well documented thanks to contracts he signed while doing his noble portrait commissions. He is sometimes seen in the contract records as "Perin" or even the Hispanicized "Pérez." After painting portraits of members of the family of the future Viceroy Peralta, Pereyns was encouraged to accompany the marquis to Mexico City as part of his official retinue. Simon Pereyns accepted and become the first European portrait artist to take up residence in Mexico.

 Simon Pereyns enjoyed great success in colonial Mexico City. As the lone European-trained portrait artist in the capital city, he was never at a loss for work or the sponsorship of wealthy patrons. One of his backers was Francisco de Morales, a man known for his lavish banquets and parties. At one of Morales' parties an interesting topic of conversation arose. The Archbishop of Mexico, Alonso de Montúfar, had announced a contest connected with the main cathedral of Mexico City which was still under construction. The contest called on all the artists of New Spain to create a portrait of the Virgin Mary for the cathedral's new *Altar del Perdón*, or Altar of Forgiveness. The Virgin would be called Our Lady of Forgiveness, or the Virgin of Forgiveness. When asked if he would participate in the contest, Pereyns waved his hand in a dismissive manner and told Francisco de Morales that he didn't want to waste his time on painting religious pictures when there was real money to be made in painting portraits of the family members of people of high station in Mexico City. The comment was overheard by many and was considered blasphemous. Pereyns had thought himself so above creating paintings with religious themes that it almost seemed as if he was mocking the Church. As Simon Pereyns had enjoyed a good life in Mexico City and commanded a high premium for his works, there were many people who were jealous of him and eager to either witness or actively participate in his downfall. His comments at the party had given his enemies the ammunition to take him down. Not only were there rumors around the city that Pereyns was a blasphemer, but others also came forward alleging that Pereyns had partaken in scandalous gossip of a more private nature. There were also stories circulating around Mexico City that Simon Pereyns was secretly a Jew.

In the 1560s in Mexico City, the formal Holy Office of the Spanish Inquisition did not yet exist, although the functions of the Inquisition did, in the office of the Archbishop of Mexico. The purpose of the Inquisition was to root out heretics and punish those who went against the Catholic Church in word or deed. Pereyns' comments at the Morales party and rumors of his secret practice of the Jewish faith were enough cause to bring him before Archbishop Alonso de Montúfar. On September 10, 1568, he forcibly "confessed" his blasphemy before a Dominican brother and 4 days later was examined formally. In the initial rounds of questioning, it was discovered that while Pereyns was not the most faithful

Christian in Mexico City and almost never made confession or attended mass, he was not a Jew. To his off-the-cuff comments of being too good to paint religious pictures, this was another matter. For these comments he was to be punished, even tortured. The archbishop's preferred method was to put those examined on a rack and have water slowly dripped into their mouths from a linen rag. Simon Pereyn had this done to him three times and the questioning and imprisonment lasted for months. It seems like nothing Pereyns could do would please the church authorities. Apparently, during his brief time in Mexico City, Pereyns had angered many people with his holier-than-thou attitude and many delighted to hear he was punished so harshly. Some were even calling for him to be burned at the stake.

Sometime in December of 1568, Simon Pereyns was returned to his jail cell after a long session with the inquisitors. While lying on his back, trying to fall asleep, a shimmering light began to glow in his cell. His quarters also began to fill with a sweet fragrance of spring flowers. The glow became much brighter which caused the dejected and demoralized artist to sit up. He then watched the light turn into a beautiful figure. It was an apparition of the Virgin Mary known as Our Lady of Mercy, and for a few moments she looked upon Pereyns with gentle eyes which had an element of sadness to them.

"Little son, why do you not love me?" The Virgin asked in a soothing voice.

Pereyns immediately got up and knelt before the blazing apparition which was described as brighter than sunlight. "Queen of Heaven," he began, "I love you with all of my heart and soul. Please deliver me from this place."

With a gentle smile, the Virgin slowly faded away and the light became dimmer. The heavenly perfume that once filled the room had gone. The only light left in Pereyns' cell was the light of the moon. In the moonlight the artist saw something that the Virgin had left behind: paints, brushes and colors in chalk. The artist's task was clear: Pereyns would give up his personal aversion to painting religious-themed art and would get to work on the back of the prison cell door with the materials at hand. By the first light of morning Pereyns had painted the likeness of the Virgin who had visited him that previous night. He used all the colors left behind and the painting seemed to radiate its own special luminescence. Pereyns called a jailer to see his work, and thinking the Flemish artists was playing a trick, two other jailers entered the cell. The painting was so marvelous, they dropped to their knees. There was no explaining how the artist had crafted such a work with no materials and so little time. The jail authorities called for the archbishop who came immediately. During a brief conversation, Pereyns told the archbishop that he would paint the Virgin for the cathedral and would not accept the prize money. The archbishop entertained Pereyns' offer and let him go. Simon Pereyns painted the painting which occupied the place over the Altar of Forgiveness in the Mexico City Cathedral for many years. Like so many of Pereyns' works, the Virgin of Forgiveness remains lost. Some say it was destroyed in a fire sometime in the 1960s, but other sources cite that it was gone a long time before that. After he painted the virgin for the cathedral Simon Pereyns, who was now in the good graces of the people of Mexico City, settled down and got married. He also continued painting religious-themed works. The few that survive include a painting of Saint Christopher and what is considered his most important work: the main altarpiece of the Monastery of Huejotzingo, which includes 6 painted panels depicting the life of Christ. Pereyns' style was said to have influenced other Mexican-born artists well into the 17th Century.

As with other stories of miracles or fantastic claims, researchers are quick to look for proof. In the ecclesiastical records of colonial Mexico City, there is documentation in the archives of the Inquisition of what happened to Pereyns. There exists a parchment signed by a "Doctor Estevan de Portillo," who was listed as Pereyns' inquisitor, that lists the artist's punishment for blasphemy. Translated into English, it reads:

"On the acts and merits of this case it is found that for the crime committed I condemn him to paint at his own cost an altar-piece of Our Lady of Mercy for the Holy Church (the Cathedral) very devout and to me pleasing, and that in the interim while he is painting this altar-piece he shall not leave this city under penalty of being punished with all the rigor as one disobedient to the mandates of the Holy Office, and I admonish and command that said Simon Pereyns that from this time forth he shall not speak such words as those for the speaking of which he has been arrested, nor shall he question any matters touching our holy Catholic faith under penalty of being rigorously punished."

Although there is no documented evidence of the miracle of the appearance of Our Lady of Mercy in Pereyns' jail cell, one must wonder what compelled the stubborn artist to change his mind and submit to authorities. Was he simply worn down by the Inquisition or was he genuinely touched by the divine?

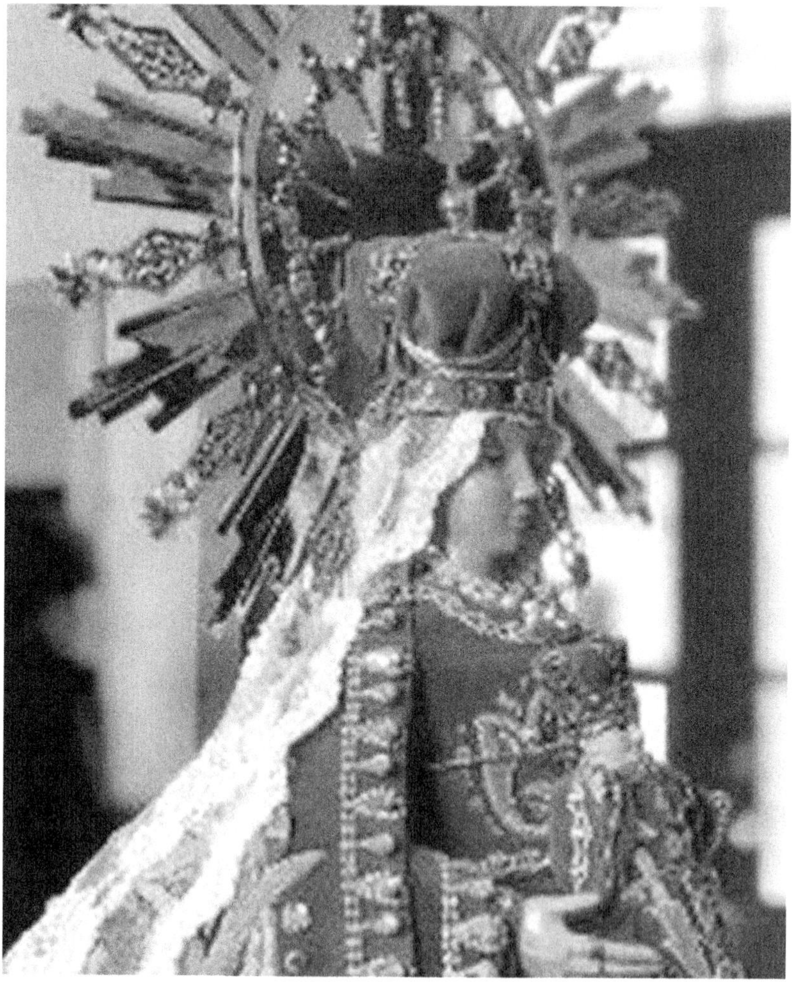

LA VIRGEN DEL BUEN SUCESO, SANTIAGO TIANGUISTENCO

La Virgen del Buen Suceso is often called in English, "Our Lady of Good Success," or "Our Lady of Good Events." The image of this Virgin and her veneration is traced back to two statues from the early days of the Spanish Empire, the mid-1500s. One statue was enshrined in Madrid while the other was taken to the town of Parañaque, located just south of Manila in the Spanish Philippines. According to the official story of Our Lady of Good Success, the statue in Madrid was found by two brothers from the Order of Saint Francis of Paola who found it in a cave while on a journey to Rome. The statue was cradling the Christ child in one arm and holding a scepter in the other. The Virgin was elaborately dressed and topped with a very intricate golden crown. The brothers carried the statue to Rome and told the pope of their miraculous discovery. The pope made the Virgin the protectoress of the Order of Saint Francis of Paola, also known as the Brothers Minor in Service of the Sick. This is how the statue ended up in the Royal Hospital in Madrid, under the care of these brothers. The owners of the Atencio Hacienda in the Mexican state of México had a small chapel dedicated to La Virgen de Buen Suceso on their property. It was a local pilgrimage site and became particularly important in 1853 when the countryside was ravaged by a cholera epidemic. As a health-related Virgin, the locals believed in her power to heal and claimed many miracles and answered prayers related to the statue. The Atencio family loaned the Virgin out to the nearby town of San Pedro Tlaltizapan in 1866 when it experienced a very devastating smallpox epidemic which especially afflicted children. The statue was placed in the local church and within two days the smallpox epidemic ended. On the morning of the third day the caretakers of the church noticed that the Baby Jesus cradled in the arm of the Virgin was covered in spots. The faithful believed that the Baby Jesus had somehow absorbed or otherwise transferred the pox from the afflicted locals. During the 1860s there was great conflict between Church and State in Mexico and many church properties were confiscated by the government. Because this famous Virgin had a gold crown and thus had monetary value, La Virgen de Buen Suceso was hidden in the town of Santiago Tianguistenco and her devotion was held in secret. In 1912 and 1913, during the Mexican Revolution, the town was captured by forces loyal to Emiliano Zapata. The people of Santiago Tianguistenco prayed to the Virgin of Good Success for their liberation and when the Zapatista forces left, she was given credit for their departure. It wasn't until 1919 that the statue itself resurfaced and public celebrations resumed with her official saint's day fixed on January 1st. In 1947 Pope Pius XII granted the pontifical coronation to La Virgen del Buen Suceso Santiago Tianguistenco in recognition of her power to cure the sick and to intercede in times of trouble. The small shrine in this town receives thousands of visitors annually.

LA VIRGEN GIGANTE DE XICOTEPEC

In the northern sierra region of the state of Puebla a sleepy mountain town called Xicotepec de Juárez is home to one of Mexico's newest Virgin Mary shrines. It is known in Mexico as "Monumental Virgen de Guadalupe," or "The Monumental Virgin of Guadalupe." For many years this town, whose unofficial motto is, "Wait 20 minutes and the weather will change," wanted to do more to attract tourists. This gigantic, colorful statue of the iconic Virgin of Guadalupe measures some 75 feet tall and is made of hollowed-out cement. It stands looming over the city on Tabacal Hill in the northern part of Xicotepec. This hill was important because it was here in 1949 that a silhouette of the Virgin of Guadalupe appeared in a broken half of a stone that was being quarried for a building project. Because of this usual occurrence, the locals decided to build a small chapel to the Virgin of Guadalupe on Tabacal Hill. The shrine received a steady trickle of visitors, especially on December 12th which is the feast day of the Virgin of Guadalupe. City officials wanted to expand the shrine and do something impactful that would draw even more tourists and pilgrims to Xicotepec. So, in the early 2000s a grassroots campaign began to raise money for a gigantic statue for Tabacal Hill. Construction on the "Virgen Monumental" began in October of 2006 and concluded on December 5, 2010. No machinery was used in the building of this statue and much of the work was done by volunteers from the town or surrounding area. As the statue is hollow, an inside staircase leads to a cramped observation deck inside the Virgin's head with her eyes serving as windows. This was closed down within a few months as local religious leaders claimed that there was too much horseplay and goofing off happening inside the statue which was not appropriate for such a solemn monument. Since its completion in late 2010 the gigantic statue – some say the largest outside statue of the Virgin of Guadalupe in the world – has attracted tens of thousands of visitors. Two years after the statue's dedication, Xicotepec was granted "Pueblo Mágico," or "Magical Town" status by the Mexican government which put it on the map as a prime tourist destination. In 2018 the town constructed a gigantic cross on another part of Tabacal Hill and built a series of stairs connecting the cross with the Plaza de la Virgen de Guadalupe surrounding the statue. If the recent increase in visitors to Xicotepec is any indication, La Virgen Gigante de Xicotepec may turn into one of the most popular religious shrines in all of Mexico.

NUESTRA SEÑORA DE TONATICO

In the Mexican state of México halfway between the silver town of Taxco and the arts and crafts center of Metepec, a small town called Tonatico has an interesting religious history. When the Dominicans, Franciscans and Augustinians were busy converting the local Nahua people to Christianity, one of the townsfolk found a wooden female statue in the woods. History does not record if the sculpture was indigenous in origin or European, only that the face of this female carving was looking down. The person who discovered this statue took it to a local Catholic priest who dressed it up in fancy silk clothes and proclaimed it to be the Virgin Mary, formally naming her Our Lady of Tonatico. In the late 1500s the religious authorities in the town built a special chapel to house the Virgin and many people from the countryside came to venerate her, claiming she was responsible for various miracles and intercessions. Sometime in the 1650s, the church at Tonatico burned to the ground with the statue of Nuestra Señora de Tonatico the only thing to survive the massive fire unscathed. Although untouched by the flames, worshippers were quick to notice that the face of the statue now looked up and had a smile instead of having a serious expression and looking down. This miraculous change in the image gave people hope for a better future and news of the transformation caused more people to come to Tonatico to pay their respects to the Virgin. By 1660 a new church was built, and this is the same place where the statue rests to this day. With its domed top, two steeples and ornate interior, the Sanctuary of Our Lady of Tonatico is an architectural jewel of the region. A special side room at the *santuario* is reserved for votive offerings and on any given day one can see a thousand or so devotional objects left by pilgrims. These may range from the personal, such as the shoes of a baby cured of an illness, to the elaborate, including everything from specially commissioned ex voto paintings to solid gold milagro charms. The fiesta in honor of Our Lady of Tonatico is considered one of the most important religious festivals in the region. It begins each year on the last Sunday of January and ends on February 2, Candlemas Day. During this time, Tonatico receives pilgrims from all corners of the municipality, and from towns nearby in the states of Guerrero and Morelos. Those from the region who live abroad often make the trip back home during fiesta time, thanking the Virgin for a safe journey and for keeping them out of harm's way in their new homelands.

NUESTRA SEÑORA DE LA SOLEDAD DE ACAPULCO

Located in the central square of Acapulco, Mexico's oldest Pacific port, is the rather out-of-place Acapulco Cathedral consecrated to Our Lady of Solitude. The building looks more like a mosque with its domed towers and other architectural elements combining Moorish and Byzantine styles. This place of worship did not always look this way. On the spot of this blue, white and gold building, one of the oldest churches on the Pacific coast was built in the early 1530s to serve the growing port which would develop into a main stop in Spain's galleon trade with the Far East. In 1556, newly crowned King Phillip II of Spain gave the city of Acapulco an important gift: a beautiful carving of the Virgin Mary as Our Lady of Solitude. The king of Spain would have the statue made into a general of the Spanish Army as a symbolic gesture of earthly protection to guard Spanish interests in the Pacific. The beautiful statue drew many pilgrims and those engaged in trans-Pacific trade with the Orient would visit her to ensure a successful and profitable voyage. In her role as protectoress of Acapulco, the Virgin has proved unconquerable. Over the many centuries of her residency in this beautiful port city she has born witness to violent tropical storms, fires, floods, pirate attacks and various degrees of civil unrest. Additionally, she has been housed in ever changing structures which have seen many renovations, partial demolitions and outright destruction. In 1909 an earthquake collapsed the roof of the cathedral. It was rebuilt, only to be destroyed again by a cyclone in 1938. Throughout all these calamities, the statue of the Virgin of Solitude survived unharmed which seemed only to intensify the faith of the true believers who saw her as a very generous giver of miracles. To this day, locals pray to her and visit her to ask for help in impossible situations. Hundreds of thousands of people across time can testify to her enduring power.

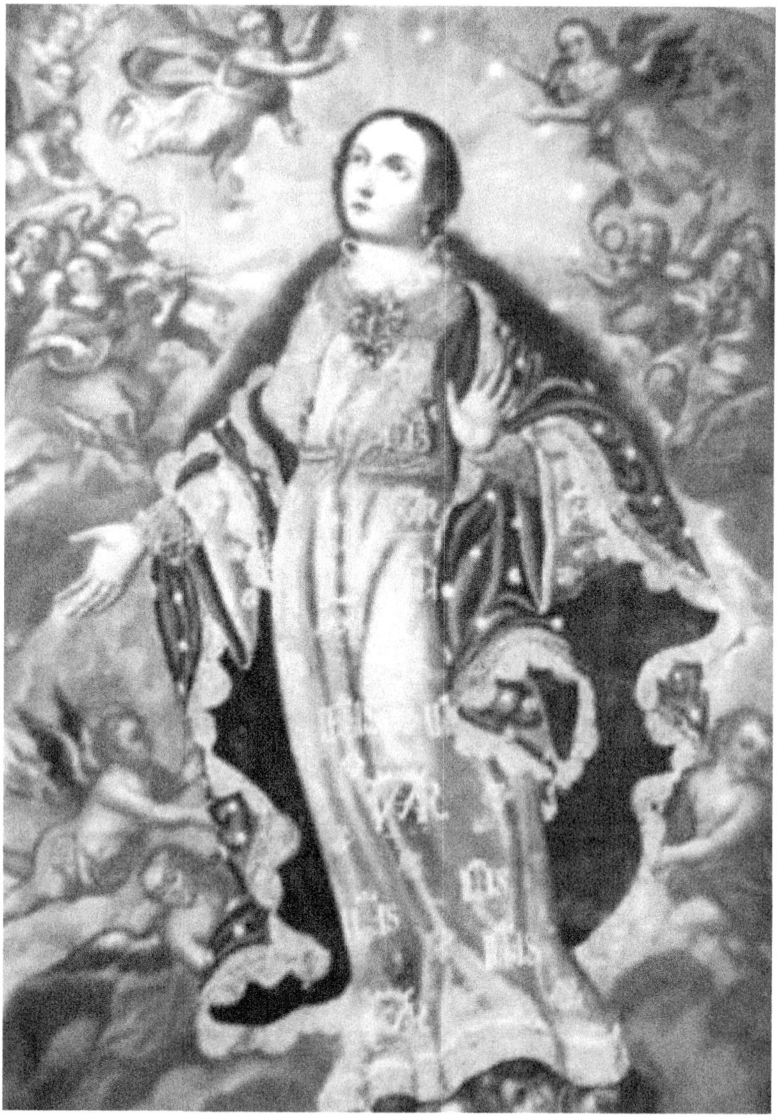

NUESTRA SEÑORA DE TZOCUILAC

A few miles southeast of the city of Puebla is the tiny town of Tzocuilac. The name of the town comes from a now-extinct Nahuatl dialect and for many years its meaning has puzzled researchers. The name Tzocuilac may come from two words, *zocuitl*, "mud", and *cuitlatl*, meaning "dirt" or "excrement" in English. Other language scholars believe the name derives from *tzocuitl*, meaning "painting", and *cuilac*, which translates to "that appears." The latter interpretation of "Painting that appears" makes more sense in the context of the story of Our Lady of Tzocuilac. From a book written in 1910 about this particular virgin, the author, Father Francisco Hernández says this about the origins of this sacred image:

"A well-stationed and pious cacique, named Antonio Abab Xilotl, had an image of the Blessed Virgin painted on the walls of his house. The cacique died when the plague called *matlazahuatl* decimated the indigenous people. As he did not leave anyone to take care of the house, it was soon ruined, the roofs collapsed and only walls were left as a den for vermin and a shelter for buzzards, which littered the walls. For many years, the image of the Blessed Virgin was exposed to rain, sun, air and frost, without the painting being damaged by the force of these elements, nor by the roots of the herbs that crumble the walls, annihilating its colors and smoothness. One day the wall of the front of the walls that kept such a beautiful relic collapsed and this circumstance led to the prodigious appearance."

The story continues with a local priest ordering that the image be erased from the wall because he did not want it to be subject to any sort of desecration. The locals complied and scraped the image off the wall. The next Sunday, the image re-appeared on the same wall. When the priest passed by, he thought that the villagers had not obeyed his orders and asked sternly that the painting be erased again. So it was, and it appeared once more on the same crumbly wall. The priest saw the image again and became angry. Why were these people so disobedient? The frustrated father decided to scrape the wall himself. The next Sunday, he walked by and saw that the image had appeared again. Unable to explain what was going on, he declared that God was the artist who made sure the image had stayed fixed on the wall.

That old adobe wall eventually succumbed to the elements and crumbled away, but not before an artist managed to recreate the image of the Virgin on a canvas which now hangs in the local church at Tzocuilac. The current painting housed in the humble church has changed since the original image was painted sometime in the 17th Century. The portrait is of a very European-looking woman, traditionally styled as the Assumption of the Virgin Mary, with the twelve fine stars, which look like jewels, radiating from her head. She has her hands open, as if in expectation, and has thick black hair that spreads over her shoulders and her flowing cloak. The accompanying angels were painted later and date to sometime in the 18th century. The two cherubs above the Virgin's head are raising their arms as if ready to hold something. Perhaps the artist who added these angels was also supposed to add a crown but did not finish his work. In the year 1825 gold was painted on the canvas by an artist known to history as Don Feliciano Tello, and this was the last revision to the centuries-old piece.

Because the Virgin on the original adobe wall was associated with appearing after a plague, throughout the years many people in the region have prayed to Nuestra Señora de Tzocuilac in times of epidemics. In the great plague of 1731 and again during a typhus epidemic in 1915, thousands of people prayed to the Virgin to end the mass sicknesses and then gave credit to her when people became suddenly cured. August 15th is her feast day, and many people make the journey to the small village of Tzocuilac to pray in front of this miraculous image and to give thanks.

LA SANTISIMA MADRE DE LA LUZ

The story of this Mexican Virgin, known in English as The Most Holy Mother of Light, begins on the Italian island of Sicily sometime in the early 1720s. An Italian Jesuit, Father Juan Antonio Genovesi, was preparing for his future missionary work in the New World and wanted to emphasize the devotion to the Virgin Mary. Father Genovesi decided he would have a painting commissioned in Italy to take with him to Mexico. The Jesuit wanted a woman to inspire the creation of the painting, and there are a few versions of the story as to who this woman was. Some say it was a nun, others say it was a very holy woman prone to having religious visions and premonitions. Others say that it was the Virgin Mary herself who would guide the painter to create the image. In either story, the artist's hand was guided by some sort of supernatural presence or heavenly grace, and the final image is an interesting one. The painting represents Mary with a slight smile on her face looking directly at the viewer. She is carrying the Baby Jesus in her left arm. The Christ Child grabs a heart in his right hand, and with his left he takes another from a basket full of hearts presented to him by a kneeling angel. The Virgin stops with her right hand a soul about to fall into the jaws of a dragon that represents the sinner and hell. Two chubby angels keep an imperial crown on the Virgin's head. Three seraphim are under her feet, and others on each side complete the picture. In the year 1732 the painting of La Madre Santisima de la Luz arrived in New Spain. Church officials conducted a lottery and whichever diocese was drawn in the contest would get the painting. The city of León in the modern Mexican state of Guanajuato was the winner. On May 23, 1849, Our Most Holy Mother of Light was officially made patroness of León. She became a regional draw as many people in the surrounding area credited the Virgin with many miracles and intercessions. On October 8, 1902, the Celestial Lady was solemnly crowned by Bishop Leopoldo Ruiz y Flores, thanks to the concession made by Pope Leo XIII, on March 23, 1901. Over the years the image of this virgin has been copied and other likenesses of the Virgen de la Luz in Mexico are found in the Franciscan mission of

Tancoyol, in Sierra Gorda, Querétaro; in the church of San Cayetano, in Valenciana, Guanajuato; in the Church of Nuestra Señora de la Luz in Puebla, as well as in the Metropolitan Cathedral in Mexico City.

LA VIRGEN DE LA IMACULADA CONCEPCIÓN DE CHIGNAHUAPAN

In the northern mountainous part of the state of Puebla near the borders of states of Tlaxcala and Hidalgo lies the small town of Chignahuapan, home to a most unusual Virgin Mary. In the local Nahuatl dialect, the name Chignahuapan means, "Over the Nine Waters." For thousands of years the hot springs outside of town have been known for their curative powers and many peoples throughout ancient Mexico made the trip to Chignahuapan as a health pilgrimage of sorts. The local thermal baths still draw tourists by the thousands to this area annually. In addition to the tourism generated by the hot springs, the town is known for its production of Christmas ornaments. Some 500 artists live in Chignahuapan and for generations the people here have made beautiful glass baubles that are shipped all over the world. A relatively more modern attraction in this "magical town" is the gigantic statue of the Virgin of the Immaculate Conception that draws more non-secular visitors than traditional pilgrims.

In 1960 Father Idelfonso Illescas Pichardo, seeing that his parish was insufficient to house the number of faithful who came, took the initiative to build a larger church to house the parishioners. Twelve years later, on May 12, 1972, the church was inaugurated and, on this day also, the largest indoor religious sculpture in all Latin America was unveiled. A sculptor from the city of Puebla named José Luis Silva carved the gigantic 39-foot-tall Virgin out of cedar wood. The original design did not include the Baby Jesus, but the final product included the Christ Child with an outstretched hand holding a dove. The Virgin Mary herself looks very contemporary to the 1970s. With high cheekbones, bright blue eyes and a Charlie's Angels feathered hairstyle, she seems more like a product of Hollywood than a sacred image of the Catholic Church. In 1999 her home, the Church of the Immaculate Conception, was given the designation of "Minor Basilica." With that upgrade, the Virgin of Chignahuapan was given a pontifical crown with the blessings of Pope John Paul the Second. Also made of cedar wood, the 3-foot-tall crown is covered in gold leaf and inlaid with dozens of precious jewels. The sight of this sculpture leaves most sightseers breathless. The Minor Basilica of the Immaculate Conception receives about 5,000 visitors per month, and this may increase to about 15,000 in December. The feast day to this gigantic virgin is December 8th and on that day the church is filled with thousands of flowers which adorn the walls and are scattered on the floor. Perhaps owing to its contemporary nature, the fiestas for the Virgin of Chignahuapan are not as long-lasting as in other Mexican villages and take place only across a few days. During this holy time more pilgrims visit the image than secular tourists. As time has passed, devotees traveling to this shrine have increased and sometime soon this massive statue may be the focal point of a strong religious pilgrimage.

CRISTOS

Although not as common as shrines to the Virgin Mary, pilgrimage sites dedicated to a local image of Jesus are found throughout Mexico. Even rarer is Christ appearing in apparitions. One of the very first and perhaps the most famous appearance of Jesus happened in Mexico in the 19th Century after a devastating earthquake. As with shrines to Jesus' earthly mother, sites dedicated to Christ attract devotees from the local areas to the rest of Mexico and beyond.

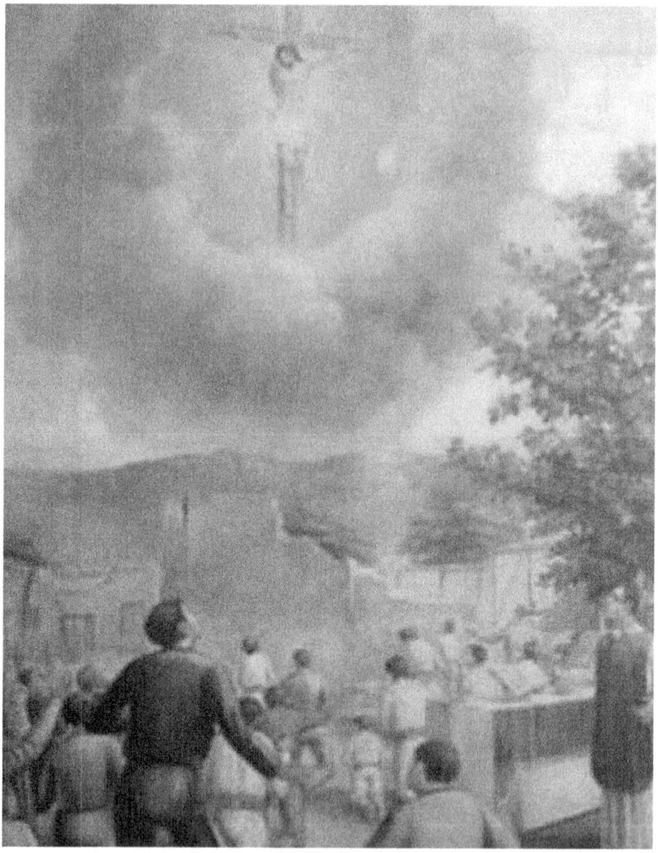

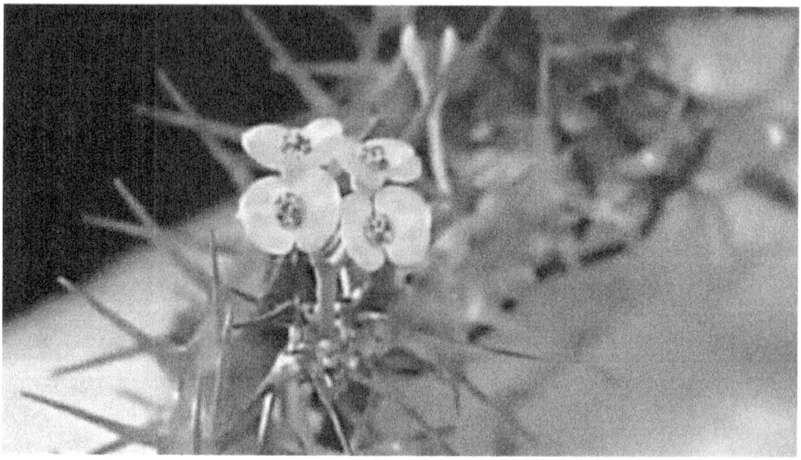

JESUS IN THE SKY AND
THE FLOWERING CROWN OF THORNS

In December of 2010 television crews from all over Latin America came to the town of Ocotlán in the Mexican state of Jalisco. Among them was Spanish-language broadcast giant Univisión which sent a film crew from their show "Primer Impacto" to cover what people throughout the region were considering to be a miracle. In the Basilica to Our Lord of Mercy something unusual was happening on the main crucifix behind the altar, the crown of thorns on the head of Jesus began to sprout flowers. The crown, which had been made from a thorny desert plant that had been twisted into a circle, had been taken off the Jesus when Father Miguel Angel González noticed a sprout which had appeared in the back of the crown in early November of 2010. By the time of the filming of the "Primer Impacto" episode about this event, the crown of thorns had been removed from the Jesus and put under glass and monitored by security cameras. When the television crew filmed the sacred object, it had several pink, trumpet-like flowers coming out of it and a few other green shoots with leaves. Faithful from the town of Ocotlán and the surrounding areas formed a line to view the crown, and the flowers seemed extra special because it was the week before Christmas. The resident priest talked briefly about the history of this specific crown of thorns. It was given to the church as a gift in 1994 by a new bride after a wedding. The crown was placed at the foot of the cross and then moved to rest on the praying hands of a statue of the Virgin of Dolores. From the Virgin statue it was moved to its rightful place on top of the *Cristo* on the main crucifix in the basilica. In addition to Father Miguel Angel, the Univisión reporter also spoke with two parishioners about what they were witnessing. Gerardo Moreno stated calmly and evenly, "It's a message because everything is pretty bad. I think that this is a sign." Juan Manuel Nuñez, an older man with tears in his eyes trembled when he told the reporter, "I am a believer, a believer in God. It's a warning, a warning of something." Like most people who visited the object, the locals interviewed were not sure exactly what they were seeing, only that it was somehow supernaturally inspired and seemed to underscore their already strong religious beliefs. Father Miguel Angel assured the public that the church was going to great lengths to investigate the phenomenon and promised to keep the relic under glass with round-the-clock monitoring by security cameras to prove that the crown was not being tampered with. The "Primer Impacto" show ended by telling its viewers that the University of Guadalajara was going to make a thorough scientific investigation of the crown and would make its findings public. The intrusion of science into the realm of faith was largely ignored by the multitudes of people who came to the basilica to witness what they were claiming was the *second* miracle at Octotlán, the first one occurring on the same spot some 153 years before.

The name "Ocotlán" comes from the language of the Aztecs, Nahuatl, and is a combination of two words, "*ocotl*," or "pine tree" in English and "*tlan*," which means "place of," in English: "Place of the pine trees." The town sits on the shores of Lake Chapala where the Zuma and Santiago rivers pour into the lake. The climate is temperate, the air is fresh, and the soils are rich. A thriving indigenous settlement existed there when the Spanish first arrived in 1530 and the area had been long occupied by the Otancas, Texuexes, Tepehuanes and Coanos. One of the first major battles of conquistador Nuño de Guzmán happened at Ocotlán and when the local native kingdom was defeated, the Spanish established a permanent presence, building a hospital and a chapel dedicated to the Virgin of the Immaculate Conception under the direction of the Franciscans. The Virgin at Ocotlán quickly became known as "The Patroness of the Indians" and the building to house her became a regional pilgrimage site. Parts of that chapel still exist today, and it is considered to be one of the oldest buildings in the Mexican state of Jalisco.

By the mid-1840s the town had become known as a place of vice and licentiousness, so the history goes. All of that changed abruptly on October 2, 1847. A massive earthquake hit the town leveling most buildings and causing the rest to be uninhabitable. There was much misery and death and the survivors in this town of 1,500 people were in a state of shock. In the day following the quake, the mayor of Ocotlán, Juan Antonio Ximénez wrote a letter to the governor of the state of Jalisco. The letter survives. The mayor writes:

"Yesterday, Saturday the 2nd at seven thirty in the morning a strong earthquake, which lasted more than five minutes was felt in this town. It did not, however, cause any damage. The repetition, happening between nine and ten o'clock on the same morning, was terrible. In an instant, some of the town's buildings were knocked down, and the others were completely destroyed or in imminent danger of collapse.
As of yesterday, 46 persons of both sexes, and of various ages, had been found dead, and it is not possible now to know with certainty the number of injured and wounded who miraculously escaped the destruction.
It was not only the town that suffered this misfortune. The same thing occurred in all the other places in the municipality. There was terror and fright everywhere, especially when rocks broke away from the hill and the wild animals were terrified."

The mayor's last paragraph in this letter surely rose the eyebrows of the governor of Jalisco. Mayor Ximénez continues:
"This morning, Your Excellency, 24 hours after the unfortunate events, the perfect image of Our Lord Jesus Christ on the Cross was seen between west and north, formed between two clouds and lasting for half an hour, in which time more than 1,500 people who were in the plaza fell to their knees, performing acts of contrition and crying to the Lord to show mercy."
What the mayor described would be later called the miraculous appearance of *El Señor de la Misericordia*, or in English, Our Lord of Mercy. According to the survivors of the town, the day after the quake, a Sunday, everyone was gathered in the Plaza de Armas of Ocotlán, to celebrate an open-air mass because the ruined church was unfit for services. An image of Jesus appeared in the clouds sometime during the 9:00 hour. The image has been described as everything from a fluffy cloud formation in the shape of a cross to a glimmering perfect image of a crucified Christ on whose face was an expression combining love and reassurance. The image was said to

have hovered to the northwest before slowly disappearing. People in the surrounding rural areas also reported seeing the image of Jesus in the clouds. Word of this miracle spread throughout the region and Ocotlán became the focus of a new pilgrimage for people wanting to venerate what was being called the Lord of Mercy. By 1875 a new church was built to honor this manifestation of Jesus and was further expanded to the basilica complex that exists in Ocotlán to this day. With time, the event became more formalized and documented. In 1897, for the 50th anniversary of the apparition, Archbishop of Guadalajara, Pedro Loza y Pardavé, felt it necessary to take down written testimonies of the remaining 30 people who witnessed the event in 1847. By the 1890s most of Mexico had heard of the apparition and the word of the miraculous appearance was gaining international interest. Local church authorities sought to formalize and further legitimize the event and on September 29, 1911, Cardinal José de Jesús Ortiz y Rodríguez, the Archbishop of Guadalajara, signed a document acknowledging the 1897 written testimonies and proclaiming the event of 1847 as "The Miracle of Ocotlán." In his pronouncement, the cardinal wrote:

"We must acknowledge as a historical fact, perfectly proven, the apparition of the blessed image of Jesus Christ Crucified...and that it could not have been the work of a hallucination or fraud, since it happened in broad daylight, in the sight of more than 2,000 people."

In addition, Cardinal Ortíz y Rodríguez established a formal feast day to recognize Our Lord of Mercy. In his proclamation, the cardinal continues:

"(Townsfolk) must gather together in whatever manner possible, after purifying their consciences with the holy sacraments of Penance and Holy Communion and solemnly swear in the presence of God, for themselves and their descendants, that year after year they will celebrate the October 3 anniversary."

The following year, 1912, the formal feast to the Lord of Mercy began, which starts every September 20th and ends on the date of the apparition, October 3rd, a full 13 days of celebration, contemplation and contrition.

What does the Vatican think of this event? While not formally recognizing it as it has the appearances of the Virgin Mary – Lourdes, Guadalupe, and Fatima – it has given its tacit recognition of its miraculous nature. In 1997, on the 150th anniversary of the appearance of Jesus in the sky, Pope John Paul II sent an apostolic blessing to the people of Ocotlán acknowledging the importance of the event. To many Mexican Catholics, the first miracle at Ocotlán is the only legitimate appearance of Jesus as an apparition in the entire world. Pilgrims continue to visit the basilica to see the place where the event took place and recently, to see the second miracle, the flowering crown of thorns. In the time since both the appearance of Jesus in the sky and the unexpected sprouting of the crown of thorns, many people have come forth to debunk or "re-explain" what has happened at Ocotlán. The University of Guadalajara did issue its scientific explanation for the miracle of the flowering crown in early 2011. In its comprehensive report, university scientists stated that the plant from which the crown was made – known by its scientific name, *euphorbia milii* – is a hardy desert plant that can go years without water. Seeds may stay dormant for decades and are activated by the slightest indications of moisture. So, after 15+ years of being "inactive," the plant the crown was made of "came to life," presumably because of humidity in the room or the coalescing of water droplets on the back of the head of the statue on which the crown rested. To the faithful, although the story may seem thoroughly explained and even well-intentioned, the flowering crown of thorns remains a miracle.

The appearance of Jesus in the sky has gotten more scrutiny over the years simply because it happened so long ago and there is nothing that exists from that event like the crown of thorns that can physically be tested. On the TV show, "Extranormal," shown on the LA-based Spanish language broadcast television network Azteca America, the hosts discussed the 1847 apparition over Ocotlán after a documentary segment presenting a timeline and describing events. The scientists – a physicist and a psychologist – came up with standard explanations of mass hallucination and tricks of light in the sky playing with the minds of a beleaguered and desperate population. The show's resident parapsychologist, Laura Rivas, had a different explanation for the events at Ocotlán. She said that the area is the site of an energy vortex and a tonal focal point, and many paranormal events have occurred in the area and will occur in the area. Indeed, the Franciscans established the very popular Virgin of the Immaculate Conception shrine at Ocotlán in the 1530s for a reason: The location had already been known to be a somewhat holy place. Whether or not either or some parts of the miracles are true or whatever scientific explanation is put forth, pilgrims will keep making the trip to Ocotlán. The Jesus in the Sky and the flowering crown of thorns will always be in the collective Mexican memory to connect the true believers to the divine.

THE BLACK CHRIST OF OTATITLÁN

From the 1920s and into the 1930s the country of Mexico was in the grips of the Cristero War. The war pit pro-Catholic forces against those of secular politicians who wanted a strict separation of church and state in accordance with the 1917 constitution. On September 8, 1931, a group of anti-Catholics under the direction of the governor of the Mexican state of Veracruz – Adalberto Tejeda – broke into the small church of San Andrés Apóstol in the town of Otatitlán. Their goal was the removal and destruction of the prime object of veneration at that small church: A black crucified Christ. Called the Cristo Negro de Otatitlán, the black carving had been the subject of countless pilgrimages over the centuries and had been credited with working an untold number of miracles. The armed men removed the *cristo* to the tears and protests of the townsfolk. It was carried away to someplace out of town. Although the carving was made of centuries-old wood, when the men tried to burn it, it did not catch fire. Even after emptying an entire can of gasoline on the black image of the crucified Christ, it would not burn. Exasperated, the men took a hack saw and cut off the carving's head, leaving the decapitated body behind. The faithful waited for the pro-Tejeda forces to leave town before they rescued their precious relic which was now headless but otherwise unharmed. The fact that the *cristo* could not burn was evidence to the faithful of a miraculous sign from Heaven. They brought it back to the church. By the end of 1931 masses were suspended in Otatitlán. The government ordered the parish priest arrested and the church locked. In 1932 the annual fiesta to celebrate the Black Christ of Otatitlán was suspended by the Tejeda government. When the Veracruz secular authorities lifted all religious restrictions in 1933, the Church of San Andrés Apóstol re-opened to the public and the veneration and annual fiesta resumed. An artist named Olaguibel carved another head and it perfectly matched the head that was sawed off. The original head of the sculpture mysteriously appeared at the front of the door of the church sometime in 1950 and was restored to the *cristo*. To this day, Olaguibel's replacement head is on view under glass at the San Andrés Apóstol church in Otatitlán.

There are two stories involving how the Black Christ ended up in Otatitlán. Both are promoted by the church, and it is up to the individual to discern which one could be the real story.

The first story takes place a little upriver from Otatitlán. It can be traced to a document written in 1746 by José Villaseñor y Sánchez who collected testimonies and investigated the archives at the Otatitlán church. According to this version of the story, two mysterious travelers showed up at the house of a local indigenous man sometime in the 1590s. The travelers saw that the man had a large piece of cedar and asked if they could use that cedar block to make a carving of Christ since they were expert carvers. The indigenous man agreed. The next morning when the man awoke that block of wood was now something else. It had been carved into the Black Christ overnight by the two strangers. They also left behind food and pieces of silver as gifts for the man. No one in the village had ever seen these two men before and immediately people claimed that they were angels disguised as men. The *cristo* traveled from village to village before finding a more permanent home at San Andrés Apóstol in Otatitlán.

The second origin story gives the *cristo* carving an earthlier provenance. This story comes from the writings of Antonio de Alcedo y Bejarano, a soldier and scholar, and the son of a Spanish colonial official who was posted to various locations in the New World. Alcedo himself was born outside of Quito in what is now Ecuador but traveled throughout the Spanish possessions in the Americas. Between 1786 and 1789 Alcedo wrote a massive 5-volume encyclopedia about the New World. He combined his firsthand experience with over 300 sources he compiled over 20 years. The sources ranged from church documents and diaries of individual clergy members to bland government records and papers from military archives. Alcedo's great work was so comprehensive and so detailed that the King of Spain, Charles IV, prohibited export of the book from Spain for fear of giving enemy nations vital information of His Majesty's overseas territories. In his encyclopedia Alcedo references the Black Christ of Otatitlán and mentions that it was one of three darker Jesus images that were sent to the New World at the same time in the late 1590s. The other carvings went to Espuipulas in modern-day Guatemala and to Chalma located in the modern Mexican state of México. Alcedo notes in his encyclopedia that in September of 1595 the king of Spain, Phillip II, commissioned an artist named Juan Donnier to carve the three black Christs. The price for each was 6,900 Marks. The sculptures were delivered to the court at Madrid on January 9, 1596, and then sent to New Spain. On April 20, 1596, the sculptures arrived at the Veracruz port of Villa Rica and went their separate ways. The one destined for Otatitlán arrived at the mouth of the Papaloapan River two days later for its journey upstream. On April 28, 1596, the *cristo* arrived at Puctlancingo, a place where missionaries were in the process of converting the indigenous locals. It remained there until February of 1597. At that time an epidemic of smallpox wiped out most of the population of Puctlancingo and the survivors moved to the small Spanish settlement called San Andrés Apóstol also known by its indigenous name of Otatitlán, which may mean either "The Place of the Tamarind Trees" or "The Place of the Bendable Bamboo." The sculpture immediately attracted pilgrims and helped convert the remaining natives in the region to Christianity. The *cristo* remained in the church of San Andrés Apóstol until it was moved to the town of Chacaltianguis in 1838 for two years. Since 1840 it has remained in Otatitlán.

Why was the image of Jesus black? Why were these three special Christ statues sent to these three specific areas? Guatemalan anthropologist and writer Carlos Navarrete has an interesting theory regarding the complexion and placement of these carvings. He noticed that the Spanish installed all three of these dark *cristos* at key spots in ancient overland trading routes of the *pochteca*, the class of Aztec traveling merchants which connected far-flung parts of Mesoamerica through commerce. The commission to create the black Christ statues came from the highest levels of the Spanish government. The king and his advisors knew what they were doing. A few generations after the Spanish Conquest many indigenous people throughout New Spain were starting to question Catholicism. They were becoming curious about their ancient religions, the belief systems of their grandparents and great-grandparents. In some parts of the Spanish Americas the clergy felt their hold slowly slipping. How could the Spanish strengthen the church's position in its colonies? The answer to that question varied depending on the region and the circumstances. If Navarrete's theory is correct, the three black Christs not only went to strategic areas, but the black color of the statues was also very intentional. As previously mentioned, these three places, Chalma, Esquipulas and Otatitlán were important way stations or hubs on the old overland trading routes. As such, they were also sites that included pre-existing shrines, shrines to the dark-colored god of trade and travelers called Yacatecuhtli.

In the language of the Aztecs, Nahuatl, "Yacatecuhtli" combines two words, *yacatl*, which means "nose" in English, and *tecuhtli* which means lord. So, this god's name literally means "lord of the noses." It was said that the god could sniff out bargains and he used his nose to point the traveling merchants in the right direction in their journeys. The god was worshipped wherever merchants stopped for the night, so key places on the trade routes has small shrines to Yacatecuhtli. Before turning in for the evening, merchants would bundle together sticks and put blood from their earlobes on the bundles as offerings to the god for nighttime protection from bandits and predatory wild animals. In iconography Yacatecuhtli was often depicted as being dark-skinned. He was also portrayed as carrying a large cross on his back, to symbolize the four directions. It's no wonder that when the carved black figures of the crucified Christ arrived at the three destinations that the locals became instant devotees and converts. The Spanish had used the former beliefs present in these three areas and brought a new god that was easy for the indigenous people to digest. This was not the first nor the last time that Christianity slightly bended to local traditions to solidify its own power over a newly converted population. Anthropologists call this blending of old and new beliefs "syncretism." This is why we have an Easter bunny and why people decorate Christmas trees with brightly colored bulbs to celebrate the birth of Christ.

Even more than four centuries later, some syncretism still exists, and indigenous traditions survive in connection with festivities surrounding the Black Christ of Otatitlán. After the mass to honor the *cristo* it is not uncommon for a Mazatec shaman to perform a cleansing ritual in the streets of the town. Besides the indigenous undertones, the celebrations for this important devotional object are typical Mexican fiesta fare. The major feast day for Black Christ of Otatitlán is May 3rd, which also coincides with the Day of the Cross on the Latin American liturgical calendar. Festivities in this town of 5,000 people usually begin on April 28th and end on May 7th. Over the course of the 10 days of the fiesta some 150,000 people attend the various events connected to the celebration. Pilgrims come mostly from the states of Veracruz and Oaxaca, but the entire nation of Mexico is represented among the multitude of attendees. In a tradition that started with the 400th anniversary of the Black Christ of Otatitlán in 1997, every year the statue is taken overland 15 kilometers between the states of Oaxaca and Veracruz. At the end of the 15-kilometer procession, the *cristo* is placed on a large raft and floated down the Papaloapan River much as it did in its early days during its first move from Puctlancingo to Otatitlán. Devotees follow along in small boats or swim partway. Since it often rains during that time of year in that part of Mexico, the Black Christ is often traveling under several sheets of plastic. Like many other saints and virgins in Mexico, the Black Christ of Otatitlán is credited with many miracles. Throughout the year, thousands of people travel from many miles to visit the shrine in this small town to give thanks to this incredible image or perhaps to seek a miracle of their own.

THE LUCKY BABY JESUS OF TLALPAN

    The year was 1806. Two young priests were walking on a remote back road in a wooded area of what would later be the Distrito Federal or Federal District of the independent nation of Mexico. The place then was part of New Spain and the monster that is now Mexico City was a long way from this remote country road. Headed to the small town of Santiago Tepalcatlalpan the two young priests heard the cries of a young boy. They were surprised because they had not seen anyone on the road in hours and the area around them was wilderness. Concerned, they began to search the surroundings. When they approached the place where the crying came from, they encountered a small carved wooden image of the Baby Jesus who was sleeping peacefully on a skull. As they got closer to this serene image, water started bubbling up out of the ground. Today, this very spot is known as "*El Ojo del Niño,*" or "*Eye of the Child,*" in English. The location around the spring would later become the site of the seminary of the Salesian Fathers. After the seminary was abandoned, the Mexican government built a tuberculosis sanitarium there. The groundwater has since been diverted and the greater Mexico City metropolitan area has grown, so now the place of the miraculous appearance of the Baby Jesus resting peacefully on a skull is part of the Niño Jesús neighborhood of the suburb of Tlalpan. What ever became of the curious statue?

    The two young priests gathered up the holy carving and brought it to Mexico City. There, they presented it to the Archbishop of Mexico, the very powerful Francisco Javier de Lizana y Beaumont who would later serve as the 58th Viceroy of New Spain. The archbishop was taken by the statue and proclaimed it a divine sign of the mercy of God. He wanted to find a special place for it so that it could be properly venerated. After consulting his council, Archbishop Lizana decided to hold a raffle to determine which religious community, church or shrine would be responsible for housing this unique artistic representation of the Baby Jesus. When the lots were drawn, the winner was the Convent of San Bernardo, run by mostly European-born Conceptionist nuns. The convent was in a state of disrepair and the nuns lived an austere, meager existence. The Archbishop of Mexico did not think this was an appropriate choice, so he ordered the raffle be taken again. In the second round, the Convent of San Bernardo was chosen again. So, the name of the convent was taken out of the contest altogether. During the third drawing, the name of the Convent of San Bernardo came up a third time, and seeing this as a sign from God, the archbishop relented and gave the statue to the nuns. The sisters of San Bernardo saw this as a gift from Heaven. The attention the statue would bring to their order would have many beneficial and long-lasting effects. Because of their good fortune in this raffle, the Mother Superior of the convent christened this holy carving "El Santo Niño de las Suertes" or "The Holy Child of Luck." Two hundred years later, it is still known as the Santo Niño de las Suertes and this unusual representation of the Baby Jesus has attracted millions of pilgrims from throughout Mexico and beyond.

The sculpture is polychrome on wood, created in the late 1700s or early 1800s and probably handcrafted in Europe. It is an image of a child of approximately four months of age, with a white complexion, eyes closed, lying on his side. Both his head and his arms rest on a skull that serves as a pillow. The baby and the skull imagery may be a curious mix to the uninitiated or to people not familiar with what this might mean. Some may see this as creepy or even bordering on the occult. Father José de Jesús Aguilar, a scholar and devotee to this holy image said this about the Santo Niño de las Suertes:

"It represents the sleeping (Christ) child lying on a human skull. It is a symbolic image that represents Christ's dominion over death. During the Baroque period, images of the Baby Jesus were created in which his passion, death and resurrection could be foreshadowed. Thus, we can see images of the Child Jesus with the cross or crucified, or with a thorn in his foot or in his hand and even with a crown of thorns on his head. The image of the Santo Niño de las Suertes would represent Christ sleeping, alluding to his rest in the tomb after his passion, a rest that would end with the resurrection and triumph over death."

In an interview with *Antropología*, the journal associated with the Mexican National Institute of Anthropology and History, a mother superior of the San Bernardo Convent further clarified the meaning of the imagery of this interesting Santo Niño. She stated:

"In the New Testament death is mentioned as one of the greatest evils, and it will be the last enemy that Christ subdues on the day of his second advent. Although Jesus died for our sins, at the end of time, when the resurrection is extended to all, the triumph over death will have been achieved. This sculpture illustrates the end of death promised by the birth of a baby. It also causes great admiration how, in such a tiny, inoffensive being, such greatness develops for human beings. The skull represents humanity; it is a redemption for us."

The nuns set up a small chapel dedicated to the Santo Niño de las Suertes that has changed little over time. Devotees can sit in rows of pews to contemplate the image or to pray, with the holy statue encased behind glass at the part of the chapel where the altar would be. A long, thin, neon bulb hanging from two wires illuminates the Santo Niño. His backdrop is made of a soft satin cloth covered in rows of milagros, the tiny metal charms given as tokens of thanks for miracles received. The baby is dressed in delicate clothing which is changed throughout the course of the year in accordance with the Catholic calendar.

As is typical of many such shrines in Mexico, faithful devotees have ascribed many miracles to the Santo Niño de las Suertes. Traditionally, he is seen as being responsible for interceding in matters of work, health, and even love. As the image represents the Christ Child, anything connected with children or pregnancy is within his realm as well. Because the word "luck" is associated with this statue, in modern times people have visited the shrine to help with gambling addictions or even for luck in winning games of chance or even the lottery, but the church frowns on those sorts of devotions. People have claimed that the Baby Jesus represented here has appeared to them incarnate, as a living, breathing being, whether it be at the edge of a hospital bed or in the desert alongside a struggling migrant crossing over to the

United States. Some construction workers building the new convent have also claimed to have seen this Baby Jesus appear at the construction site. Those who frequent the chapel or who have made various pilgrimages to see the Santo Niño, claim that his complexion changes color from pale white to bright pink depending on his mood. When asked about the statue's changing colors, one of the nuns remarked, "perhaps it is because he is sad for humanity." As with other shrines in Mexico, devotees leave behind toys, candles, ex voto paintings, handwritten letters and other assorted objects as offerings to the Baby Jesus. The area near the statue is cleaned of these objects periodically with toys donated to charity and devotional objects and other items of meaning carefully stored away.

In recent years, the Santo Niño de las Suertes has been confused with, mixed with or paired up with Mexico's most popular folk saint, the Santa Muerte. The Santa Muerte is not recognized by the Catholic Church and is the personification of death itself in the form of an image very reminiscent of the Western European concept of the Grim Reaper. Possibly because of the skull imagery of this unique Santo Niño, there has been a growing connection to this famous underground folk saint of death. The nuns taking care of the Santo Niño de las Suertes chapel noticed this connection in the early 2000s, which was coincident with the meteoric rise in the popularity of the Santa Muerte throughout Mexico. February 2 on the Catholic calendar is Candlemas, or in Spanish, "Candelaria," often called The Feast of the Presentation, when Mary and Joseph brought the Baby Jesus to the Temple in Jerusalem 40 days after his birth. In many parts of Mexico on February 2 people who have household Baby Jesus statues clean them, dress them up and take them to a church for a special Candlemas blessing. On Candlemas each year the nuns at the Santo Niño de las Suertes chapel started noticing people bringing in their Baby Jesus statues dressed as the Santa Muerte in a black or red hooded garment accompanied sometimes with a scythe and a skull. Some have also been bringing into the Santo Niño chapel candles and small statues of the Santa Muerte, much to the disappointment of the nuns. The current Abbess has a policy that anyone presenting Santa Muerte imagery of any kind be asked about their devotion to the folk saint and where they stand regarding traditional Catholicism. In a recent interview, the abbess explained that many worshipping the Santa Muerte are unaware that the Santo Niño de las Suertes has no connection to this folk saint of death and when confronted by the nuns the visitor usually withdraws their items with Santa Muerte imagery. This connection between the powerful folk saint of death and this unique Santo Niño cannot be controlled by the nuns in this convent, however. In shrines to the Santa Muerte throughout Mexico, icons and statues of the "Lucky Baby Jesus" are starting to appear with more frequency. As with everything, perhaps this Santo Niño is evolving and taking on new meaning as it leaves the bounds of traditional Catholicism. The future of this unique holy image may take on a life of its own and develop into something quite unexpected.

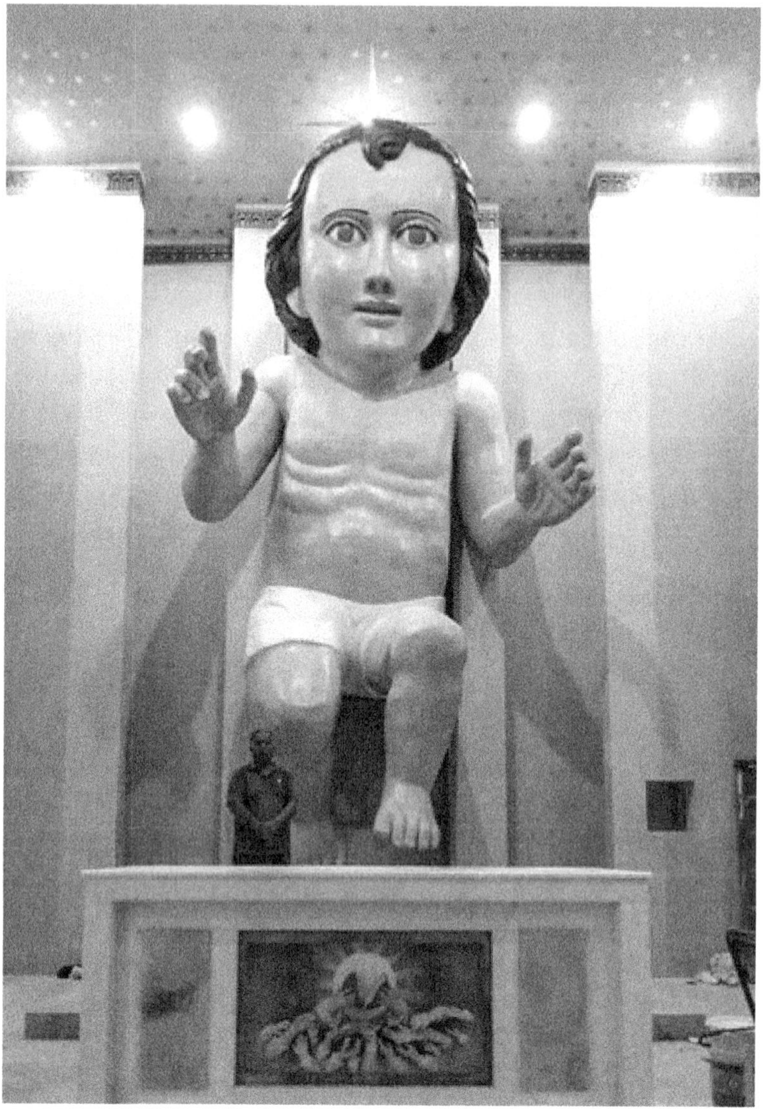

THE GIGANTIC BABY JESUS OF ZÓQUITE

"Congratulations Zóquite and congratulations to the Christian communities that form this parish. I know this place will become famous around the world thanks to your fiesta, thanks to this image which represents your faith, your eternal great faith."

Thus spoke Sigifredo Noriega Barceló, Archbishop of Zacatecas on January 6, 2020, on the Feast of the Epiphany, also known as "Tres Reyes" in Mexico. The holiday – observed to honor the arrival of the Three Wise Men in Bethlehem – usually marks the end of the Christmas season in most Latin American countries. This special celebration in the town of Zóquite, however, marked a new beginning for the town, in a sense. The archbishop of Zacatecas led the religious festivities for this small parish in part to bless formally the installation of the largest Baby Jesus sculpture the world has ever seen.

The Spanish came to the region surrounding the town of Zóquite in the mid-1500s when silver was discovered nearby. At the time of European contact, the town had already been established as an indigenous village with several hundred people living there. The town's name derives from the Nahuatl word zoquitl which means "mud." "Zóquite" means, "a place where there is no mud," owing to the arid conditions of the surrounding countryside. The town has 4,300 inhabitants and is located in the Mexican state of Zacatecas about 14 miles east of the state capital near Zacatecas' border with the state of San Luis Potosi. In 2008 the Catholic Church established the parish of Our Lord of the Epiphany in Zóquite to serve the communities of Santa Mónica, La Blanquita and Colonia Osiris. With this new parish, the construction of a new church was not far behind. With the enthusiasm and dedicated energy of parish priest Father Manuel Haro Campos, the parishioners raised 6 million pesos for the building project which was the biggest such endeavor the town had seen in many years. The following year, 2009, Zóquite had a brand-new church, called in Spanish, El Templo de la Epifania del Señor. The enthusiasm built up around the new church did not end when masons fitted the last stone in its place in this *templo*. The parishioners wanted to make their new church a special place, a site that would draw outside visitors, including pilgrims and tourists. Less than 45 minutes from Zóquite is a major Mexican pilgrimage site at the town of Plateros just north of the capital city of Zacatecas where a statue of the seated Christ Child is venerated, drawing millions of visitors per year. Perhaps hoping to get some spillover from the other Santo Niño site, the people of the new parish in Zóquite came up with an idea to put themselves on the map: they would create the largest sculpture of the Baby Jesus found anywhere in the world and house it in their new church.

It wasn't difficult to research their competition. In the year 2014 a parish in the city of Nezahualcóyotl in the Mexican state of México shared with the world a massive, blue-eyed Baby Jesus sculpture that measured sixteen and a half feet long and weighed over 1,100 pounds. Mayor of Nezahualcóyotl Juan Hugo de la Rosa García bragged that this Santo Niño would be in the *Guinness Book of World Records* because it beat the largest Baby Jesus sculpture in the world, found in Germany, by about two and a half feet. The people of Zóquite watched all of this unfold and took notes.

The parishioners in this small Zacatecas town started fundraising again with the same zeal they had when raising money for their new church. This time they gathered 218,800 pesos for the creation of their own gigantic Baby Jesus sculpture, the biggest of them all. To make the statue, they commissioned an artist named Román Salvador Barrueto who has his workshop in the town of Chimalhuacán in the Mexican state of México some 375 miles away from the Church of Our Lord of the Epiphany in Zóquite. Barrueto and his team of craftsmen spent months creating this colossal Christ Child starting with a metal frame and mesh and then covering it all with silica sand, ceramic pastes and resins. The final product was a 21 ½-foot long, 1,700-pound giant. It traveled the 375 from Barrueto's workshop on the back of a flatbed truck with its arms detached. When it arrived at Zóquite on November 13, 2019, it took 12 men to unload this massive religious icon and bring it to the altar section of the church. There, local artists attached the arms and put the finishing touches on this sculpture that looks, at first glance, like a gigantic baby in diapers. The Zóquite artists added color to the Santo Niño's cheeks and then painted his eyes blue. Under objections from some people in charge of the project, the eye color was repainted to a coffee-color brown. With the finishing touches complete, it took 20 men to screw the 1,700-pound sculpture to the wall behind the altar. Zóquite artist Hilario Fuentes then painted pictures on either side of the gigantic Baby Jesus. Facing the sculpture to the right is the baby's earthly father, Joseph, wearing a carpenter's apron over a golden-colored shirt. The left side features a painting of the Virgin Mary with a stern but somewhat perplexed expression on her face. Fuentes also painted the Three Wise Men on the wall of the church.

    The enthronement of this huge Baby Jesus by the archbishop of Zacatecas in early January 2020 seemed like a good start for this monumental undertaking that took years of planning and effort. Visitors started coming to Zóquite as expected and things were going better than hoped as the economic ripple effect was felt positively throughout the town. A few months after the dedication, however, the church was closed to visitors due to COVID-19. With less travel even after some of the restrictions were lifted, the oversized Santo Niño has not been receiving the adoration and veneration the locals had initially expected. Despite the lull in visitors, parishioners and others in the surrounding areas have been praying to this new Christ Child and have claimed that he has answered prayers and worked miracles. The town of Zóquite has endured little sickness and death from the global pandemic and many credit the protection of the Santo Niño for this. In an interview with a Zacatecas television station a Zóquite resident claimed that the statue serves as a reminder of when Christ was the most vulnerable, when he was a little baby, and faith in this powerful image helps protect the most vulnerable among us from disease or from any other of life's maladies and misfortunes.

    Seriousness aside, when news of the "Gigantic Baby Jesus of Zóquite" hit the internet, the largest Christ Child statue in the world became the butt of jokes and the subject of many memes. Some claimed that the face of the sculpture looked eerily like that of the British musician Phil Collins or to American actor Nicholas Cage. To others, the face of the Baby Jesus, along with his posture and outstretched arms, were reminiscent of deceased Mexican wrestler Perro Aguayo. A conspiracy theory arose claiming that the sculptor played a joke on the town when he fashioned this massive icon to look like the famous former *luchador* who was one of his personal favorites. Other memes pair the statue with Godzilla and Rodan attacking Tokyo or some other major city. Some internet commenters also compared the likeness of the gigantic Baby Jesus to that of Chucky, the evil doll from hell as seen in the American horror film series "Childsplay." There seems no end to the creative showcasing of the human imagination online these days.

With pandemic restrictions gone and as more miracles are attributed to the Santo Niño Gigante of Zóquite, perhaps the town may become one of Mexico's main pilgrimage sites attracting the curious, the faithful and those desperate for some sort of divine interventions in their lives. Only time will tell.

BABY JESUS OF THE LITTLE PEANUT

In the dry dusty highlands of the state of Jalisco, just north of Guadalajara, a community called Mezquitic de la Magdalena has existed since before the arrival of the Spanish. No one knows the exact meaning of the word "Mezquitic" but it originates from the Tecuexe language which saw its last speaker walk the earth sometime in the 1850s. The completely Mexicanized descendants of the Tecuexe still live in this town of less than two thousand people today. Besides DNA there is very little linking the current residents to their colorful past. This sleepy town is not completely under the radar, though, at least not to the deeply religious. Devout Mexican Catholics know this place as the home of the third most visited holy shrine in the state of Jalisco, behind the basilicas devoted to the Virgins of Zapopan and San Juan de los Lagos, respectively. Even though the town is a mere 10 miles from the shrine of the Virgin of San Juan de los Lagos, just 5 minutes on a modern road, many people throughout Mexico and even in the larger cities of Jalisco have never heard of the biggest draw to Mezquitic de la Magdalena: The Shrine to the Santo Niño del Cacahuatito. In English this translates to, Holy Child of the Little Peanut.

The story of the Santo Niño begins on the eve of Mexican independence, in the year 1810. Pedro Alanís and Juana Gallardo had very little water on their property and often asked their neighbors for water in times of drought. Their neighbors got tired of always helping them out and one of them told Pedro to leave everyone alone and dig a well. Pedro knew his land would probably not yield much water, so he and his wife prayed to the Virgin of Guadalupe to give them a sign on where to dig. Along with those prayers for dowsing advice, according to the story, the couple also prayed that their neighbors would be more charitable toward others in the future. In the ensuing days Pedro wandered his property looking for a sign. While out one afternoon he noticed an unusually healthy and green young tree which he had never seen before. At the base of the tree the ground was somewhat damp. It was here where he would dig his well. Pedro went to his neighbors to ask for assistance, and they were eager to help him. This was encouraging to him because part of his prayer was to have his neighbors' hearts soften to the idea of giving help. With enthusiasm, a group of village men began to dig the well. They would eventually hit an overabundance of water, but about 10 feet down they found something curious in the dirt. It was a figure of a baby measuring about 4 inches long and 2 inches wide. It was made of mud and wood, with one arm resting on its chest and one arm resting on its belly. It was devoid of clothing but had delicate features on its face, including eyelashes. Some insist that this is a small devotional item from the time of the Tecuexes made centuries before the Spanish arrived, possibly a representation of a god or natural spirit.   How it ended up so deep in the earth is unknown. Perhaps it was intentionally buried for some ceremonial purpose. Others faithfully believe that it is a small Christ Child, and it is responsible for the miracle of bringing the neighbors together and for providing water in a time of dire need.

Pedro and Juana were among the faithful. They cleaned up the tiny statue and dressed it up in fancy clothing. They put it on the small altar inside their home along with other devotional objects. It wasn't long before word spread throughout the town of this curious discovery and people came knocking at the door of Pedro and Juana's home. The couple opened their humble house to those wishing to see what would be soon called the Santo Niño de Mezquitic. People seeking miraculous interventions in their lives also came for the well water. The crowds grew and within their lifetimes Pedro and Juana received returning pilgrims who told them of the many miracles attributed to praying to the statue or to drinking or otherwise using the water from their well. Because the town of Mezquitic de la Magdalena is so close to the Basilica of the Virgin of San Juan de los Lagos, the Alanís-Gallardo home became a short stopover for San Juan devotees. The crowds grew over time.

In 1884, the small Santo Niño statue was moved. That year a small chapel was built in the town dedicated to the Virgin of Guadalupe and this became the sculpture's new home. That same year, the Archbishop of San Juan de los Lagos, Pedro Loza y Pardavé intervened and declared that the statue was not officially miraculous in the eyes of the Catholic Church and neither was the water from the well. One of the problems the archbishop had with the statue was that it was too small, about the size of a peanut. The archbishop was afraid that devotion to this Santo Niño was turning into a cult and taking people away from the real officially sanctioned worship that should have been happening at the basilica. Nothing could stop the pilgrims from coming, however, and the primary focus of the new Guadalupe chapel became this unusual tiny statue which visitors now affectionately called El Santo Niño del Cacahuatito, or the Holy Child of the Little Peanut, due to its size. The caretakers of the Guadalupe chapel took special care of this miraculous statue. They topped it with a golden crown and dressed it up in a fancy flaring yellow robe. Most people not familiar with Mexico's take on Catholicism might think it strange that the Baby Jesus looks like a pretty little girl in an elegant party dress, but this is the custom, as seen with many Santo Niño statues throughout the country. In addition to the fine stitchery, the statue is housed in an ornate oval silver nicho surrounded in delicately hand-fashioned silver roses. This oval nicho sits atop a shiny silver base that looks somewhat like a championship sports trophy. The elaborate silver nicho is kept in a glass box flanked with small twisting pillars carved of wood and rests on a wooden base flanked with cherub heads. This display case is located beneath the statue of the Virgin of Guadalupe in the part of the chapel where an altar normally would be located. Visitors can get within inches of the glass to see the small slouchy figure inside the display case. The Baby Jesus appears to have a rather drowsy expression on his delicate face, despite his rosy cheeks. The statue never leaves the shrine, and it is not paraded through the streets as devotional figures often are in Mexico. There are two dates on the ecclesiastical calendar that have special celebrations centered around the Santo Niño in Mezquitic. These are February 1st on the Eve of the Catholic holiday Candlemas, and on September 17th.

  The devotion to this sculpture was mostly local until 100 years after the Santo Niño was gussied up and given a permanent home. The veneration of the Baby Jesus of the Little Peanut has increased tremendously since 1985, when the priest Maximino Rodríguez arrived at the parish of Sangre de Cristo in Mezquitic de la Magdalena and decided to remodel the chapel and promote worship. In 1993, Father José Inés Rodríguez appointed Francisco Padilla de Luna to oversee the chapel, who through photographs promoted the image by calling it the more endearing El Niño del Cacahuatito.

Today, thousands of parishioners from all over Mexico and from abroad worship him. In León, in the neighboring state of Guanajuato, religious pilgrimages are organized to the area that include a visit to the Niño del Cacahuatito. One can enter the small chapel to visit the tiny statue and sit in the pews reserved for contemplation and prayer. Beside the glass cubicle home of the Baby Jesus figure people often leave toys and other gifts of thanks for prayers answered or miracles performed. This is only a small taste of the great devotion this shrine exudes. Off to the left of the statue the chapel has two rooms. These rooms are reserved for objects left by pilgrims. The walls from floor to ceiling are covered with small tokens of thanks left behind by the devout. Because many people pray to the Niño del Cacahuatito for intercessions in the lives of children there are many articles related to children in this part of the chapel. Toys, clothing and devotional paintings called ex votos describing miracles hang somberly on the walls. There are also several designated areas on which the faithful can pin tiny metal charms called milagros to pray for a miracle or to give thanks for a miracle received. A pilgrimage stop at Mezquitic de la Magdalena also includes a visit to the sacred well. There is the original brick-lined well that Pedro Alanís and his neighbors built back in 1810 now covered with a metal grate. Near the old well is a larger and more modern pump that extracts water from the original source. The caretakers of the shrine and volunteers make water available for free in large barrels. Visitors can come with little bottles and fill their containers by dipping pitchers into the barrels. Donations are accepted, but not required. There is also a legend involving coins. Visitors to the well are supposed to throw three coins in the sacred well. One coin will ensure a return to the town. The second one is for finding true love. The third one is so that the person making the wish would one day live in the town. Outside the shrine and the well area vendors sell the typical Mexican devotional items found at most shrines, and trinkets and images specific to the tiny Christ sculpture. This place, though, has something unique to it not found at any other Mexican religious shrine, or perhaps anywhere else in the world of holy places: Sacred peanuts! Because peanuts are grown locally and the object of devotion is nicknamed the Baby Jesus of the Little Peanut, it was only a matter of time before an enterprising local started selling bags of nuts and calling them miraculous. There is a myth that the tiny statue was found inside a peanut shell, but according to the generally accepted story of the sculpture's discovery, this was not the case. We are still left with a series of mysteries around the Santo Niño's true origins and age. Was it a tiny indigenous idol or offering buried for a specific purpose and never to be unearthed? Was it a hoax, something created by the townsfolk to increase tourism and trade in the area? Or was it a true miraculous manifestation of the Christ Child appearing in a time of need and to reassure the faithful? Whatever the answers to these questions may be, the devotion to the Baby Jesus of the Little Peanut continues to increase and tens of thousands of people believe in his miracles.

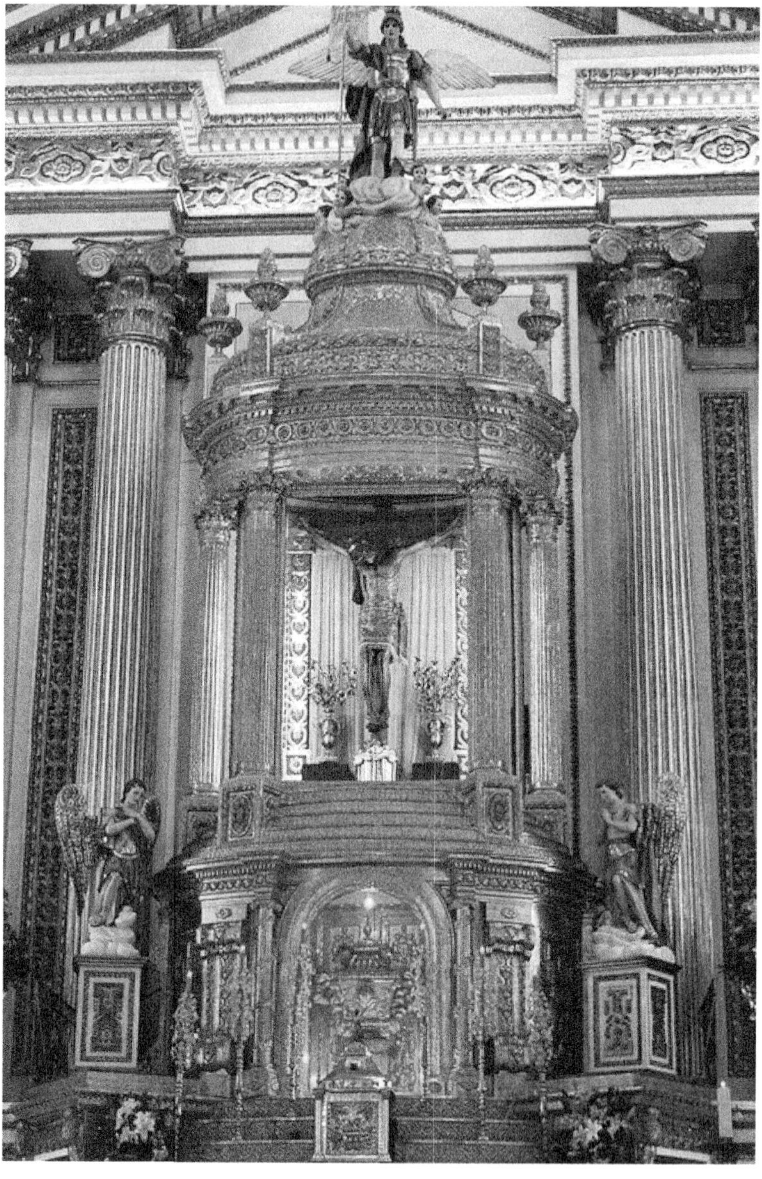

THE BLACK CHRIST OF CHALMA

    In a dark and damp mountainside cave in central Mexico, a young Italian Augustinian friar named Sebastián de Tolentino covered his nose with the fringe of his cloak. His companion, Brother Nicolás Perea did the same. The stench of blood from human sacrifices was too much for the two men to bear. They had both been sent by their order to evangelize this region of New Spain and had heard about the pilgrimages the local people had made to these caves, the caves dedicated to an aspect of the Aztec god Tezcatlipoca, also called "The Smoking Mirror." The year was 1537 and the place was near the modern village of Chalma in the state of Mexico. The friars approached a mysterious figure at the end of one of the main caves, it was a large, black cylindrical monolith, a carved likeness of Tezcatlipoca about the size of a man. The two Europeans felt somewhat afraid, as if they were making first contact with an alien or demonic presence. The brothers left the cave and returned to their monastery nearby to regroup and formulate a plan. The two friars reasoned that the key to claiming the surrounding country for Christendom would depend on the destruction of that idol in the cave. They vowed to return to the cave three days later with implements to smash the idol, to literally and figuratively break the power it had over the local people. The monks spent a few days in prayer and contemplation before embarking on their trek. By the time they had reached the base of the small mountain in which the caves were located they had realized that something important had happened as there was a great commotion among the pilgrims who had come to visit the monolith statue. From their limited knowledge of the local language, Brothers Sebastián and Nicolás had understood that something happened to the statue, so they ascended the rocky crags to the cave to have a look for themselves. The two fell to their knees when they saw the sight: in the place of the pagan black monolith was a crucifix. On the crucifix was a black rendition of Jesus. Nothing remained of the life-size idol, except for fine shards and rubble around the large crucifix. The Augustinian brothers believed they had witnessed a miracle and now had their powerful tool to convert the Indians.

Whether you choose believe in what happened in that cave in the remote area of New Spain, the Black Christ of Chalma – in Spanish *El Señor de Chalma* – still exists today and the shrine dedicated to Him is the second most popular religious destination in Mexico, right behind the Basilica of the Virgin of Guadalupe. The modern-day town of Chalma is a small community in the Mexican state of Mexico about 40 miles from the state capital of Toluca and about 60 miles from Mexico City. Many Mexican Catholics believe that three visits to Chalma are necessary to have one's specific prayers answered, and the small town becomes inundated with the faithful around Easter when hundreds of thousands of people, mostly on foot from neighboring states walk to the shrine in hopes of being on the receiving end of a miracle. Anthropologists and historians believe that the cave in which the Black Christ appeared was dedicated to an aspect or form of the Aztec "smoking mirror" god Tezcatlipoca called Oxtoteotl which has been associated with a wide range of concepts including discord, temptations, war, evil sorcery, jaguars, the night winds, the night sky, the earth, hurricanes and volcanic glass, also called obsidian. The "Smoking Mirror" nickname of the god comes the Aztec term for the volcanic glass polished to a high sheen used in divination. The earliest known formal Spanish description of the caves of Chalma came from the Jesuit priest Francisco de Florencia who called the place the Cave of Ostoc Teotl, which translates to "The Dark Lord of the Cave." Prior to the Conquest the caves around Chalma had deep spiritual significance and attracted pilgrims from throughout the Aztec Empire. Many of the rituals and celebrations surrounding the pilgrimage to the caves still survive in some form of another today. The Jesuit Florencia described people arriving to the area wearing flowers and carrying incense, and bathing in the local springs and streams as part of a cleansing ritual. Tezcatlipoca devotees would also drink a type of purified holy water before entering the caves. Human sacrifice was not uncommon here, but, of course, it did not survive the Spanish takeover. No one knows who carved the large black monolith, which was venerated in the cave, how it got there or how old it was. As it was allegedly destroyed, we will probably never know anything more about it.

When the Black Jesus appeared in the cave to the Augustinian friars, a mass conversion occurred, and thousands of people in the surrounding area converted to Christianity almost instantaneously. Visits to the shrine in the cave continued almost uninterrupted, but the people began coming to see a new god and to receive favors from a new divine entity. According to the popular story, when Tezcatlipoca left, so did the jaguars with which he was associated, as well as other predatory animals, thus making the journey to Chalma safer for the pilgrims. Sometime in the 17th Century the entrance to the main cave was enlarged and a small shrine to Saint Michael was installed. Almost 150 years after the Christ appeared, two other Augustinian brothers – Bartolomé de Jesús María and Juan de San José – founded a monastery near the cave site which attended to the many pilgrims visiting the caves. Later, a church was built near the monastery and the image of the Black Christ was moved out of the cave and to the church. The sanctuary complex has been modified over the years with various remodels and expansions. Sometime in the 1700s the shrine complex suffered a massive fire, and the original Christ figure was damaged in that fire. A new figure was created in what remained of the old and that newly modified Black Christ can be seen in the church of Chalma today. In 1783, King Charles III of Spain, who took great interest in Chalma, put the shrine directly under his protection. With patronage from the king came many more improvements to the shrine, including a new elaborately carved altar, beautiful works of art depicting the Virgin of Guadalupe and Saint Michael, and a new neoclassical façade for the church. King Charles proclaimed that the shrine was to be called *El Convento Real y Sanctuario de Nuestro Señor Jesucristo y San Miguel de las Cuevas de Chalma*, which in English translates to The Royal Monastery and Sanctuary of Our Lord Jesus Christ and Saint Michael of the Caves of Chalma. While the shrine complex is located on the canyon floor, the cliffs and caves overlooking the complex are still considered holy. There are large crosses on the cliffs overlooking the town which are taken down during various times of the year to be rededicated in the Chalma church, a custom that dates to at least the time of King Charles' patronage.

As the second most visited religious site in Mexico, Chalma receives over 2 million visitors per year. Chalma is your typical Mexican pilgrimage site. Outside the sanctuary complex we find almost a carnival atmosphere with vendors hawking religious trinkets, and food of all kinds being sold, from fast food and snacks to elaborate sit-down meals. There is a place on the path to the river outside the church where people can leave folk art paintings called *retablos* detailing in graphic form thanks for miracles received. Alongside the retablos are other typical offerings of thanks: locks of hair, photos, and so on. This wall has to be cleaned periodically as it gets crowded with devotional items from the thousands and thousands of miracles and prayers granted which are attributed to the Black Christ of Chalma.

Pilgrimages to Chalma are often a group effort. Villages or towns may sponsor a small contingent from their municipality to make the trek to Chalma. Although there is now a paved road leading through the winding canyons and rugged terrain to get to the sanctuary, many pilgrims prefer to make the journey on foot as they have done for hundreds of years. When they get to Chalma pilgrims participate in a number of ritual activities. Many wear flowers, much as the Aztecs did. Many also dance at the shrine, which is another ritualistic behavior traced back to the pre-Hispanic times. Just as the Aztecs had done, visitors to Chalma purify themselves in the springs and small streams surrounding the caves and rocky outcrops. After bathing, it is said, one is spiritually clean and can wear a crown of flowers to dance at the shrine. Of special note is a spring that comes directly out of a centuries-old cypress tree. Many women believe that the water from the spring will help with fertility, and they splash it all over their bodies. During festival days, primarily around Easter, artists in the town of Chalma construct intricate panels comprised of flowers and seeds. The townsfolk also make arches constructed of colorful tissue paper or papier-mâché. During festival days all the streets of Chalma are filled with people and vehicles are prohibited. The whole town explodes in celebration.

No one knows how long people have been visiting the area of Chalma seeking guidance and grace from the divine. We know that it goes back at least to the 13th Century with the coming of the Aztec Empire but may even go back before then. Whether one believes the story of how the Black Christ came to be, there is no denying the power and the comfort that the image generates. The origin and original meaning of the venerated black monolith in the cave that preceded it is still unknown. At Chalma we have a miracle, magic and mystery all wrapped into one.

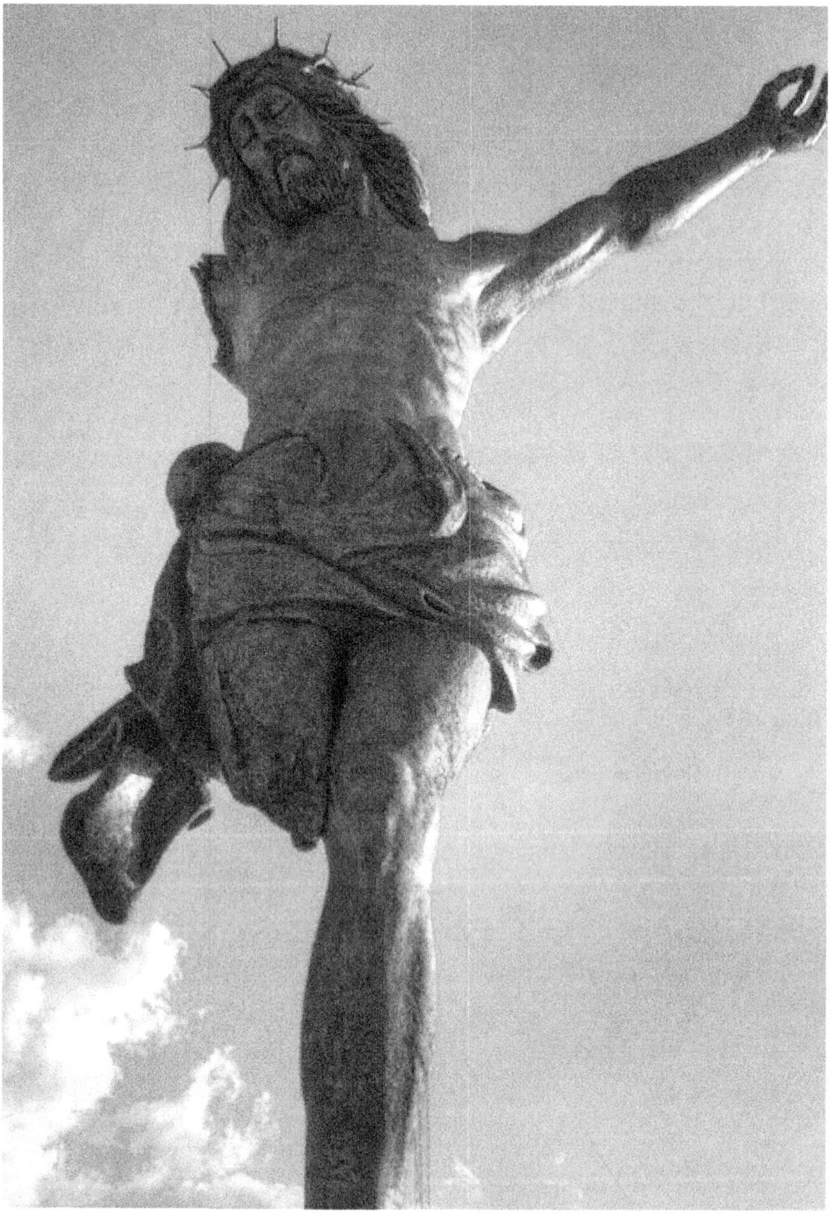

EL CRISTO ROTO
THE BROKEN JESUS OF AGUASCALIENTES

On a bleak island in a manmade lake in the middle of a semi-arid wasteland there stands a gigantic statue of Jesus. His right arm is broken off by the shoulder and his right leg is also missing halfway down the thigh. Although a classic image of the crucified Christ, the sculpture is that of a mutilated corpus only and does not include a cross. Beneath this statue there is a plaque with an inscription on its surface. The inscription starts off with "Déjame roto," which means, "Leave me broken," in English. Here is the plaque's complete translation from Spanish to English:

"Leave me broken...
I want myself to be seen as broken. Remember so many of your brothers who are like me, broken, crushed, homeless, oppressed, sick, mutilated...
Without arms, because they have no possibilities or means of work; without feet, because they have blocked their paths; without a cross, because they have taken away their respect, honor, and prestige. Everyone will forget them and turn their backs on them even though they are like you...
a broken Christ."

El Cristo Roto, or "The Broken Christ," stands 82 feet tall on an island aptly named La Isla del Santuario del Cristo Roto, or "The Island of the Sanctuary of the Broken Christ". The island is located in an artificial lake behind Plutarco Elias Calles Dam in the northwestern part of the Mexican state of Aguascalientes about 50 minutes from the capital city of the state, also called Aguascalientes. The closest town to the shrine is San José de Gracia on the eastern shore of the manmade lake. For 40 pesos round-trip, which is about two US dollars, the island is just a five- to ten-minute boat ride away. The statue is made of concrete and steel and painted with a finish to make it look like bronze. The sanctuary includes an open-air plaza in front of the gigantic Jesus. Around the perimeter of the plaza are several shrines. Within the glass-enclosed niches are replicas of the Christ statues of all the major churches in the state of Aguascalientes. The plaza plays host to various celebrations and religious observances, especially during the Semana Santa, or Holy Week, preceding Easter Sunday. Although the Christ statue is broken, it was made on purpose to look this way. The whole shrine is relatively new, only being constructed in the year 2006. Since they built the sanctuary, El Cristo Roto has received many thousands of visitors from around Mexico and beyond. A great many of these visitors are simply curious tourists while many come here in search of miracles and divine guidance.

    So, what is the history of the area and how did this sculpture come to be? As mentioned previously, the statue and sanctuary are located on an island in the reservoir behind Plutarco Elias Calles Dam. This dam was the first such project ever undertaken in Mexico. It was built in 1928 and took about 3 years to completely fill up to current levels. Before the dam, the town of San José de Gracia was located in the future lake bottom surrounded by thousands of tall, shade-giving cottonwood trees that the locals used as an endless supply of wood.

    Centuries and thousands of years before the dam, the region was inhabited by roaming indigenous people collectively known as the Chichimeca. The Aztec Empire and even the Tarascan State tried to either conquer or make peace with the Chichimeca but were repelled. When the Spanish arrived in the Aguascalientes region in the middle of the 1500s, they met with similar resistance from the indigenous. The area was finally subdued about a hundred years later in the 1660s. By the middle of the 1670s all the nomadic Chichimeca were stripped of their way of life and forced to settle in towns or to work on haciendas. Between the years 1673 and 1675 the town of San José de Gracia was formed by families who formerly worked at the Hacienda de Garabato. In the records of colonial New Spain, after its founding San José de Gracia was declared to be an "Indian Town." The population lost its "nativeness" over the years and slowly adopted the general mestizo national culture found throughout Mexico today. For four days San José de Gracia played host to Father Miguel Hidalgo, the famous leader of Mexican Independence, who was passing through here with a large band of insurgents on what is called by historians, "The Freedom Route." Hidalgo's forces engaged with the Spanish army on a bridge in the middle of town called the Puente de Calderón, on January 19, 1811. The rebels suffered a defeat, so they retreated. The bridge had such a drop into the canyon below that it was said that men could not ride horses across it because the horses would be spooked. The bridge, along with the rest of the town would disappear completely under the waters of the Calles reservoir by 1932. Before the waters overtook San José de Gracia, the small town had three neighborhoods: Patio Blanco, Cajon del Muerto and Barrio Hidalgo. The back of the Cristo Roto statue faces what would have been the highest part of the Cajon de Muerto neighborhood. The new town built on the eastern shores of the new lake took a few years to establish with some 20 families from the old town making up most of the new town's population. Other families from the flooded town decided to make their ways to the capital city of Aguascalientes or to the neighboring state of Zacatecas.

There are a few versions of the Broken Christ story that may have inspired the sculpture. One story has a poor parish priest buying a broken Christ because he could not afford one for his church that was intact and nailed to a cross. Another story claims that a donkey carrying a box showed up in front of the San José de Gracia church many years ago, and inside the box was a wooden crucifix with the body of Jesus broken in several pieces. The priest at the church wanted to fix it and the night before he was to pass it off to an artist to make repairs, he heard a voice that said this:

"I don't want you to restore me. I am the Broken Christ. I want it to hurt you when you see me and to remember all the people who don't have a path."

The priest then kept it at the church and occasionally allowed the Cristo to be paraded around in times of drought or pestilence. The only problem with these two stories is that they are not verifiable historically, and only seemed to start to circulate in the early 2000s when plans for the sanctuary on the island were being hashed out. Some say that the sculptors of the piece – Erasmo Aguilar and Miguel Romo Santino – became inspired to create the Cristo Roto after hearing about a statue with the same name in Spain that was missing its head. The municipal authorities of San José de Gracia thought that a gigantic Jesus with a missing head was too gruesome but liked the idea of a Broken Christ in some other form. The town fathers were hoping to cash in on an increasing trend spreading throughout Mexico: that of the gigantic religious statue created to draw in the tourist trade. Some examples of these types of monumental sculptures already talked about on Mexico Unexplained include the Gigantic Baby Jesus of Zóquite in neighboring Zacatecas and the largest indoor religious carving in Latin America, the Virgin of Chignahuapan located in a minor basilica nestled in the remote mountains of the State of Puebla. Essentially, the Cristo Roto is akin to the American roadside attraction or "tourist trap" of days past. Instead of a gigantic fiberglass jackrabbit with a saddle on its back or poorly made metal dinosaurs looming from the cliffs above a desert highway, we have a huge disfigured Jesus statue in the middle of a lake. At the island shrine itself, and on the shore, vendors hawk touristy items like shot glasses and keychains as souvenirs with the image of the Cristo Roto on them. And who could pass up exact replicas of the Broken Christ made of painted resin measuring almost a foot tall selling for only 50 pesos? Now, that's a deal.

As a relatively new Catholic shrine, there have not been thousands of miracles attributed to the Cristo Roto of Aguascalientes just yet, but pilgrims are pouring in and so are the claims of healings and other assorted divine favors granted. Now that the town of San José de Gracia is "on the map" after being granted "Pueblo Mágico," or "Magical Town" status by the Mexican national government, more people are likely to visit here in the coming years. It will be interesting to see what happens at San José de Gracia or how the Cristo Roto will be outdone by another town building something bigger and more elaborate to rope in the tourists.

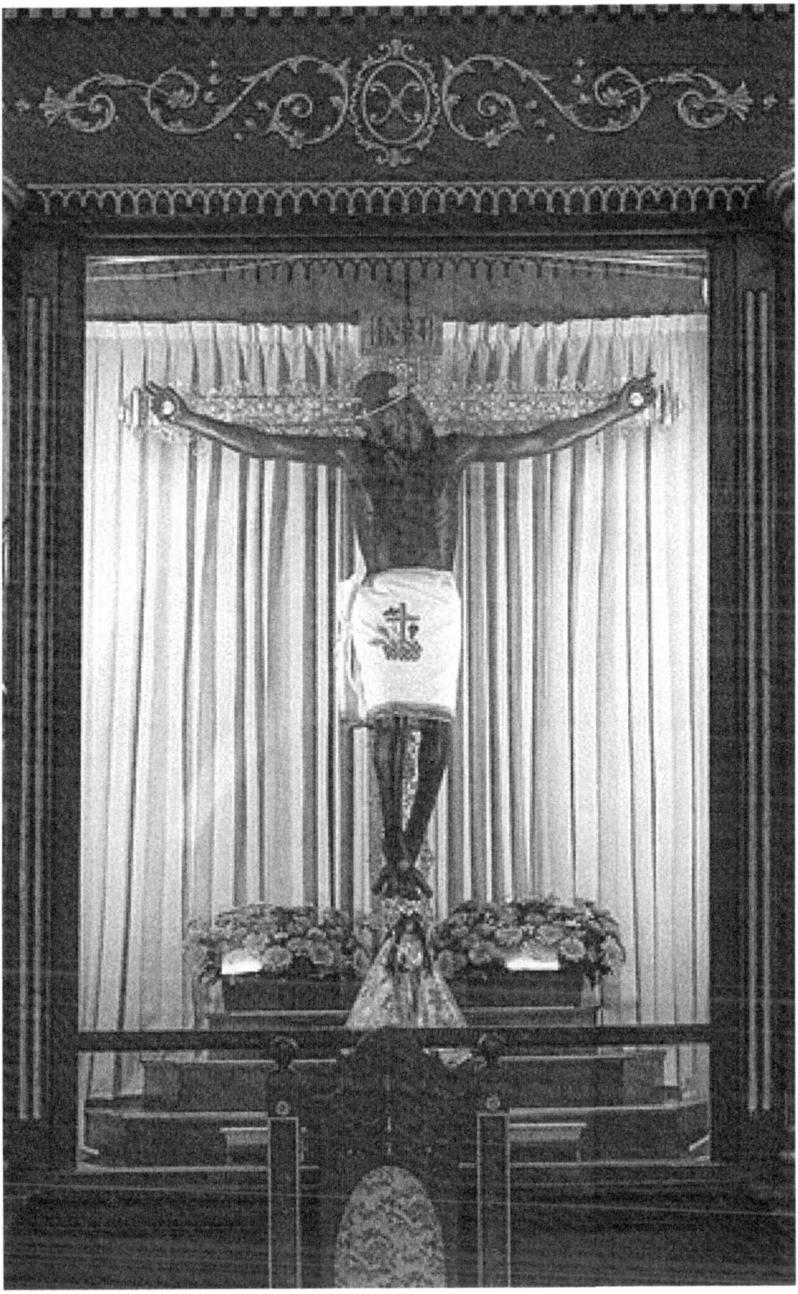

THE BLACK CHRIST OF SAN ROMÁN

The date was August 9, 2020. The Bishop of Campeche, José Francisco González González presided over the annual taking down or descent of one of the region's most venerated religious objects, the Cristo Negro de San Román. Every year at noon on August 9th for the past 455 years, 11 faithful people would take down the black statue of Christ from its place above the altar and move it to the center of the church for public veneration. This was done to commemorate the martyrdom of the statue's patron, Saint Romanus, a Roman soldier in the legion of Emperor Valerian who converted to Christianity and was beheaded on August 9th in the year 258. The solemn ceremony in the Campeche church taking place in the year 2020 was unlike any other in the previous 454 years. The life-size black Christ was put in an enclosure, and for the first time in its history the faithful were not allowed to touch it or kiss it, as in other years. Ushers in surgical masks shepherded pilgrims and the curious through a sanitization tent outside where people were asked to wash and disinfect their hands. The bishop, the statue's 11 chosen attendants and everyone else in attendance wore masks and tried – albeit unsuccessfully – to adhere to social distancing protocols. Believers had to be satisfied with being able to be in close proximity to the crucifix only. The ceremony went on, however, and even with hundreds of visitors that day, no one who attended came down with COVID 19. Was this yet another miracle, in centuries of miracles, to be attributed to the Black Christ of San Román?

The story of the Black Christ begins in the 1560s. The city of Campeche was founded by the Spanish who built the city at the site of a Maya town called Can Pech or Akh'iin Pech in the year 1540. In the 1550s the Spanish brought a group of Tlaxcalans from central Mexico to settle a little to the west of the main square of the city of Campeche. Their *barrio* was called Naborios. The name of the settlement was telling. A *naborio* in colonial New Spain was a free indigenous person. In the early decades of the Spanish colonization of Mexico, many natives were either slaves or worked in a sort of indentured servitude. A *naborio* was neither slave nor indentured servant. For their help given to the Spanish in the overthrow of the Aztec Empire, the Tlaxcalan people were afforded many privileges in colonial society. Unlike most other indigenous peoples, they could ride horses, possess firearms and most of them were *naborio*, or free. This little Tlaxcalan colony, hundreds of miles from home, was mostly agricultural. The Tlaxcalans grew bountiful crops in the Campechean soil. By 1563, though, this *naborio* community suffered a calamity that spread throughout the Yucatán and surrounding regions. Swarms of locusts of biblical proportions destroyed everything imaginable. The local religious authorities reasoned that the community of Naborios was lacking proper religious protection. The priests and friars in Campeche built a small chapel that was no more than a shack in the middle of the Tlaxcalan community. They called this little house of worship La Iglesia de San Román Mártir and later changed the name of the settlement from Naborios to San Román. The small church was lacking an image, so in 1565 the local priest commissioned a merchant by the name of Juan Cano de Coca Gaitán to sail to the port of Veracruz, two days by sea from Campeche, to buy a Christ figure. During his next regular run to Veracruz, Gaitán met with a religious objects merchant and purchased a beautiful large crucifix with a nearly life-size Christ carved out of black ebony wood. The crucifix came from Civitavecchia, the Italian port closest to Rome, and was carved by an unknown Italian artist. Although the figure of Jesus was black, he had European and not African facial features. The merchant Juan Cano de Coca Gaitán loaded the Black Christ on his ship with other cargo purchased in Veracruz and set sail. Within hours his ship encountered a terrible storm, a hurricane, that tore apart some of the masts and almost sank the ship. According to the sailors serving in Gaitán's crew, a mysterious dark-skinned man appeared on deck in the midst of the worst part of the storm and helped the sailors square away the ship. This mysterious man was reported as having a very kind face and was said to have been extraordinarily strong. The sailors would say later that the ship would not have survived without the help of this man who was not part of the crew. Something else happened connected to this sea voyage that was very curious. Despite the storm,

Gaitán's ship arrived back to Campeche in less than 24 hours, not the two days it normally took.

Some modern-day historians and armchair researchers claim that the priests requested a dark Christ instead of a light-skinned one to appeal to the Tlaxcalans' racial sensitivities. The priests wanted the natives to identify more with the image, these researchers say, and would be more apt to worship a Christ that looked more like them. The Tlaxcalans had already converted to Christianity decades before and were devout enough not to need any sort of extra "push" to get them to accept the imported religion. There was no apparent reason why Gaitán purchased that specific *Cristo* while in Veracruz. There is evidence that the darker Christs were somewhat fashionable in New Spain at the time and prized because they were unusual and uncommon. In the early 1500s there were four other churches in the Yucatán that had black Christs in them. All the churches containing this type of Cristo were destroyed during the Caste Wars of the mid-1800s, except for the San Román church in Campeche which was located away from the bulk of the fighting. The "Dark Skin to Appeal to the Natives Theory" seems to be just 21st Century academic thinking applied to a situation that took place centuries ago.

Over the hundreds of years of its existence, there are many stories and miracles associated with The Black Christ of San Román. In the 1600s and 1700s the city of Campeche was often besieged by pirates. In one story involving the Cristo, a group of English or Dutch pirates attacked the city and upon hearing of the famous crucifix, a band of buccaneers tried to loot the Church of San Román and make off with the famous Black Christ. When a pirate approached the altar, the crucifix began glowing and let out an electrical charge that "zapped" the pirates. Needless to say, they scurried away, and the Cristo remained safe and sound in the humble church. Perhaps related to the story of the mysterious dark-skinned man that helped the merchant ship during the hurricane, many people around Campeche for hundreds of years have seen a dark-skinned helper whom they believe is the Cristo come to life, wandering about the city making miracles happen. It's important to note this is not the first reported incident in Latin America of a religious figure animating itself and being seen to intercede in the human world. The Church at San Román, like so many other pilgrimage sites throughout Mexico is full of offerings made to the Black Christ for prayers answered or miracles received. These are in the form of candles, handwritten letters, devotional or personal objects, or typical small ex voto paintings illustrating miraculous events or healings. During the annual August 9th "Taking Down" ceremony involving this crucifix, bouquets of flowers are passed over the body of the Black Christ. The faithful believe that anyone who touches one of these holy flowers will be cured of any disease and their homes will be protected.

The Descent of the Cristo Negro on August 9th marks the beginning of the Fiestas de San Román. The Black Christ is not only seen as the protector of the city of Campeche but he is also the patron saint of the entire Mexican state of Campeche. The formal fiestas intensify from September 14th to September 28th. In addition to traditional religious processions and special masses, the fiestas include rodeos, agricultural exhibitions, beauty contests, dance competitions, boxing matches, concerts, craft fairs, fireworks displays, and many celebrations in private homes from low-key to extravagant. The fiestas attract people from around Mexico and it is a time for locals living away to come back home. During the fiestas, devotees make the pilgrimage to the crowded Church of San Román sometimes with the last few yards done on their knees. The church itself is not elaborate. It has one low bell tower and a whitewashed exterior with no ornamentation. Over the centuries the Black Christ has been perfectly preserved with no cracks or bore holes from insects. Some may consider this one of the statue's biggest miracles, surviving the centuries intact. In its 455 years it has endured a shipwreck, pirate attacks, human handling and the march of time. There is no doubt the Black Christ of San Román will be around for many years to come.

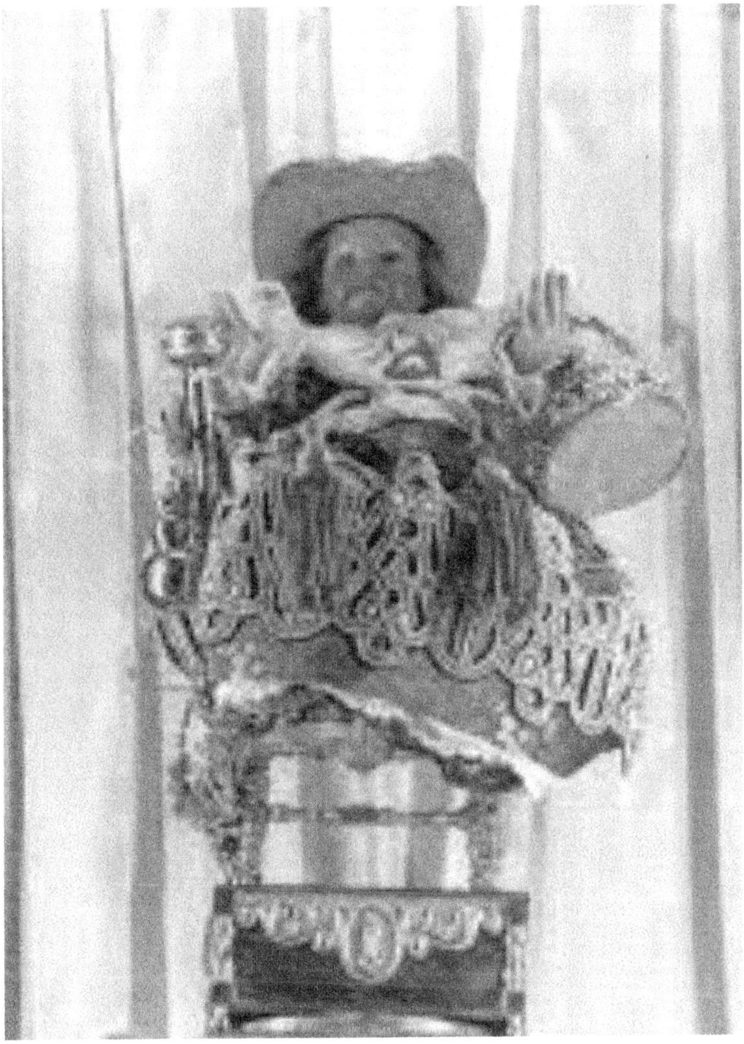

THE SANTO NIÑO AND THE MIRACLES OF PLATEROS

The date was April 8, 1566. In the northern fringes of New Spain, a small band of miners was traveling from the Gulf port of Veracruz to the frontier town of Durango delivering supplies. They were caught in a rainstorm and had to stop and make camp in the rugged hills outside the modern-day Mexican city of Fresnillo, Zacatecas. In their wagon of provisions was a large wooden crucifix intended for a new church in Durango. The men wanted to strike it rich in the newly discovered silver mines in the region, so they took the crucifix out of its large box and prayed to it, hoping that God would reward them for their veneration and piousness. That night it continued to rain heavily, and when the men woke up the next day, they saw a newly revealed vein of silver on the side of a cliff. The little caravan never made it to Durango. The men stopped there, made a more permanent camp, and established their own silver mine. They discovered the vein on April 9, the feast day of Saint Dimitri, an early Christian martyr killed by the Roman Emperor Diocletian. Because of their good fortune, they decided to name their town San Demetrio. The men cherished that large church crucifix that they felt was responsible for their newly found riches and built a small chapel around it. The local indigenous population, the mountain-dwelling Huichol people who had only partially converted to Christianity, seemed to be drawn to the Christ. Rumors circulated throughout the area that the *Cristo* had special healing powers and emitted a distinct positive energy. It only took a few decades before the little chapel became a pilgrimage site for Spanish and Native alike. The people of the region nicknamed the crucifix, El Señor de los Plateros, or in English, the Lord of the Silver Miners. Over the years the people in charge of the chapel added silver overlay to the Christ figure and other embellishments, making a more elaborate presentation to visitors who started to come from all over colonial Mexico. In 1621, the town even changed its name from San Demetrio to Plateros to pay homage to the important shrine. In the 1780s, the town began construction on a more impressive stone church to replace the smaller chapel that had been in use for some 200 years.

Although this is the official story told in modern-day brochures and on the official Plateros web site, there are two different oral histories of the miraculous Christ of Plateros. In one version of the story, the Christ carving was being transported overland on the back of a mule, part of a supply transport for a wealthy hacienda. The large crucifix had been specially made in Spain for use in the hacienda's private chapel. The mule carrying the cross somehow made its way into a small house of a miner. No one could explain how the mule carrying the large crucifix was able to fit through the door to get into the house because a group of men could not get the object back out through the door. So, the Señor de los Plateros had to remain in the tiny town of San Demetrio in that miner's house. People came to visit the Christ and eventually the small house was converted into a chapel, then torn down, with a larger church built on the same spot sometime later.

In another version of the story involves the miraculous appearance of the large cross in the deserts outside the town of San Demetrio right after the town was built in the mid-1500s. News of the beautiful crucifix drew people out to the desert to see it and had many people in the town debating about how it got there and what to do with it. Some people reasoned that it had probably belonged to a frontier mission or church that had been raided and looted by marauding Huicholes or Chichimecas. The Indians had no use for the crucifix, so they just dumped it in the desert. Should they bring it into town? Some people cautioned against it for fear that the object was a sort of evilly charged Trojan Horse. Those who believe this thought the object was carrying a Native curse on it and it was left in the desert as a sort of bait. The intention of those who left it there was for it to be brought into town so it would infect the Spanish settlement with all the bad mojo the Indian shamans instilled in it. The ones who thought the Christ could have possibly been cursed lost out to the others who wanted to bring the beautiful crucifix into town. As the Señor de los Plateros has been credited with many miracles and healings over the centuries, to the faithful, the native curse camp was proved wrong.

After a few centuries of silver mining the region became very prosperous, and as previously mentioned, the town of Plateros started constructing a new, much larger church in the 1780s. A wealthy silver miner in the region wanted to contribute to the construction of the new church, so he donated a large statue of Nuestra Señora de Atocha, or in English, Our Lady of Atocha. This statue, or rather an element of it, would later surpass the Señor de los Plateros crucifix in its importance at this pilgrimage site. The Virgin of Atocha had been venerated in Spain since the 13th Century when a great deal of territory of that country was under Muslim rule. In the town of Atocha near Madrid, a chapel housed a beautiful carving of the Virgin Mary with a small Christ Child which drew pilgrims from the immediate area. When Atocha fell to the Muslims, many Christians were taken prisoner. The prisoners were not fed by jailers and were only given food by their families when they were allowed to visit. The visitation laws became stricter with time and only children were allowed to see prisoners and bring food. Those imprisoned men who had no small children could therefore not get any food. According to the story, the women of Atocha prayed to the statue of the Virgin Mary and asked her for her help. It was said that in the middle of the night the Christ Child, or Santo Niño, attached to the statue, would walk around, and give food to the prisoners who needed it. The stories were verified when people started noticing that the shoes on the Santo Niño were scuffed, as if from excessive walking. The image of the Santo Niño de Atocha is easily recognizable as he is currently popular in many countries throughout Latin America. He is dressed as a pilgrim wearing a blue robe and brownish-red cloak. He has a feathered hat, and he carries two things: a basket of food and a staff with a water gourd attached. In artistic renditions he is usually pictured comfortably seated and wearing sandals. On his cape there is a scallop shell, symbolizing a pilgrimage to the shrine of Saint James. Smiling cherubs are suspended above the Santo Niño and fancy flower vases are at his feet. His hair tends to be curly and at shoulder length and his facial features are always soft and delicate, almost feminine.

    In the Mexican church at Plateros the imported replica of Our Lady of Atocha donated by the wealthy miner had a detachable

Baby Jesus. Caretakers and priests at the new church would remove the Santo Niño and honor it with festivities and special masses on December 24th and 25th. By the beginning of the 1800s devotion to the Santo Niño started to become the main draw to the church. The Santo Niño de Atocha was permanently detached from the Virgin Mary statue and moved from the side of the church to a glass box placed right under the main crucifix, the much older Lord of Plateros. The elevation of his status occurred when something happened like the feeding of the prisoners in Muslim-occupied Spain centuries before. In the first decade of the 1800s there was an explosion in one of the mines outside the town of Plateros. There were many miners who were trapped, and it was well over a week before they were rescued. During the time the miners were in peril, visitors to the church noticed that the Santo Niño statue was missing. Believers attested that it was the Baby Jesus himself who was tending to the trapped miners and was seeing them through the crisis. When the Santo Niño statue appeared again in the church it was dusty and dirty, as if it had been down in the mines assisting with the rescue efforts. While this seemed to be a fantastic story, throughout north-central Mexico, the healing powers of the Santo Niño became legendary. He became the unofficial patron saint of miners, the sick, prisoners, and those facing immediate danger.

    Some researchers believe that the story of the disappearing statue helping the miners may have been made up decades later to serve specific political purposes. After Mexican independence in the 1820s, the Catholic Church in Mexico found itself with an uncertain future. Often associated with Spanish imperialism, the Church in a newly independent Mexico had to find its way and was often met with contempt from ambitious politicians who saw the Church as either a threat to their power or just a relic from the old power structure that needed to be done away with. While anticlerical politicians turned up the heat on the Church, many within the Church saw the need to consolidate or enhance their own power. In 1820s and 1830s Mexico, this promotion of power often took the form of elevating certain saints and virgins to local protector status. Encouraging important shrines and sanctuaries was part of the Mexican church's plan to have power over the people in a more divine way. It was hard for the government to compete against an institution that derived its authority from the Almighty and the Church localized its power through the shrines. People could connect directly with a manifestation of heavenly power that was more personal because it was intimately tied to their immediate geographical area. As the promotion of the Santo Niño grew, so did the pilgrimages. Pilgrims were encouraged to bring offerings in the form of personal objects or ex votos, painted stories depicting a miracle or other event for which the devotee is thankful. A big development in the expansion of the devotion of the Santo Niño at Plateros came in the promulgation of a novena, or formal nine days of prayer, in which 9 miracles taken directly from ex votos left by pilgrims were incorporated into the prayers. The novena to the Santo Niño was published by a local press in a Mexican version of Spanish that was less formal than the European Spanish the churchgoers were used to. The Santo Niño had thus become the patron and helper of the common person. The Church had won their battle with the government for the hearts and minds of the people, at least in this region of the Republic. Over the years the Santo Niño would be credited with many miracles from healing the sick to helping with finances to interceding in situations involving incarcerated persons.

Today, the Plateros church is one of the most-visited religious shrines in all Mexico. The delicate Santo Niño still has his place in a glass box directly beneath the crucifix depicting the Lord of Plateros which is now almost 500 years old. Over the years the Baby Jesus statue has gotten many make-overs and wardrobe changes, and he is still celebrated every Christmas. The devotional painting, the ex votos, encouraged to be brought to the sanctuary as testimonies of the faithful have now overwhelmed the church complex. Thousands of these artistic representations of thanks are on display for the public in the colonnades and hallways flanking the main church. Millions of people attest to the many miracles of

Plateros.   The devotion continues.

OUR LORD OF WONDERS
A TALE OF TWO JESUS SHRINES

In Mexico there are many pilgrimage sites to many different virgins, saints and other apparitions and miraculous occurrences. Many of these devotions are not known outside Mexico or even outside their respective regions to other Mexicans. Many saints or virgins have multiple shrines set up to them. Nuestro Señor de las Maravillas, or Our Lord of Wonders, is one such devotion, having two major pilgrimage sites set up in the Mexican states of Hidalgo and Puebla, respectively.

Hidalgo

The origins of the image currently venerated in Hidalgo are unknown, and it is not known when it was made or who made it. Some say that the carved Christ came on a galleon from the Spanish Philippines, but this is just speculation. What is known is that in 1806 an old woman from Atotonilco el Chico in the state of Hidalgo arrived in the city of El Arenal carrying a sculpture of the crucified Christ. She called this *cristo* El Señor de los Laureles or "Our Lord of the Laurels" in order to sell it. After not finding a buyer, and given the poor financial situation of the woman, the family of Don Andrés Pérez carried out a collection in the town and acquired the *cristo* for 30 pesos. Another version of the story maintains, however, that a group of pilgrims from Atotonilco was heading towards Actopan with the statue when, after arriving at El Arenal, it began to become so heavy that they decided to stop and rest, proceeding the next day to put the carving up for sale. The sculpture was purchased and put in a small hermitage, and then ended up at its current location, the Sanctuary of the Lord of Wonders built in 1812 right before Mexico became an independent country. Soon people began to allege that miracles were associated with the statue, which led to the decision to move it to the town of Actopan. Each time they tried to move the carving, a storm prevented it, so it was finally decided that El Arenal would be its permanent home. There is a popular legend that states that a wife cheated on her husband with another man while he was working in the fields, the woman having the habit of bringing a basket of food to her secret love when she committed adultery. Her husband, warned of his wife's behavior, decided to keep an eye on her. After intercepting her one day while she was on her way to see her lover, the man asked his wife what was in her basket. The woman, aware of the violent character of her husband, entrusted herself to the Lord of Wonders and lied to her husband, saying that she brought items for the monks at the hermitage where the image of Christ was venerated. The man, believing that his wife was lying to him, threw the basket to the ground and instead of food, religious articles fell out, including devotional candles, communion wafers, sacramental wine, rosaries and saintly amulets. This story caused the image to acquire great fame and devotion and pilgrimages to the shrine increased.

So, what does this image look like? The statue is made of polychrome wood, has a straight-haired wig and beard, and shows Christ immediately after his death on the cross, with his head fallen to his right side and his body covered with various bleeding wounds. The one on the right side stands out the most. He is cloaked in real cloth, usually an unadorned lilac color, although sometimes he is dressed in a purple cloak with fringes and gold-colored embroidered details. On his head he wears a royal crown instead of the characteristic crown of thorns. Behind the cross several golden rays form the shape of an oval. This Señor de las Maravillas rests on a stone altarpiece and is encased in protective glass. On the fifth Friday of Lent, the feast of the Lord of Wonders is celebrated, which includes a religious procession, masses and pilgrimages. Also, the dance of the Concheros is performed. This dance has indigenous origins, and its original significance is unknown. The Lord of Wonders has a special prayer said to him, first thanking him for life and for providing the believer with a unique destiny on earth, following with a petition for forgiveness and usually a request.

Puebla

The shrine to the Señor de las Maravillas in the city of Puebla is somewhat different from the one in El Arenal, Hidalgo. The building was initially a shelter for Spanish wives, then an orphanage for girls and later converted into the Convent of Santa Monica. It was built in the year 1606 and underwent renovations in the 18th century, the second half of the 19th and the beginning of the 20th. In 1934 the Augustinian nuns who inhabited it were secularized by virtue of Mexico's Reform Laws. In the following year the building became a museum and in 1940 it fell under the administration of the National Institute of Anthropology and History.

There is a legend about the creation and veneration of the image of the Lord of Wonders as found in Puebla: Centuries ago, outside the Templo de San José, located somewhere in the historic center of the city, a leafy tree once stood until one day lightning struck it down. The parish priest of the church of San José ordered an artisan to carve the image of Christ out of the wood from the tree. The image was to be of Christ in one of the falls of the Via Crucis. The skillful hands of the artisan produced an image that represented great piety and compassion. The image was originally called Nuestro Señor de los Rayos or Our Lord of Lightning. Later, this *cristo* was obtained by the Augustinian nuns in a raffle, who took it to their convent, which is now the current location of the shrine. Originally, the carving was accompanied by two Roman soldiers who held whips. In the convent, it is said that a novice heard groans and whip noises one night. In the company of the mother superior, she discovered that the Jesus statue was actually being whipped. The news of this event spread everywhere and in this way the image acquired fame and devotion. Sometime later, the carved Roman executioners were withdrawn and burned. There is another popular legend connected with this *cristo* which is like the one told in Hidalgo. A woman went every day to visit her husband, confined in the San Juan de Dios prison across the street from the Convent of Santa Monica. During her visits, she noticed the presence of a poor inmate whom no one would ever see, so the woman, moved, decided to secretly visit that man every time she went to see her husband. When her husband was released, the woman continued to go to the jail to visit the man, always bringing him a basket full of food. Her husband, alerted to the activities of his wife and suspecting that she was unfaithful to him, decided to wait for her one day at the gates of the prison. After intercepting her, he asked his wife what was in her basket, to which she replied that she was carrying only religious items. The man, suspicious, uncovered the basket and found exactly what his wife said would be in there: devotional candles, communion wafers, sacramental wine, rosaries and saintly amulets. In some versions of the story, when the husband uncovers the basket, it starts pouring out roses, much like what happened to San Juan Diego when he unfurled his cloak to reveal the image of the Virgin of Guadalupe. The woman, herself surprised, entered the grounds of the convent with her husband, where she confessed the truth. Both went immediately to the prison to see the inmate, although they could not find him or obtain any news about him, so they assumed that this man was Christ, who had put the couple's love to the test. This story caused the carving, initially known as Lord of Lightning to come to be called the Lord of Wonders.

How does the image in Puebla differ from the one in Hidalgo? The Puebla *cristo* is dressed finely and dons a wig made up of ringlets. It shows Christ fallen on the ground with the cross on his left side, resting on his knees and arms, his head turned to his right with a bleeding wound on his left cheek. The carving is life-size and weighs about 145 pounds. It is housed next to the choir gate inside the shrine. The image is often decorated with metal heart milagros, most of them made of gold or silver, given as gifts by the faithful. Next to the statue is a place for candles which was apparently the cause of a fire that occurred in the shrine on January 1, 2013. Miraculously, the image was unharmed. The Puebla version of the Señor de las Maravillas has three annual festivals: July 1, Good Friday and the third Friday of Lent. On the festival of July 1, it is a tradition that a mariachi performs "Las Mañanitas" at the entrance of the shrine where it is common for there to be food tasting. On Good Friday the image is removed from the shrine and becomes part of a procession along with other images of the area, such as the Virgen de los Dolores, Jesús de Analco, Jesús Nazareno and the Virgen de la Soledad. One of the most famous rituals related to the Lord of Wonders is the *limpia*, consisting of approaching the image with a yellow candle, making the sign of the cross and then proceeding to "clean" the whole body or a part with the same candle, which is later lit and deposited, either next to the image, or in the private home. The *limpia* is often performed by a trained practitioner for a fee. Also on the festival days, the nuns sell bagged fragments of cloth from garments that used to adorn the *cristo*, as devotees believe the cloth has special curative powers. The shrine in Puebla has more visitors from a larger geographical area, and the one in Hidalgo is seen as a humbler place to honor this interesting depiction of Christ.

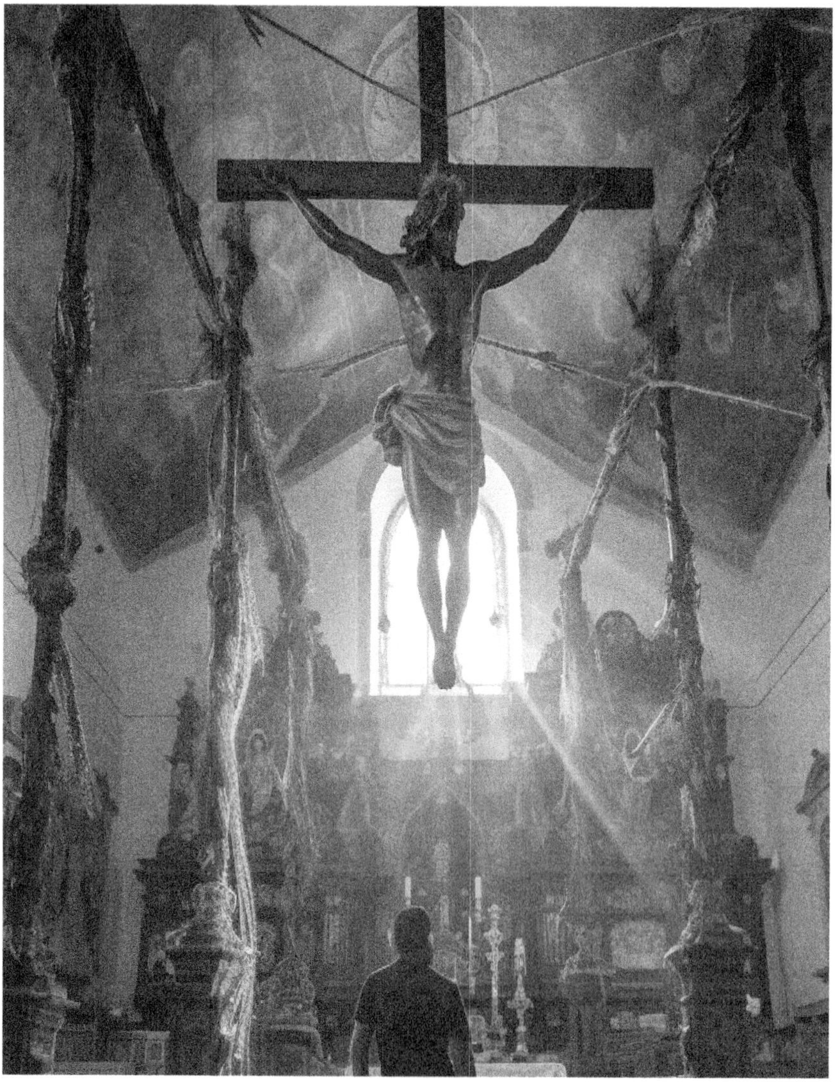

THE STUBBORN JESUS OF GIL DE LEYVA

This brief legend takes place in a tiny town south of Monterrey called Gil de Leyva, now a suburb of a larger town called Montemorelos. The former Misión de la Purificación which had been founded in 1715, was serving as a church for the small town just a few decades later. In this church was a venerated image Jesus, a carved *Cristo* of Tlaxcalan origin, crafted by skilled indigenous hands sometime in the mid-1500s. The pious inhabitants of Gil de Leyva and the surrounding countryside attributed numerous miracles to this beautiful wooden carving, and many made pilgrimages to the small church to give thanks. A few decades before Mexican independence, an unbelieving Spanish army captain came to the town and heard about the miracles attributed to the statue of Jesus in the modest church. The captain wanted to show the townsfolk that the venerated icon did not possess any power. Mounted on his horse, he entered the church, amid the astonishment and fear of the faithful, who were devoutly listening to mass, and lassoed the sacred image, pulling strongly on it with the intent of removing it from the chapel. Overwhelmed with terror, the captain felt the image pull back harder than he was pulling. So, he then decided to make a superhuman effort to rip the Jesus off the altar. He whipped his horse to pull harder and then his horse suddenly slipped. The incredulous captain was violently thrown to the ground and died immediately.

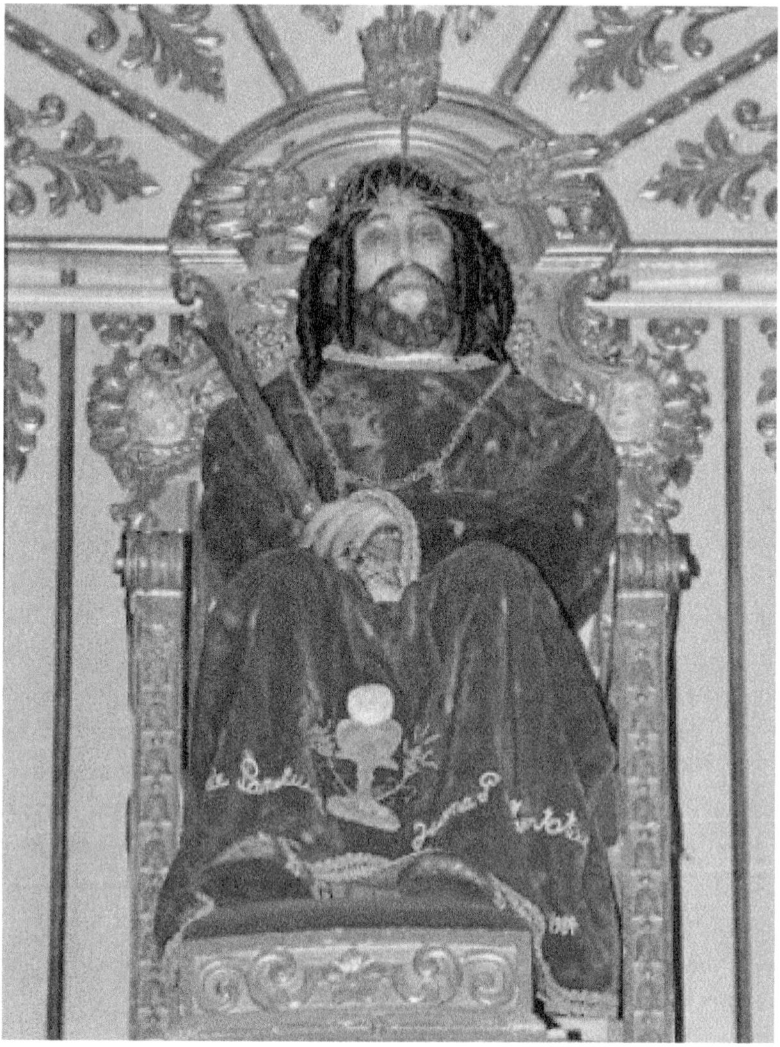

EL SEÑOR DE LA SANTA ESCUELITA

In a small town in the state of Jalisco an old woman sat at her spinning wheel turning wool into thread, wiling away her time. She enjoyed her golden years and was very happy, but her room was lacking something special: a statue of Jesus. The old woman couldn't venture very far away from her home, so she prayed that one day a traveling salesman would come to her remote area and sell her the perfect Jesus statue. One day, this very thing happened. Her grandchildren alerted her of a traveling salesman in town and told him to visit the old woman's house. He arrived and she was delighted to see him. From his sack he pulled out a beautiful statue of Jesus, with long curly hair flowing well past his shoulders. She examined the statue and said she would buy it and asked the peddler if he could wait outside while she fetched her money. He told her she could take the statue inside with her and she did. When the old woman went back outside to pay the traveling vendor, he was gone.

Months passed and she forgot about the salesman, but since the day of the sale she had built an altar in the corner of her room with the spinning wheel and had clothed her precious statue in a fluffy blouse. One day, the old woman fell asleep at the wheel and while she dozed a candle on her altar caught the blouse of her precious Jesus on fire. She awoke in time to put out the fire, but the statue was damaged. She took it down to the stream to clean it, but the damage was so great that she had to send it off to Guadalajara for repairs. When the woman received the statue back, the paint and plaster from the repairs fell off. She sent the Señor away two more times, but whenever she got the statue back the paint and plaster would fall away, revealing the horrible burn marks. It didn't matter because not only did the woman have faith in her statue, but people living around her did, too, and sometimes she would receive visitors who would pray and make offerings at her little altar in the spinning wheel room.

When the old woman died, she left money for a small chapel to house her precious statue. The shrine soon attracted people from hundreds of miles away. Thousands of people had faith in this image of Jesus, now called El Señor de la Santa Escuelita. During a drought which lasted months, the statue was paraded throughout the countryside to help make it rain. After two more processions there was still no rain. One of the wealthiest men in the community – a rich *ranchero* who owned thousands of acres of land – doubted the powers of the Señor and made a proclamation that if a gussied-up wood carving can make it rain, he would drink every last drop of water. As soon as he said this, the sky grew dark, and it started raining. The rain came hard, and it rained day and night, coming down buckets. After the third day of rain, the ranchero's property resembled a swamp. As the rain continued for weeks, everything the man owned was slowly being washed away. At the end of the second month of non-stop precipitation the wealthy man went to the shrine of El Señor de la Santa Escuelita and knelt before the statue he once ridiculed. There were many people there and he led the group in prayer. Within a few hours the skies calmed down and the following morning the sun shone through the clouds. The people in the area were now tasked with a hefty cleanup. The *ranchero* returned to his flooded home and vowed never again to doubt the power of El Señor.

OUR LORD OF POISON

Deep within the heart of Mexico City's historic center, inside the magnificent Metropolitan Cathedral, lies an enigmatic and somewhat macabre figure, yet another *Cristo negro*. Known as "El Señor de Veneno," or the "Lord of Poison," this mysterious statue has captured the imaginations of the faithful and the curious alike. With a history shrouded in legend and folklore, the Señor de Veneno stands as a testament to the complex interplay between faith, history, and superstition in Mexico.

The legend surrounding El Señor de Veneno is inextricably tied to the wealth amassed by the church during the Spanish colonial era. As the story goes, a large sum of gold was secretly hidden within the walls of the Metropolitan Cathedral. The statue of El Señor de Veneno was said to have been crafted to protect this treasure, which was rumored to be tainted by the blood of indigenous people who had been exploited and enslaved during the colonial period.

The statue was believed to serve as both a guardian and a warning. It was said to hold the curse of the poisoned gold and to punish anyone who sought to steal or desecrate it. Those who dared to tamper with the statue, the legend foretold, would face dire consequences.

Despite the ominous tales associated with El Señor de Veneno, the statue has garnered a dedicated following of the faithful. Every year, on the first Friday of March, a procession is held to honor this enigmatic figure. Pilgrims from all corners of Mexico gather at the Metropolitan Cathedral to pay their respects, and many fervent believers attribute miracles to the statue.

The faithful often pray to El Señor de Veneno for protection and guidance in their lives. They believe that the statue, despite its fearsome reputation, is a source of comfort and aid, helping them through their trials and tribulations. This blend of fear, reverence, and hope is a testament to the complexity of a uniquely Mexican relationship with religious icons.

In the modern age, the legend of El Señor de Veneno has evolved. While some may still fear the statue's alleged curse, it is largely seen as a symbol of Mexico's complex history, where the legacies of colonization, resistance, and faith intertwine. It has become a unique representation of the nation's cultural and spiritual identity.

El Señor de Veneno, the Lord of Poison, stands as a singular and enigmatic figure within the hallowed walls of Mexico City's Metropolitan Cathedral. Whether one sees it as a guardian of cursed gold, a source of miracles, or a symbol of Mexico's intricate history, the statue captures the imaginations of those who encounter it. In a country known for its vibrant religious traditions and complex cultural tapestry, El Señor de Veneno serves as a testament to the enduring power of faith and folklore.

MEXICAN CATHOLIC SAINTS AND HOLY ONES

By the 2020s the Catholic Church had recognized a total of 11 saints who had some connection to Mexico, having either been born there, lived there or died there. There are dozens more people whom the church has declared "Blessed," "Venerable" or a "Servant of God," who are on the path of sainthood. These are common people who lived extraordinary lives who either dedicated their lives to holy causes or gave their lives for them. The country of Mexico has more saints, blesseds, venerables and servants of God than any other country in the Western Hemisphere and the list of Mexicans on track to sainthood is most likely to grow.

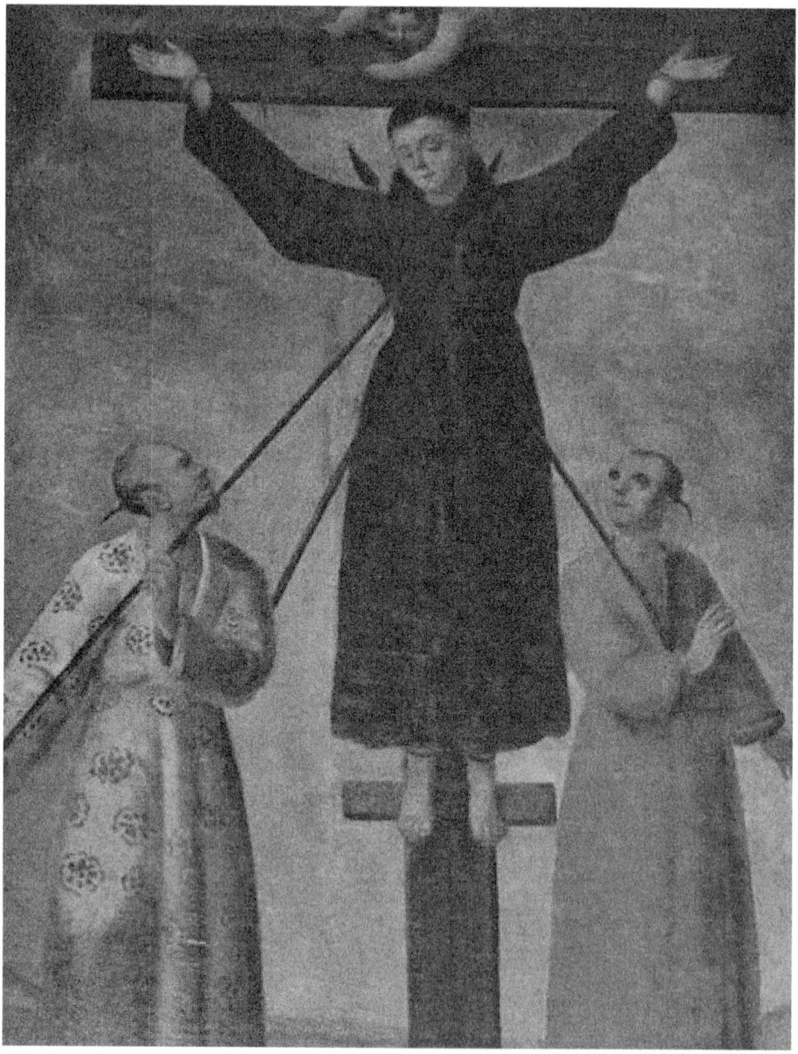

FELIPE DE JESÚS
MEXICAN MARTYR IN JAPAN

Dressed in black with her head covered in a dark lace cactus shawl, Antonia Martínez Fernández, made her way as part of the procession to Mexico City's metropolitan cathedral. Antonia was almost 80 years old and was moving slowly, as was this long march of people to the religious heart of New Spain. The elderly Mexican woman was flanked by some of the most powerful people of the Spanish Empire in the New World, notably, the viceroy himself, the Marqués de Cerralvo, and the Archbishop of New Spain, Francisco Manso y Zúñiga. It was the morning of February 5, 1629. Antonia could not believe that she was part of such a grand spectacle, having left Spain for the New World as a girl some 70 years before. It was a jubilant but sad day for this woman whose son was being honored by a city for acts committed a continent and an ocean away some 2 decades before. In August of the previous year, the head of the Franciscans in Mexico, Francisco de la Cruz, had presented a bull of beatification signed by Pope Urban VIII, to various dignitaries in Mexico City: the archbishop, the viceroy and the members of the city council. The pope had honored the city by beatifying one of their own, the Mexico-City-born Felipe de las Casas known thenceforth as the Blessed Felipe de Jesús. Felipe's mother, the elderly Antonia, had prayed the night before for the strength to participate in the solemn ceremonies and festivities to honor her son. She was too tired to take part in the masquerade held that night or to view the fireworks to be set off in her son's honor. The officials of the city were proud of Antonia's son and spent a great number of resources to mark the first official feast day of the first person born in the New World, and the first Mexican, to be recognized by the pope in Rome to be put on the track for sainthood. Felipe de las Casas would eventually be canonized by Pope Pius the Ninth 233 years later in 1862.

No one knows exactly where in Mexico City Felipe de las Casas was born or when, as no baptismal records exist. His year of birth is recognized as 1572. His parents were *peninsulares*, or those born in

Spain, and both had immigrated to the New World less than a half century after the Conquest of the Aztecs and the fall of Tenochtitlán. It is unclear whether Felipe's parents had come from moderate wealth or if they were members of the merchant class of New Spain. As a youth in colonial Mexico City, Felipe has been noted as having several different professions from silversmith apprentice to soldier. Much of his early life has been taken from secondhand accounts written many years after his death. The future saint was said to have had a kind of "bad boy childhood" and has been described as restless or mischievous, and got into more than his share of trouble. Early church biographers struggled to piece together the saint's early life which included very little "saintly" material. The young Felipe joined the Franciscans in Mexico City to bring a sense of order and discipline to his life but grew disenchanted with monastic life a few months after entering the friary. It was around the age of 17 or 18 in the year 1591 that Felipe's father gave him some money to sail to Manila in the Spanish Philippines in hopes that his son would start a business there. Felipe's early years in Asia are unclear and early biographers note that he took advantages of all the liberties that a bustling port city had to offer. By 1593, the listless Felipe de las Casas longed for a sense of discipline and perhaps some meaning to his life, so he decided to enter religious life again.

Documents show that Friar Vicente Valero, the master of novices at the Santa María de los Angeles Friary in Manila, admitted Felipe de las Casas on May 21, 1593. Felipe would have been 21 years old. He had chosen a particularly severe order, a group of "discalced" Franciscans who embraced a strictness in dress, work and prayer and who ministered among the poorest of the poor of Spain's fledgling colony of Asia. This order of Franciscans was so regimented and thorough that King Phillip the Second of Spain put them in charge of evangelizing the Philippines in 1576 with wider aspirations for Asia. The Santa María friary where the young novice Felipe resided was the center for the Franciscans greater ambitions in Asia. It was from there that they sent out unsuccessful missionaries to China and it was there where they strategized and formulated their plans for expansion into Japan which began the same year Felipe entered the order. The Jesuits had already established a beachhead in the Japanese home islands and other Christian orders looked to this ancient country to expand into. The Japanese government, then headed by the regent Toyotomi Hideyoshi, had allowed a limited number of foreigners into the country and had tolerated the new practices of the Christians, although they were closely watched.

Felipe's life at the Santa María de los Angeles friary in Manila was a quiet one and he was described as contemplative and hard-working. He showed great talent helping in the infirmary, a later biographer would note. His life as a novice was ending and soon Felipe wanted to be a priest. Because the bishop's seat in Manila was vacant, Felipe asked permission to return to Mexico City to take his vows. Permission was granted to him and in July of 1596 he left Manila bound for Acapulco on a Spanish galleon with other passengers and cargo. The ship, ironically, was named the *San Felipe*. Onboard ship was another discalced Franciscan named Juan de Pobre who kept a diary on the voyage. Much of what survives about what happened after Felipe de las Casas left the Philippines comes from Juan de Pobre's writings. As soon as the galleon *San Felipe* left the South China Sea, it encountered a series of bad storms. Between August and October of 1596, the ship was tossed about, severely damaged and unable to navigate. By mid-October the ship found itself off the southern Japanese island of Shikoku and put into port at Urado. The officials on Shikoku did not know what to do with these foreigners who they suspected as being part of some sort of scout force of a Spanish invasion. For weeks the local Japanese officials squabbled with the passengers and crew of the *San Felipe* and the situation for those shipwrecked became worse. They decided to travel to Osaka to meet with the Spanish ambassador, another fellow discalced Franciscan by the name of Pedro Bautista who also had a small mission there. The young Mexican Felipe de las Casas undertook the journey to Osaka with Juan de Pobre and two merchants who were passengers on the ship. They wanted to obtain guarantees from the supreme leader of Japan that they could affect repairs on their ship and be let free to continue along their way to Mexico, with all of their cargo returned to them intact. When the four arrived in Osaka and met with the Spanish ambassador Pedro Bautista, Bautista assured them that the ruler of Japan, Toyotomi Hideyoshi, would put pressure on the local officials at Urado to let the *San Felipe* continue its journey. The Franciscan overestimated his influence at the Japanese court. Hideyoshi was already distrustful of foreigners. He had heard that the cargo of the galleon was worth over a million and a half pesos, and there were also arms onboard. The Spanish ambassador had no other allies in Japan to whom he could go for help. Not even his fellow Christians, the Jesuits, would assist in their cause because, as previously mentioned, they saw Franciscan encroachment in Japan as a threat to their total domination over Christianity in the region. With only 7 other Franciscans in the whole country, no allies and no money to bribe the local officials on the island of Shikoku, the young Mexican friar and his entourage were at the mercy of their Japanese captors. The situation soon escalated, the *San Felipe* was formally impounded by the Japanese government, and the castaways from the ship, along with the few Japanese Christian converts from the Franciscan mission, were jailed in early December of 1596. Hideyoshi, once sympathetic to the Franciscans, eventually ordered the execution of those jailed. The Japanese ruler explained, "Some years ago Fathers came to this realm preaching a diabolical law of alien kingdoms … introducing the customs of their lands, troubling hearts of the people, and destroying the administration of this kingdom." After weeks of imprisonment, on January 3, 1597, guards cut off the left ears of the prisoners and paraded them around the city of Kyoto in wooden carts. The parading of the prisoners also took place in a handful of other Japanese cities. In addition to suffering through the extreme cold of winter, the prisoners suffered abuse at the hands of the Japanese public. Ordinary people came out to greet the parade with a volley of stones and angry citizens would shove weeds down the throats of the prisoners. The last stop on the grisly procession was the city of Nagasaki. On a hill outside of town on February 5, 1597, the prisoners were taken out of their wooden carts and promptly crucified. The young Mexican man who had lived a short life of piety in Asia was the first to die.

    News of the martyrs soon spread outside Nagasaki. Christian converts and a few remaining Spaniards and Portuguese had heard of the execution and had visited the site soon after. As is standard in stories about the saints and martyrs of the Church, the bodies of those crucified were untouched by scavengers and showed no signs of decomposition. Christian subjects throughout the Spanish Empire became outraged when hearing the news of what had happened in Japan. The Franciscans used the outrage to encourage devotion to the slain Christians and proposed martyr status for Felipe de las Casas and his companions. They sent a surviving Franciscan who had eluded Hideyoshi's capture, a Portuguese named Marcelo de Ribadeneira, to Rome by way of Mexico City to plead the case of martyrdom to the pope. Ribadeneira carried with him personal effects of the martyrs to be used as relics of devotion to further the cause of recognition. While there was initial interest in the case for martyrdom for Felipe and a growing devotion to him in Mexico City, by the time Ribadeneira left Mexico, interest in the home-grown holy man waned, and people returned to their traditional devotions to European saints and manifestations of the Virgin Mary that had proven track records of miracles and intercessions. It took a great deal of lobbying in Rome to get Felipe recognized and later beatified, and the elites of Mexico City in the early 17th Century used the fact that their town had produced a man on his way to becoming a saint to foster a sense of pride, thus elevating their city's status within the Spanish Empire. The local people, though, had a hard time accepting the young Mexican martyr as a saint they could rely on even though Felipe de las Casas, renamed Felipe de Jesús, was one of their own. With time and a large PR campaign in the early days, this martyred man who died so far away from Mexico became an important part of the Catholic pantheon and Mexican religious life and has thousands of devoted followers centuries after his death.

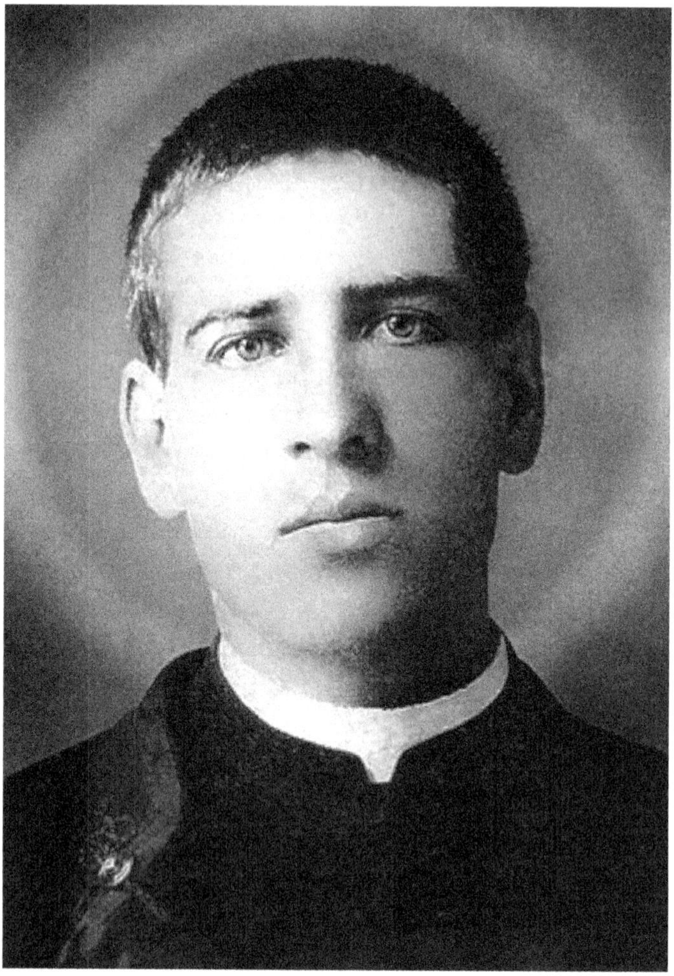

TORIBIO ROMO
MEXICAN MARTYR AND ANGEL TO MIGRANTS

Santo Toribio Romo – in Latin, Saint Thuribius – was a humble parish priest born in the Mexican state of Jalisco who has become one of the most venerated saints among the Mexicans. Saint Toribio was canonized by Pope John Paul II in the year 2000.

In the American Southwest in the early 1980s a young man from Zacatecas named Jesús Buendía Gaytán found himself stranded in the desert somewhere north of the US Mexico border near Mexicali. After a few days of wandering, lost, exhausted from the heat and with no water, a truck approached Jesús when he thought all hope was lost. Out of the truck emerged a blue-eyed Mexican man in his 20s, who offered Jesús water and food and told him of a place to get work. When Jesús asked the stranger what he wanted for payment, the young, man told him that when he had enough money to return to Mexico, to look for him at a small church in the town of Santa Ana de Guadalupe in Jalisco where he served as a parish priest. Years later, Jesús did just that and was amazed to see the portrait of his desert savior hanging over the altar of town's church. The only problem here was that the Good Samaritan who had helped him had died some 50 years before that desert encounter. There are many other stories of a man who fits Toribio Romo's description helping migrants in the desert. Sometimes he appears to offer tangible things like water or money. Sometimes he appears to console the travelers or encourage them to keep going. Sometimes he has even been known to encourage people to return to Mexico. Other times he appears fully frocked as a priest and sometimes wearing the simple clothes of a Mexican cowboy. In all cases, he is there to help with the journey.

No one knows how Toribio Romo became the de facto patron saint of border crossers or those undertaking perilous journeys. While the Catholic Church recognizes him as a saint, they do not recognize him as the patron saint of migrants, a role he has assumed seemingly spontaneously. The Vatican's official saint for migrants, ironically, is the first American citizen to become a saint, Mother Frances Cabrini, an Italian nun who helped Italian immigrants in the US in the late 19th Century. As Mexicans have a hard time identifying with Mother Cabrini, Santo Toribio has filled the void and has been growing in popularity as the patron saint of Mexican migrants ever since his canonization.

So, who was Toribio Romo, the man? He was born in the year 1900 in the small farming town of Santa Ana de Guadalupe in Jalisco a little way off the main road leading from Guadalajara to San Juan de los Lagos. He was from a very poor family, but early on young Toribio stood out from the other children for his intelligent and contemplative nature. From an early age he wanted to go to seminary and become a priest, but his family hesitated in sending him away. In 1912 Romo entered the Auxiliary Seminary about 25 miles away in San Juan de los Lagos. Ten years later he became a priest, one of the youngest to be ordained in Mexico which required special permission from the Vatican.

Toribio Romo has been described as a deep thinker and scholar, constantly challenged by matters of faith and always examining his conscience. He was known for having a fine mind and gentle nature. He also loved writing. In an ironic twist, in 1920, while still in seminary, Toribio Romo published a play called "Let's Go North!" a comedy about the perils of crossing the border to find work in the United States and what would happen to a man after spending too much time on the other side of the border. Like many Catholic priests of the time, Romo discouraged people from leaving their small towns to seek work in the United States. His one-act play consists of two characters, the Americanized Mexican Don Rogaciano who returns to his town with money and fancy clothes, and an attitude of superiority and worldliness, and Sancho, a smart-mouthed local who never left Mexico. Don Rogaciano tries to impress the townsfolk with his command of English and his city ways and denounces village priests as "money-grubbing retrograde obscurantists." In the end Sancho gets the best of Rogaciano by beating him with a cane, but Toribio Romo's main message of the play can be found in some of the final words of the Sancho character when he says this: "Take a good look at what becomes of the Mexican who goes north. He ends up a man without religion, without a country or home… a coward, a feminized man who is incapable of feeling shame for having abandoned his responsibilities to his family. Despite this, the roads are packed with Mexicans headed toward the United States in search of bitter bread. Everywhere you hear the rallying cry: 'Let's go north!'"

To understand the saint's life and death, we must examine the times in which he was alive. Toribio Romo lived during a dark and often unexamined period in Mexican history. As a young priest Father Romo found himself in the middle of the Cristero War also known as the Cristero Rebellion or La Cristiada, a brutal internal conflict that lasted between 1926 and 1929 and pitted rural Catholic lay people and clergymen against the forces of the anti-Catholic, anti-clerical central government in Mexico City headed by President Plutarco Calles. Calles sought to enforce the anti-clerical articles of the new Constitution of 1917 produced by the Mexican Revolution and enacted legislation to reduce the power of the Church. This so-called Calles Law was seen as a continuation of the long struggle of Church versus State that dated back to La Reforma of the mid-19th Century. Under this law restrictions were placed on the Catholic clergy and the power of the Church was further limited. Popular religious celebrations were suppressed in local communities along with the number of priests allowed to serve in Mexico as a whole. A few uprisings happened in 1926 and full-scale violence ensued by 1927, most notably in the countryside of the states of Zacatecas, Jalisco and Michoacán. By 1927 all priests were prohibited from celebrating the mass and ordered confined to their residences or to relocate to urban areas. Most clergy did not take part in violence, although many, like Father Toribio, defied the authorities and continued performing Catholic rites. The Church hierarchy in Mexico tacitly supported the grassroots rebellion and the authorities in Rome condemned the Mexican government. Curiously, two groups from the United States involved themselves in this war. The Knights of Columbus, a service arm of the Catholic Church, donated money to the Cristero movement. When the first donation of the Knights was announced, another group of Americans calling themselves knights – the Ku Klux Klan – offered President Calles $10,000 to fight against the Cristeros. By 1928, Dwight Whitney Morrow, the US Ambassador to

Mexico at the time became involved and eventually helped broker a truce between government forces and the Cristeros. In the end, approximately a quarter million people died in the fighting, and Toribio Romo was among them. On Friday, February 24, 1928, just a year before the end of the war, soldiers broke into the bedroom of Father Romo who had been taking an afternoon nap. A few tense moments and two bullets later, the humble priest, who never took up arms or antagonized any uprising against the authorities, was dead. He was 27 years old.

Father Toribio Romo later became one of the 25 Mexican Martyrs of the Cristero War honored by the Catholic Church. He was later beatified and then canonized. Since his canonization in the year 2000 great interest has developed in the saint and thousands of people flock to the tiny town of Santa Ana de Guadalupe to visit his shrine and to see where he spent his youth. As with many shrines in Mexico, supporting businesses have grown up alongside the attraction to serve the multitudes of pilgrims who come each year. Where there were no restaurants in Santa Ana, there are now 3, along with an ice cream shop and many other stores to cater to visitors. It was said by one of the locals that Santo Toribio managed to accomplish in death what he couldn't in life: the local population is more permanent now. The people of Santa Ana are not forced to go to the United States looking for work, rather, they now live off the steady income that the tourist trade provides.

The official saint statue of Toribio Romo went on tour to various Mexican-American parishes in California in 2013. The statue includes a relic of the saint, a piece of Romo's ankle bone, encased in glass affixed to the torso of the statue. People flocked to Indio, Hawthorn, Reseda and other cities to catch a glimpse of the saint, to thank him or to ask for a miracle. The traveling saint proved more popular than the Church could have imagined with thousands of pilgrims showing up at events.

Returning to the migrants in the desert, alone, beaten by the sun, dehydrated, running from the authorities and threatened by rattlesnakes, this question comes to mind: Who comes to them in the middle of the wasteland when all hope is nearly lost? Is this angelic coyote a mere hallucination or a product of wishful thinking, or is this mysterious blue-eyed man sent by the divine to help those unfortunate people along to live a life on earth that for him was cut short?

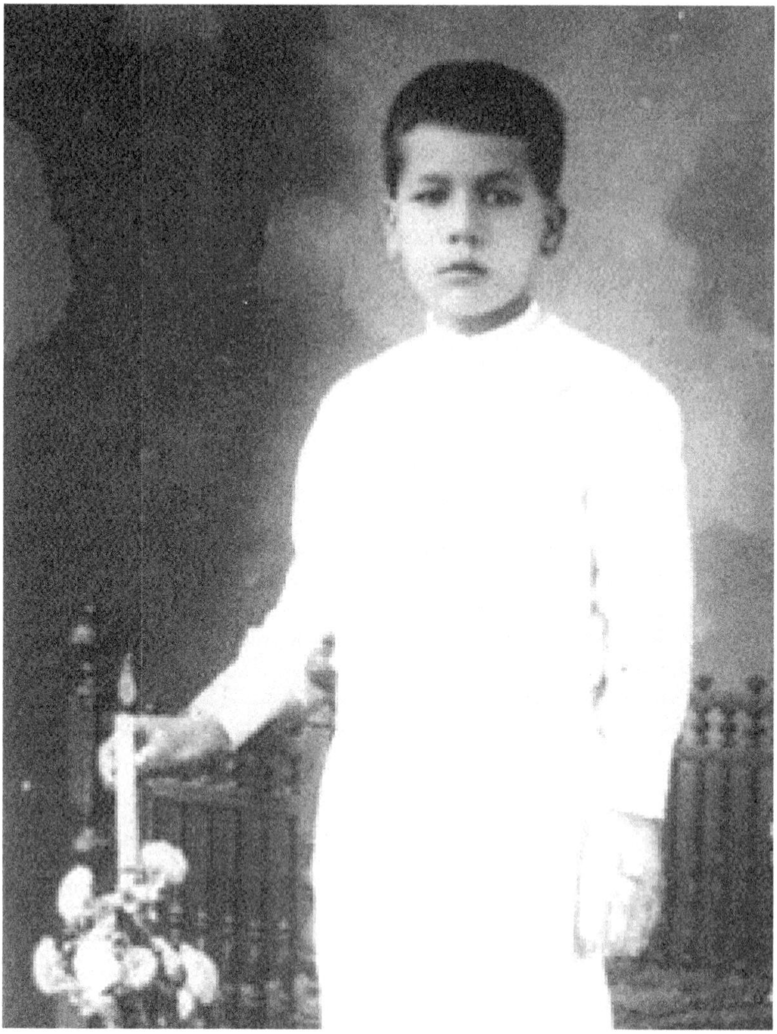

JOSÉ SÁNCHEZ DEL RIO
MEXICO'S BOY SAINT

The date is October 16, 2016. A teenage boy wearing headphones helps his grandmother off a bus. She tells him to put away the headphones out of respect as they walk toward the magnificent *Piazza San Pietro* – Saint Peter's Square – in the heart of Rome, in the very heart of the Catholic world. The two had traveled far from their small town in Michoacán, Mexico, to witness the canonization of a 14-year-old boy named José Sánchez del Río who had been martyred in their home country at the hands of the *federales* in 1928. The Mexican grandmother is dressed in black and wears on her head the lace *mantilla* made of finely woven cactus fibers that her own grandmother had given her. She approaches St. Peter's with awe. For a woman who had never flown on a plane before and had never left her home state in Mexico, the event would be one of the highlights of her life. Among the 80,000 people in the square this sunny day, besides the pope and all his cardinals, is Argentine president Mauricio Macri and many pilgrims, like the Mexican *nana*, who had traveled thousands of miles for the outdoor canonization ceremonies. Hanging on the front of the Basilica are the banners bearing the likenesses of the 6 other people to be granted sainthood along with Mexico's newest saint, among them an 18th Century French nun and Argentina's "guacho priest" who ministered to the poor and eventually died of leprosy.

José Sánchez del Río was born on March 28th 1913 in the town of Sahuayo, Michoacán, in the central part of Mexico near Lake Chapala. His parents were Macario Sánchez Sánchez and María del Río Arteaga. Little José had two older brothers who had joined the Cristero movement. After witnessing the execution of a local Cristero leader whom he admired, the 13-year-old José was determined to join up with the Cristeros to fight for his faith. He asked permission of his parents and they reluctantly agreed. José left town with a childhood friend, Trinidad Flores, and in the mountains, they met up with a band of Cristero fighters. The men thought the boys too young to fight and told them they could be a part of their group but only serve a supporting role. José and Trinidad wanted to take up arms against the enemy, so they left the group and found another band under the leadership of General Luís Guizar which took them in and trained them to fight.

The boy was soon battle-tested, but his military service would not last long. In early February of 1928, the Cristeros ambushed the *federales*, somewhere between the towns of Cotija and Jiquilpan. The government troops opened fire with machine guns and a bullet hit General Guizar's horse. With the enemy fast approaching, little José gave the general his own horse and told him that he was more important. The general rode off encouraging him to run but the boy stayed and fought and was soon captured. Many of the surviving Cristeros from that battle were offered deals to surrender or were executed on the spot. José and another boy of his same age named Lorenzo, were given the opportunity to fight for the anti-Catholic side. The future boy saint told the officers that he was only captured because he ran out of ammunition, but he vowed to keep up the resistance. His friend Lorenzo stood by him, and they were both taken to a prison in Cotija.

While in prison, José was allowed to write to his parents. The letter he wrote to his mother dated February 6, 1928, survives. It reads:

My dear mother:
I was made a prisoner in battle today. I think I will die soon, but I do not care, mother. Resign yourself to the will of God. I will die happy because I die on the side of our God. Do not worry about my death, which would mortify me. Tell my brothers to follow the example that their youngest brother leaves them, and do the will of God. Have courage and send me your blessing along with my father's.

Send my regards to everyone one last time and finally receive the heart of your son who loves you so much and who wanted to see you before dying.
— José

The day after he wrote the letter José was transferred to the Catholic church in the town of Sahuayo where he was baptized. The government had transformed the church into an annex of their local military headquarters. The altar and pews were destroyed and used for firewood, the main body of the church was used to house military supplies and as a stockade of sorts for all types of animals. José's town church, which was once a beautiful place of worship, had turned into a defiled and vandalized skeleton of its former self.

News of the boy's imprisonment spread throughout the town and attempts were made to obtain his release. The soldiers would not relent. The mayor of Sahuayo, Rafael Picazo, just so happened to be José's godfather. Picazo was a federal sympathizer and firmly against the Cristero movement. He visited his godson in the makeshift prison at the former church and offered him a deal: he would let José go either if he would renounce his allegiance to the rebels, attend military school and then become an officer in the Mexican Army, or if he would agree to live in exile in the United States. The boy looked at Picazo and yelled:

"I'd rather die first! I will not go with those monkeys! Never with those persecutors of the Church! If you let me go, tomorrow I will return to the Cristeros." He ended his diatribe with the usual Cristero mantra: "Viva Cristo Rey! Viva la Virgen de Guadalupe!" which, in English means, "Long live Christ the King! Long live the Virgin of Guadalupe!"

Picazo's frustration with the boy increased as did pressure from the town for the boy's release. The last straw happened on February 9th when José was allowed to leave his cell for a bathroom break. Disgusted at what his church had become, the boy broke the necks of all the fighting roosters that were roaming around his former place of worship. The prized fighting birds belonged to Mayor Picazo. When the man heard of what happened to his property, he issued the order for the execution of the young José Sánchez del Río.

The boy was scheduled to be shot at 8:30 on the night of February 10, 1928. José was allowed one final letter to his family, which he wrote, and one final meal, delivered to him by his Aunt Magdalena. In the dinner she smuggled in a small wafer of the Blessed Sacrament, so the future saint could have his final Holy Communion. When his aunt visited him, José seemed calm and resigned to his fate. He told the tearful Magdalena, "We will see each other in Heaven soon."

Before the execution, Picazo wanted the boy to suffer. He instructed the soldiers to lash the bottom of José's feet, and they beat him repeatedly. With each beating, the boy cried out the Cristero cry, "*Viva Cristo Rey!*" Picazo wanted the boy to be killed quietly, away from the eyes of the townsfolk, so they made him walk with his bloodied feet to the cemetery at the end of Constitution Street – the boy's own Via Dolorosa – where they gave him one last chance to deny his faith. The boy refused and was hit in the jaw with a rifle butt. Another soldier stabbed him repeatedly, and with each thrust of the knife, the boy professed his loyalty to Christ. Moments before his death, José drew a cross in the dirt and kissed it. His life finally ended when one of the soldiers shot him behind the ear. His body was thrown into a shallow grave and covered with dirt. The caretaker of the cemetery later contacted a local priest, Father Ignacio Sánchez, who exhumed the boy's body, wrapped it in white sheets and prayed over him. Thus, the boy José Sánchez del Río became a Catholic martyr with the path to sainthood paved by Pope Benedict XVI who beatified him on his visit to Mexico on November 20, 2005. After a medical miracle was ascribed to the intercession of the Blessed José Sánchez del Río in 2015, Pope Francis declared him a saint on October 16, 2016, telling a congregation of thousands that little José would always be remembered for his fortitude, valor, hope and his holy audacity. A very sad story, it seems, has given Mexicans and other faithful people cause to reflect upon and celebrate the brief life of an extraordinary young boy.

MADRE LUPITA
ANGEL TO THE POOR

It was a sunny spring day in Rome. The date was Sunday, May 12, 2013. Pope Francis had been head of the Catholic Church for only a month and was already participating in a canonization ceremony which had been scheduled months before by his predecessor, Pope Benedict XVI. The Argentine pope scanned the crowd at Saint Peter's Square and noticed many humble looking people clad in bright sarapes and indigenous dress alongside nuns wearing the crisp white habits of their order which seemed to radiate their own light in the midday Italian sun. The sisters and colorfully attired Mexicans had made the long journey to Rome to witness one of their own made into a saint, a nun who lived an extraordinary life, a woman born Anastasia Guadalupe García Zavala, in the Guadalajara suburb of Zapopan in 1878. "Madre Lupita," as she was also known, would share the stage that day with many others whom the pope would declare saints: a Colombian woman who set up jungle missionaries to minister to the indigenous, and the 800 Martyrs of Otranto, a group who died at the hands of Ottoman invaders of the Italian town of Otranto in 1480, choosing death by beheading instead of a forced mass conversion to Islam. While the ceremonies surrounding the proclamations of saints can sometimes be solemn affairs, the Mexicans in Saint Peter's Square that day felt a light sense of joy in their hearts upon seeing Madre Lupita getting the recognition she deserved. By the end of the day the Mexicans had their second female saint: Saint María Guadalupe García Zavala, Angel to the Poor.

    The future saint was born to an upper-middle-class merchant family in the state of Jalisco on April 27, 1878. She was named Anastasia, but went by María, one of the names assigned to her at her christening. María's father, Fortino García, owned a store selling religious merchandise located next to the Cathedral of Zapopan, now the Basilica of Our Lady of Zapopan. As a young girl, María would accompany her father to the family's religious goods store and would always stop into the cathedral to pray to the Virgin there or to take contemplative walks on the cathedral's grounds. María's daily visits to one of the most visited Catholic shrines in Mexico exposed her to many aspects of humanity. People came to the shrine to pray out of desperation for a loved one or for an impossible situation. The extremely poor, the handicapped, or indigenous people newly arrived from the countryside were regular fixtures at the front steps of the building, begging for assistance and hoping for miracles. María witnessed the extremes of generosity and poverty daily and what she experienced would influence her for the rest of her life. No one else in the García family had the enthusiasm for visiting the cathedral as did the young María, and she became known for her devotion and deep faith, even at a young age. Through her adolescence she maintained her religious devotions and grew into a beautiful young woman. At age 23, María was engaged to a handsome up-and-coming young businessman named Gustavo Arreola. At a dance, right before she was to be married, she called off the engagement and told Gustavo that she had a different calling and wanted to pursue a life of religious devotion. It was at this point when María contacted her spiritual advisor, Father Cipriano Iñiguez and talked to him about her change of plans and told him of a strong urge she had for service within a religious order. Father Iñiguez told María that for the longest time he wanted to establish an order to help in hospitals to tend to the sick and dying. After months of planning together, on October 13, 1901, Father Iñiguez and María García Zavala founded a new order officially named The Congregation of the Handmaids of Saint Margaret Mary and the Poor. The patroness of the congregation, Saint Margaret Mary Alacoque, was a 17th Century French nun who was part of the order of The Poor Ladies, Sisters of Saint Clare, known informally as The Poor Clares.

From the patron saint of the order Sister María drew her example of living a simple and humble existence. She joyfully embraced poverty and was often heard saying, "Be poor with the poor," while ministering to the sick and needy. In the early days of the new order, María worked out of a small run-down building that served as their hospital. She welcomed patients who had no money to pay for their care and tended to them both physically and spiritually. As news of her good works spread, more young women showed interest in joining the Handmaids. Father Iñiguez soon made María the Superior General of the order and she was thereafter known as "Madre Lupita." True to her motto, "Be poor with the poor," Madre Lupita and her sisters would often beg on the street to raise funds for their medical facilities. The sisters would retire to the hospital when the basic needs of the facilities were met and didn't ask of others any more than they needed. As the Handmaids of Saint Mary Margaret and the Poor grew, they expanded their reach out of their hospital and into the community, often working in the local parishes to teach catechism classes or to assist with elderly or sick parishioners.

By 1911, with Madre Lupita's order financially stable and things finally looking up for the sisters, the political situation in Mexico changed for the worse. There was much uncertainty in the early days of the Mexican Revolution, especially regarding the status of the Catholic Church. For most of Mexico's history there has existed a struggle between secular and clerical power. The government historically had always sought to limit the power of the Church and throughout the 19th Century the Church was subject to halfhearted attempts to limit its power and wealth. By the beginning of the 20th Century, those who overthrew the old order ruling Mexico wanted to have a much stricter control over church authority and many restrictive provisions were written into the new constitution. Church and state relations remained uneasy at best until the Cristero War in the 1920s. Madre Lupita found herself in the middle of this brutal conflict also known as the Cristero Rebellion or La Cristiada, which lasted between 1926 and 1929 and pitted Catholic lay people and clergymen against the forces of the anti-Catholic, anti-clerical central government in Mexico City headed by President Plutarco Calles. Calles sought to enforce the anti-clerical articles of the new Constitution of 1917. Under these laws restrictions were placed on the Catholic clergy and the power of the Church was further limited. Popular religious celebrations were suppressed in local communities along with the number of priests allowed to serve in Mexico as a whole. Consequently, Madre Lupita and the Handmaids gave up wearing the nun's habit and dressed as modest laypeople, but continued their hospital work unabated. A few uprisings happened in 1926 and full-scale violence ensued by 1927, most notably in the countryside of the states of Zacatecas, Jalisco and Michoacán. Most clergy did not take part in violence, although many defied the authorities and continued performing Catholic rites. The Church hierarchy in Mexico tacitly supported the grassroots rebellion and the authorities in Rome condemned the Mexican government. During the Cristero War, Madre Lupita did two things of note. She sheltered "rebel" priests in her hospital facilities, including the Mexican government's most wanted man, the Archbishop of Guadalajara, Francisco Orozco y Jiménez. Madre Lupita, as a consummate humanitarian, also did not take sides in the fight; she opened her hospital facilities to everyone and even treated injured and dying government soldiers who had fought against the Catholic Church. It was this gesture – of welcoming and treating anyone in need – that afforded her the protection of the local government garrison which should have been her sworn enemy. By 1928, the Cristero War ended and hundreds of thousands of people were dead on both sides. Madre Lupita's order emerged from the conflict even stronger than before. In the 1930s and 1940s the order expanded throughout Mexico and ministered to the poor and helpless in the most desperate areas of the country. Nuns continued to live in the new convents as per Madre Lupita's motto, "Be poor with the poor," with an emphasis on tireless, compassionate care for those in most need.

After a 2-year illness, Madre Lupita passed away on June 24, 1963 at the age of 85. In her 6 decades of service to the underserved, she helped hundreds of thousands of people. At the time of Madre Lupita's death, her order operated 11 facilities throughout Mexico. By 2017 that number had doubled and has expanded to countries outside of Mexico. The Handmaids of Saint Margaret Mary and the Poor now have hospitals in Peru, Italy, Greece and even Iceland.

Soon after Madre Lupita's death, people who prayed to her had claimed to have experienced the spirit of Madre Lupita or had a visit from her. A patient in one of the Handmaids' facilities named Abraham Arceo Higaresa who had suffered from pancreatitis was one such person. After intense prayer to Madre Lupita for her help in curing him, Abraham reported smelling a sweet fragrance and then felt 100% better. He astounded doctors by being completely healed. This was one of the two required miracles needed for Madre Lupita's promotion to sainthood. The miracle was reviewed by the Congregation for the Causes of Saints and approved after a lengthy process by Pope John Paul II on December 20, 2003. In a ceremony in Saint Peter's Square on April 25, 2004, the pope pronounced Madre Lupita "beatified," which is the last stop before canonization. To a large crowd, Pope John Paul II declared: "With deep faith, unlimited hope, and great love for Christ, Mother 'Lupita' sought her own sanctification beginning with the love for the Heart of Christ and fidelity to the Church. In this way she lived the motto which she left to her daughters: 'Charity to the point of sacrifice and perseverance until death'."

Today, Saint María Guadalupe García Zavala enjoys great veneration throughout Mexico and her popularity is growing especially among the youth of Mexico who look upon her as a grandmotherly figure. Many more miracles are ascribed to her intercession and many people throughout Mexico continue to be inspired by her example of piety, sacrifice and dedication to those most in need.

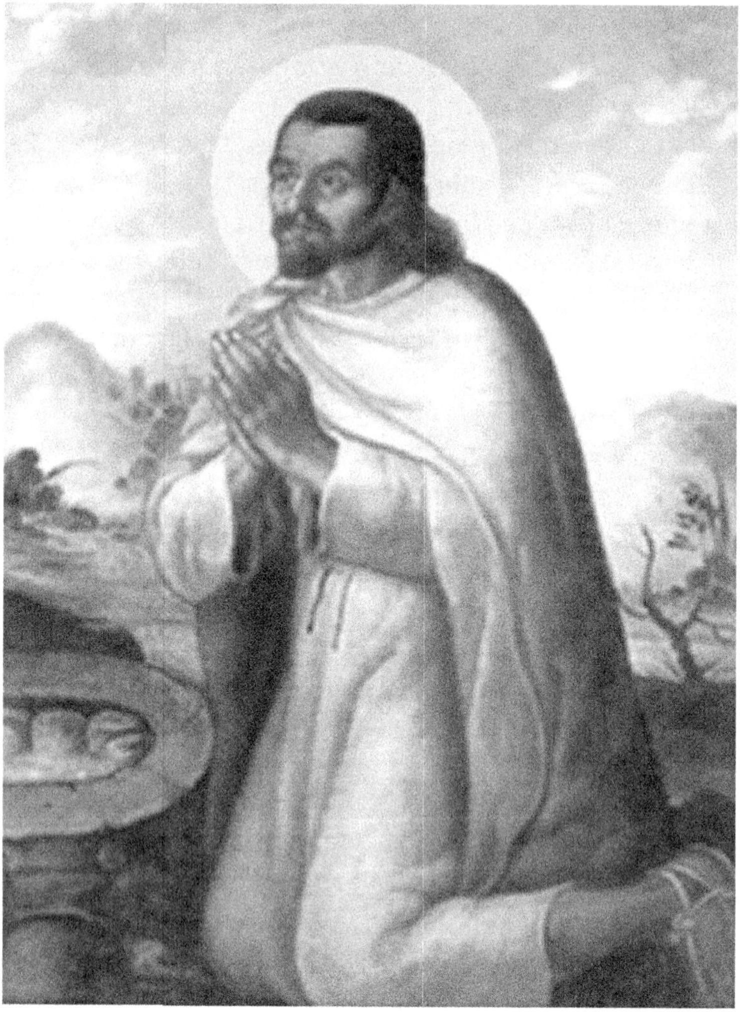

GUADALUPE'S MESSENGER
JUAN DIEGO CUAUHTLATOATZIN

    It was a warm day in Mexico City. The date was July 31, 2002. The aged Catholic pope, John Paul II, arrived at the Basilica of the Virgin of Guadalupe, after passing hundreds of thousands of people lining the streets to catch a glimpse of the 82-year-old pontiff. Hunched over, *Su Santidad*, or His Holiness, slowly made his way to a special altar set up in front of the image of the Virgin of Guadalupe. That holy place, the destination of tens of millions of pilgrims throughout the years, was the setting for a very special event: the canonization of the first indigenous saint of the Americas by the aged Polish pope who was loved by all Mexican Catholics. Although his body was frail, the pope's voice was surprisingly strong, and he read flawlessly in Spanish his prepared speech. It was his 5th visit to Mexico and by the end of the day, Mexicans had their 4th saint, officially known as San Juan Diego Cuauhtlatoatzin.

    So, who was Juan Diego and why did the Catholic Church make him a saint? In short, he played a crucial role in the story of the apparition of the Virgin of Guadalupe, a series of miraculous events occurring just 10 years after the Spanish conquest of the Aztecs. As all of this happened nearly 5 centuries ago, much of the story of Juan Diego's life and times is shrouded in mystery. Some people today allege that Juan Diego never existed, and although the Catholic Church investigated his life thoroughly and people within the church still had serious doubts, after the 2002 proclamation of sainthood, according to the Vatican the case is officially closed.

    The man known now as San Juan Diego was born in the year 1474 with the name Cuauhtlatoatzin, which means in Nahuatl, "Eagle Who Speaks." According to the official story, he lived in the town of Cuautitlán which is presently located in the Mexican state of México just north of the northern tip of the Federal District. Cuautitlán, which means, "The Place Between the Trees," was once a village of Chichimecas who had since given up their nomadic ways for a more sedentary existence. A few generations before Juan Diego's birth the future saint's hometown was conquered by the Kingdom of Tlacopan, whose capital city lay on the western shores of Lake Texcoco. When Tlacopan joined with the city-state of Tenochtitlán and the Kingdom of Texcoco to become what scholars call the Aztec Triple Alliance, Juan Diego's place of birth became part of what would later be considered the Aztec Empire. By the time he was born he would live in a fully Aztec world, and he grew up speaking Nahuatl. The house in which Juan Diego lived with his wife, María Lucia, still stands in the town of Cuautitlán and today is visited by many tourists and pilgrims alike. In the early 1520s, when Juan Diego was already in his mid-40s, the Franciscans arrived in the area and started baptizing the natives. According to the story, Juan Diego and his wife were among the very first people baptized in Cuautitlán. María Lucia died in 1529. After his wife's death Juan Diego, now in his 50s, moved to a small village near Tepeyac Hill, closer to Mexico City, and lived with his uncle Juan Bernardino. It's important to note that just a decade before, Tepeyac was a sacred place, said to be the home of the Aztec goddess Tonantzin, an earth deity also known as "The Bringer of Corn" or "The Mother of Sustenance."

    On December 9, 1531, Juan Diego was walking near the hill at Tepeyac Hill on his way to Mexico City when he heard beautiful music that sounded like the singing of birds. A cloud appeared and then an image of the sun formed around what appeared to be a young woman dressed like an Aztec princess wearing a cloak full of stars. The woman spoke to Juan Diego in his own language and told him not to be afraid. She also requested that a chapel in her honor be built on the top of the hill. Juan Diego went down into Mexico City to tell the Bishop of Mexico, Juan de Zumárraga, of what he saw and heard, which would be later referred to as the First Apparition.

    The Second Apparition occurred later that day when Juan Diego returned to the hill. He told the Virgin that he had failed on his mission to the bishop, but she told him to persist. The Virgin was emphatic that a temple devoted to her must be built on that hill and that he could not fail again. Juan Diego promised to try again and then retired to his home.

The next day Juan Diego returned to the bishop's residence to plead with him again to do as the Lady on the hill had requested. Zumárraga told Juan Diego that he needed a sign from this mysterious woman, something that would prove to him that this was Mary, the mother of Jesus Christ. When Juan Diego left, the bishop had him followed but the people following him lost track of him when he crossed a ravine. Juan Diego's trackers went back to the bishop with no information about the hill or the mysterious woman. When Juan Diego returned to Tepeyac, the Virgin was waiting for him there. This is known as the Third Apparition. Juan Diego expressed his regret for not being able to convince the bishop for the second time and told the shimmering woman that Zumárraga requested some sort of sign to prove that what he was saying was true. The Virgin then told Juan Diego to return in the morning and she would provide him with what was needed.

   Juan Diego did not return in the morning, however. His uncle, Juan Bernardino, was very sick and Juan Diego tended to him and even arranged for a doctor's visit. The visit to the lady on the hill was on his mind, but he couldn't tear himself away from his family responsibilities. The following morning, Juan Bernardino was not feeling better and asked Juan Diego to go into town and get a priest to make his last confession and to absolve him of all his sins before he died. Juan Diego did as his uncle wished, but to go into town, he had to pass by the hill at Tepeyac. He was a little reluctant to do so because he missed his meeting time with the lady on the hill the previous morning. When Juan Diego skirted the hill the woman appeared again, behind the rays of the sun and in a cloudburst as she had done the other times. This encounter is known as the Fourth Apparition. The Virgin consoled Juan Diego and told him that there was no need for him to get a priest or any more doctors because his uncle had already been healed. On the matter of the sign to present to the bishop, the lady told Juan Diego to climb to the top of the hill and to gather the flowers at its crest. Juan Diego ascended Tepeyac Hill and was surprised to see vibrantly colored Castilian roses in full bloom at the top of the hill. This was strange because it was December and the frosts had already come and the area was desolate and devoid of flowers. Juan Diego gathered some of the beautiful dew-covered roses in his cactus-fiber cloak, known as a *tilma*, and went down to the heart of Mexico City to deliver this celestial sign to Bishop Zumárraga. When he got to the bishop's palace to request an audience, the people there knew him as "the pestering Indian," and refused to acknowledge him. When one of the guards saw that Juan Diego was carrying something bunched up in his cloak, he went towards him and saw the beautiful flowers. The guard reached in to take one but couldn't. The rose he tried to grab looked more like an illustration than a real flower. Convinced that Juan Diego had something of importance, the guard granted him access to the bishop. When Zumárraga asked Juan Diego what he had for him, the humble indigenous man unfurled his cloak and a variety of beautiful roses cascaded to the ground. The bishop and those present dropped to their knees, not just because of the flowers but because of the image that appeared on the front of Juan Diego's cloak: the image of Our Lady of Guadalupe, the one known to reverent Catholics to this day. The church authorities removed Juan Diego's cloak, and that same piece of cactus cloth, which should have lasted no more than 20 years, hangs now in the Basilica of the Virgin of Guadalupe which now stands on the top of that hill at Tepeyac where the apparitions appeared.

    Soon after a small church was built on Tepeyac in 1532, masses of Indians converted to Christianity and word spread throughout New Spain of the miraculous apparitions, the curing of Juan Diego's uncle, and the beautiful roses that served as the sign from Heaven. Critics claim that the whole story was made up and that the image is a fake. The fact that the "lady on the hill" appeared in a place that had been connected to a former Aztec goddess, that the woman supposedly spoke the Indian language and looked like a Native has some people wondering if this wasn't an elaborate trick to make the process of conquest easier. To the world's billion or so Catholics, there is no doubt that the Mother of God, the "mother of us all" appeared to a humble servant that day on a hill in Mexico.

    In 1984 the Archbishop of Mexico, Ernesto Corripio Ahumada, appointed a Postulator to start an inquiry to initiate the formal process to make Juan Diego a saint. The making of a Catholic saint is a lengthy and complicated procedure. The saintly candidate goes through many stages. Juan Diego was pronounced "venerable" on

January 9, 1987. He was moved to the level of "beatified" by Pope John Paul II on May 6, 1990, during the pontiff's second visit to Mexico. To make it to the "beatified" stage, a prospective saint must have a miracle attributed to him or her. The Vatican overlooked this detail stating that since Juan Diego had been revered by Mexicans for so long, the investigation into miracles was unnecessary. A miracle connected to Juan Diego involving the survival of a drug addict who tried to commit suicide in Querétaro was later investigated and confirmed which led the pope to put Juan Diego on a list for canonization in December of 2001. The next year, 2002, the aged pontiff arrived in Mexico City for the formal sainthood ceremonies, and it was one of the most popular visits of the 100+ foreign trips that John Paul made during his nearly 27 years as pope. With his canonization, interest in San Juan Diego grew and many more miracles have been attributed to him since. While some may debate this man's very existence, no one doubts the enormous faith San Juan Diego continues to generate among true believers.

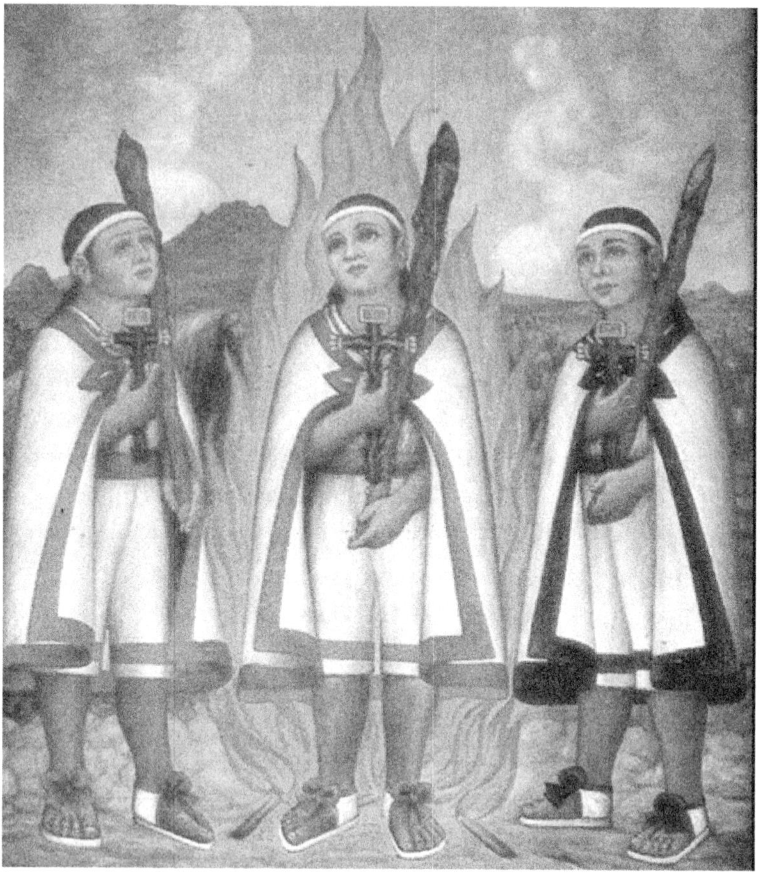

THE CHILD MARTYRS OFTLAXCALA

Pope Francis had made his decision. The date was March 23, 2017. This first Latin American pope, the outgoing and unconventional Jesuit *argentino* decided he would fast-track to sainthood three Mexican indigenous children who died in the early decades of the 1500s. The Christian names of the three who would be known to the world as the "Child Martyrs of Tlaxcala" were Cristobal, Antonio and Juan. The case for sainthood for these three began on January 7, 1982, when Pope John Paul II declared them to be "Servants of God." On his second visit to Mexico in May of 1990, Pope John Paul II furthered the cause of the Tlaxcalan martyred children and announced their beatification at the Basilica of the Virgin of Guadalupe in Mexico City. The Congregation for the Causes of Saints met in Vatican City on March 4, 2017, to approve the cause and to continue the children along the path to sainthood. This would require further investigation into their lives and whether they were associated with any miracles. The Congregation knew that Pope Francis had taken a special interest in the cause of sainthood for these children and its members were not surprised when the Holy Father bypassed the normal route taken for Catholic saints by issuing a papal decree stating that no customary confirmation of associated miracles would be required. The children had been killed in what is termed *in odium fidei* – in hatred of the faith – and had thus become the first people in the New World to die as martyrs for Christendom. That, apparently, was enough to warrant such special consideration for sainthood.

To understand the Three Martyred Children of Tlaxcala it is important to examine the world in which they lived. Where did they come from? What was life like in the area known as Tlaxcala? What was it like to be an indigenous child in the early days of colonial New Spain?

At the time of the first Spanish contact in 1519, Tlaxcala was an independent state and had been for about 150 years. It consisted of the cities of Tepetícpac Texcallan – also called Tlaxcala – Ocotelulco and Tizatlán just east of the Valley of Mexico, and the city of Quiahuitzlan which was founded later within the boundaries of the Valley of Mexico. The surrounding lands were fertile and supported a rather large population. The Tlaxcalan people were originally a conglomeration of 3 different ethnic groups speaking Nahuatl, Otomi and Pinome. Early on, the Nahua people dominated the state of Tlaxcala. This group of Tlaxcalans were closely related to the Aztecs whose empire nearly surrounded them. Tlaxcalan government was a very early example of a republic. As in the Aztec Empire there existed two classes in Tlaxcalan society, the *pilli*, or noble class, and the *macehualli*, or commoners. Whether *pilli* or *macehualli*, Tlaxcalans could be elected to the government council of *teteuctin*, which consisted of anywhere between 50 and 200 men who proved their loyalty through service to the state. The Tlaxcalan council of *teteuctin* made a variety of decisions based on popular vote and is one of the earliest examples of representative government in the Americas. A constant in pre-Hispanic Tlaxcalan society was perpetual war with the Aztecs. Historians theorize that the small state of Tlaxcala could have easily been gobbled up by the Aztecs who had one of the most powerful military forces in the world, but the Aztec Empire preferred the never-ending state of war with their smaller neighbor. One of the captains of Spanish conquistador Hernán Cortés named Andres de Tapia once asked Emperor Montezuma why his empire just didn't defeat this small state and be done with them. The Aztec emperor replied that wars with Tlaxcala provided excellent military training for his soldiers and ample captives for human sacrifices. Anthropologists refer to these series of conflicts between the Aztecs and Tlaxcalans as the "Flower Wars." Both sides would fight according to a set of conventions including predetermined spots for battles and limited use of weapons so that fighters would engage in more hand-to-hand combat. For whatever reasons these wars occurred, the Tlaxcalans were worn down by them and when the Spanish arrived in their territory asking for men to march to the Aztec capital of Tenochtitlán to take on the Aztec Empire, thousands of Tlaxcalans volunteered to join the fight. As history shows, with Tlaxcalan help, the Spanish were the ultimate victors.

    Colonial life in Tlaxcala, the context in which we find the three martyred children, was slightly different from most of the rest of

New Spain. As a reward for their help during the conquest of the Aztecs, the Spanish king granted the Tlaxcalans special privileges. The old republic of Tlaxcala remained somewhat intact for the next 300 years with the practice of limited self-government within the structure of the *teteuctin* which was allowed to continue. The Spanish had divided the Tlaxcalan homeland into 4 fiefdoms or, in Spanish, señoríos based loosely on the administrative regions that already existed in connection to the main cities of the old Independent Tlaxcalan state and renamed the capital city of Tepetícpac Texcallan, Nuestra Señora de la Asunción. The Tlaxcalans were given the highest status among all the indigenous people of New Spain. They had the right to carry guns and to ride horses. They could retain their noble titles and indigenous names. The first archbishopric established in colonial Mexico was in Tlaxcala, and the first archbishop, a 73-year-old Dominican from Aragón named Julián Garcés, assumed the post in 1525 when the martyrs Cristobal, Antonio and Juan were still alive. In addition to his primary mission of evangelization, Archbishop Garcés fought for the rights of the indigenous, established welfare services, built a hospital, and started construction of the cathedral at Puebla. Much of what Julián Garcés wrote in his diaries and letters survives to this day. He wrote this general statement about the children found throughout his immediate ministry in Tlaxcala:

"The children of the Indians... learn more rapidly and with greater joy than the Spanish children the articles of faith In their order and the other prayers. They are not chattering or quarrelsome, nor stubborn, nor restless, nor arrogant, nor disapproving, nor ill-tempered, but agreeable, and very obedient to their teachers.
"They are very intelligent, so that they can be easily taught anything. When they are ordered to count, or read or write, paint, perform any type of manual or artisan work or art, they show great clarity, quickness and facility of mind in learning the basic principles.
"No one objects, no one mumbles, nor complains because all of the care and concern of the parents is to make sure that their sons

make good progress in teachings of Christianity. They learn perfectly ecclesiastical song, as well as that of the organ and Gregorian chant and harmony to such a degree that foreign musicians are not needed."

It was the Spanish king himself who suggested that the clergy in New Spain start the evangelization process with the children of native noble houses first and that their conversion to Christianity would set an example for others living under Spanish rule who had not yet completely accepted the new faith. Great effort was made by early missionaries to focus on children with two primary objectives in mind: Conversion to Christianity and to transmit useful knowledge and skills. The first thing clerics did was to try to learn the local indigenous languages by day through playing with the children, then compiling dictionaries and grammars at night. There were some 20 major and 100 minor languages in New Spain at the time of the conquest and this was a formidable task for the friars and priests, but this group was very well educated and very patient. One of the first of the clergy to arrive was a relative of the king of Spain himself, a Franciscan from Flanders named Pedro de Gante. De Gante came up with a catechism for the Indians done in the style of the old Aztec bark-paper pictographic books called codices. He also set up the first school to educate indigenous children called San José de Belén in the former Aztec capital of Tenochtitlán. Many native noble families did not follow the Spanish king's orders and instead of sending their sons off to be educated by the Dominicans and Franciscans, they sent young household servant boys in their places. This had the unintended effect of evangelizing the lower classes along with the upper classes. The king of Spain's idea had the intended effect. As Archbishop Garcés said, the youngsters were quick learners and helpful, obedient students. More learned children often instructed other children. Bilingual children often worked closely with the clergy when it came to translation. And so, the children of New Spain adopted their new faith with zeal and spread it to their families. The evangelized became the evangelists. The newfound faith included with it the complete rejection of the old, and this caused strife within indigenous families. Here is where the story of the three Tlaxcalan martyrs begins.

Cristobal was born into a minor Tlaxcalan noble family in about 1514 or 1515, just a few years before the Spanish arrived in Mexico. When he was a young boy, Cristobal's father, Acxotécatl, reluctantly sent him away to a Franciscan school. Acxotécatl didn't concern himself too much with Cristobal's evangelism until the boy started to destroy idols to the old gods that were still being venerated in the home. At that point, the boy's father told him to stop immediately, but Cristobal continued with his personal crusade to eliminate all physical representations of the Nahua belief systems in the house. Acxotécatl grew more infuriated with his son the more "Spanish" he became and had thoughts of killing him. These thoughts were further encouraged by his second wife, Xochipapalotzin, Cristobal's stepmother. After one of Cristobal's idol-smashing tirades, sometime in the year 1527, Acxotécatl took his son by the hair, dragged him through the house and beat him terribly so as to cause many broken bones. In his fury, the father took his son outside and threw him onto a pile of burning wood. Cristobal did not die immediately but suffered with his wounds until the next day. From his deathbed, Cristobal's last words to Acxotécatl were, "Father, I forgive you." Acxotécatl hastily buried Cristobal's body in a room in their house but word quickly spread among the Tlaxcalans about what he had done. The Spanish authorities got involved and then sentenced Cristobal's father to death for his crime.

The martyring of the second and third Tlaxcalan children – Antonio and Juan – happened together two years later. Antonio was the grandson of a prominent Tlaxcalan noble named Xiochténacti, and as the eldest grandson, Antonio was set to inherit his titles and lands. Juan was a servant to Antonio and around the same age; both boys were born in 1516 or 1517. Both also converted to Christianity at the same time and were evangelists for their new faith. They found themselves in a similar situation as Cristobal: The two were destroying indigenous idols in the name of Christianity and they were caught by disapproving adults. An angry mob formed, surrounded the two and clubbed the boys to death. This was 1529. Their bodies were hurled off a high cliff but were later recovered by a Domincan friar known to history only as Bernardino.

In a gathering of cardinals at Vatican City on April 20, 2017, it was announced that Cristobal, Antonio and Juan would be canonized in Rome on October 15, 2017. It was decided by the Pope that they would be the patron saints of Mexican childhood, serving as an example of piety for generations to come.

JUNIPERO SERRA
SAINT OR VILLAIN?

The date was June 20, 2020, and the place was downtown Los Angeles, California. A few dozen people gathered at Father Serra Park, just south of Olvera Street, in the heart of old Mexican Los Angeles. Alan Salazar, an elder of both the Taviam and Chumash tribes of southern California, burned sage and invoked the spirits of his ancestors before he grabbed the megaphone. Near the end of Salazar's speech, the crowd began to chant, "Tear it down! Tear it down!" and turned their focus to the bronze statue of Junipero Serra, the 18th Century Franciscan friar who is credited with starting the California mission system in the late 1760s. The members of the crowd grabbed sturdy ropes, wrapped them around the statue and began pulling. The bronze sculpture began to rock back and forth before it came crashing to the ground. Father Serra's cross – held up above his head in his right hand – broke off as the statue hit the cement. Two members of the protesting group splashed red paint on the toppled statue. As the Franciscan lay there, two little girls climbed on his back and posed for photos. Their parents would post the images on social media later that day. The day before, a similar event took place up the coast in San Francisco. A group of nearly 100 people gathered at Golden Gate Park near the De Young Museum and the California Academy of Sciences at a place known as the Music Concourse. There, protestors tore down statues of President Ulysses S. Grant, "The Star-Spangled Banner" author Francis Scott Key and Father Junipero Serra. Statues of Spanish author Miguel Cervantes' characters Don Quixote and Sancho Panza were also vandalized, but not taken down. In comments to news media later that day, San Francisco mayor London Breed would not take sides in the statue debate and would not seek to prosecute any of the people involved in the protests. She did say, "I have asked the Arts Commission, the Human Rights Commission, and the Recreation and Parks Department to work with the community to evaluate our public art and its intersection with our country's racist history." It's not likely that the statues of Father Serra will ever return to Golden Gate Park or to the park named for him in downtown LA.

Who was Junipero Serra? He was born Miquel Josep Serra y Ferrer to a humble farming family on the island of Mallorca in the Mediterranean Sea off the coast of Spain on November 24, 1713. At age 16 he enrolled in a Franciscan school in the island's capital, Palma de Mallorca, where he studied philosophy. A few days before his 17th birthday, the young aspiring priest joined the Franciscan Order at Palma. This branch of the order was called the Alcanterine Branch, also known as the "Observant Franciscans," who strictly observed St. Francis' teachings. The teenage boy adopted the name Junipero after an early follower and companion of St. Francis of Assissi known in Catholic history as Brother Juniper. In the 7 years it took for Serra to become a priest, he immersed himself in the usual tasks of monasterial life and studied philosophy, metaphysics, theology and cosmology. In the years immediately after Serra became ordained as a priest, he taught philosophy at the Convento de San Francisco and later worked on a doctorate on theology. By 1748, Serra had decided that he wanted to pursue the life of a missionary overseas and in 1749 he was on a ship with a group of other Franciscans bound for the New World.

Serra landed at the Mexican port of Veracruz in late 1749. True to his vows, instead of using a horse, he walked to Mexico City on the Camino Real which stretched from Veracruz to the capital city through jungles and deserts and over mountains and high plains. He traveled with no money or supplies and depended on the kindnesses of those he encountered along the way. Before he left the tropical lowlands, he was bitten by a mosquito on his foot and that bite became infected, something that would remain with him for the rest of his life. Serra hobbled into Mexico City and took up residence at the Colegio de San Fernando de México, a training center for Franciscan missionaries. Serra was assigned to the missions to the Pame Indians located 90 miles north of the city of Querétaro in the town of Jalpan, nestled in the rugged Sierra Gorda mountains. Serra found the missions in disarray, and along with other newly arrived missionaries he started to spruce up and develop the missions and surrounding lands. To Serra, his predecessors had been lax in converting the local indigenous people, so he endeavored to learn their language and preach the Gospel in Pame. Serra also oversaw the construction of a beautiful church which still stands in the town of Jalpan. He not only used local indigenous laborers and craftsmen to build the church, but he also had some of the finest carpenters and artists from Mexico to come to the remote outpost to work on this ornate place of worship. In 1752, on a return trip to Mexico City, Father Serra asked that a representative of the Holy Inquisition be appointed to the Sierra Gorda to help combat a rise in witchcraft and other non-churchly practices in the area. In a surprise move, Inquisition officials appointed Serra himself to the position of Inquisitor and gave him the power to enforce the Holy Inquisition in all lands he served in or traveled to that did not already have a representative from the Inquisition working there. Serra returned to the north and filed reports – two of which survive to this day – of people whom he condemned for practicing sorcery. As indigenous people were exempt from the Inquisition unless they were already Christianized, the records show that Serra filed reports on two people of Afro-Mexican descent, a group which has been shown as overrepresented in the records of the Holy Inquisition in Mexico City.

In 1767 Serra's life changed once again when the King of Spain, Charles III, issued a proclamation expelling the Jesuit Order from all Spanish territories. The Viceroy of New Spain, the French-born Carlos Francisco de Croix, carried out the king's decree swiftly, but it took a while to expel all the members of the Order from the viceroy's jurisdiction. For the previous 70 years the Jesuits had pretty much total control over the remote peninsula of Baja California. The Jesuit expulsion left a huge vacuum in the missions and towns of that region. Back at the Franciscan headquarters at the Colegio de San Fernando in Mexico City, the Franciscan friars drew up plans to fill that void left by the forced evacuation of the Jesuits. They quickly named Father Junipero Serra as President of the Missions of the Californias. Serra was soon on a ship from the Pacific port of San Blas to sail up the coast to the mission at Loreto on the eastern side of the Baja Peninsula. He was welcomed warmly by the governor of the province known as Las Californias, a man named Gaspar de Portolá, who had recently been appointed to his post. Again, Serra arrived at a place that was severely mismanaged. Since the expulsion of the Jesuits, the Spanish military had been in charge of all 13 Baja California missions. In 1768, New Spain's Inspector General, José de Gálvez, who was appalled at the misadministration of the missions by the military, gave full control over the missions to the Franciscans. Inspector General Gálvez had grander plans for this remote corner of the Spanish Empire, and Serra would play an important role in these plans.

    By the 1760s Spain grew concerned over the fragile hold they had over their claims to the western parts of North America. Russians from Alaska had established forts and trading outposts as far south as the northern part of the modern-day US state of California. The English, too, had stepped up their activity in the region. While Spain technically claimed those lands north of the peninsula of Baja California, they never settled any of it. From his offices in Mexico City, Inspector General Gálvez formulated plans to extend the mission system found in Baja up the coast, all the way to Monterey Bay. At the time, the territory of the present-day American state of California was known as Alta California, to distinguish it from the peninsula known as Baja California. The Spanish sent two ships up the California coast to scout for mission locations, and then a formal expedition of settlement and colonization began in 1769. Serra traveled overland from Loreto with his destination at San Diego Bay, where the city of San Diego, California is now located. It took him 52 days to make the overland trek and he almost died as the infection from his foot, from that mosquito bite in the jungles outside Veracruz, spread up his leg. Serra asked one of the indigenous young men who accompanied him on the trip if he could help with the infection. The young man gathered local plants, ground them up, mixed them with sheep fat and rubbed the ointment into the infection. While some call Serra's recovery a miracle, others credit local indigenous plant knowledge with this rapid healing. Nonetheless, the 52-year-old friar reached his destination on July 1, 1769, and set to work on building a mission.

    Serra's job proved difficult as the indigenous Kumeyaay people wanted nothing to do with the San Diego mission. In the first six months of operation, with not a single native baptized, the two ships attached to the expedition plied up and down the California coast looking for other sites that would be perfect to establish more missions according to the directives of the inspector general. On April 16, 1770, Serra boarded one of those ships to head north to Monterey Bay to establish the mission there. It took 6 weeks on rough seas to get from San Diego to Monterey. The mission they would establish there would be called Mission San Carlos Borromeo, located in modern-day Carmel, California. Serra would be responsible for founding many of the 21 missions in the area and would later be called The Apostle of California.

21st Century people and history itself do not know what to make of the Spanish mission system. Contrary to popular belief, the Franciscan friars in California under Serra's leadership never rounded up nor enslaved any of the indigenous people they encountered. Critics would argue that many of the natives were forced into the mission system – which they could never leave – through pressures put on their environments due to the Spanish presence. A small famine, for example, might drive natives to seek shelter in the mission system, but once in, they could not leave. On the other hand, the missions gave all who would accept the mission lifestyle food, security, and the opportunity to learn skills like new farming techniques or a trade, like carpentry. Those examining the system may also point to the cruelty involved that seemed to be built into it by course. In Serra's defense, the Franciscan priest spoke out against abuses by members of the Spanish military who accompanied the missionaries. In many examples, the priests separated the missions from the military presidios, often relocating them away from the military presence to prevent abuses. The cruelty visited upon the Indians, some note, was the same visited on the Europeans at their own hands. The strict branch of the Franciscan order to which Serra belonged was known for its self-abuse to enact penance, including flagellation, the wearing of thorny garments, sleep deprivation, and so on. This is not to excuse any abuses brought upon the native populations of the Californias, only to put it all into context. This context and the overall history of the mission system in colonial New Spain is constantly being reexamined and reinterpreted.

In September of 2015, Father Junipero Serra became the first person to be declared a saint on American soil when Pope Francis made his first visit to the United States. In his speech about the new saint, the pope even suggested that Serra be considered as one of the Founding Fathers of the US for all his work done in California. The canonization of Junipero Serra was not, of course, without its share of controversy. While some members of California Indian tribes attended the canonization ceremonies and praised Serra's works among their people's ancestors, others did not hold such positive sentiments. in October of 2015, a week after Serra was declared a saint, his statue in Monterey was decapitated. This was the beginning of years of protests and statue destructions that continue to this day. In Mexico, Father Serra is more universally revered than in the United States. He is seen as a holy man who earned the right to be called "saint." As times change and history continues to be reexamined, the final chapter may never be written in the legacy of Father Junipero Serra.

THE MIRACULOUS LIFE OF RAFAEL GUÍZAR Y VALENCIA

Outside the town of Cotija de la Paz in the Mexican state of Michoacán, a teenage boy was wandering about his family's landholdings which numbered into the thousands of acres. The boy's name was Rafael Guízar y Valencia, one of the eleven children of Prudenzio Guízar and Natividad Valencia. It was a summer day in the year 1894 and as was typical of that time of year, a sudden thunderstorm started to pour down rain and fill the sky with lightening. The storm was particularly ferocious, but the young Rafael was intrigued by nature's violent display and sat on a hill watching the storm. Amid the dark swirling clouds and lightning bolts, the teenage boy claimed to see an image of Jesus. The sighting so alarmed him that he ran to seek refuge from the storm and entered a chapel dedicated to the Virgin of San Juan de los Lagos on his parent's property. He prayed to the statue of the Virgin and according to what Rafael would tell his parents later, the statue appeared to emit its own bright luminescence. It was at that moment in the chapel that the young blue-eyed Rafael decided to become a priest and devote his life to God. Rafael's story is very closely intertwined with the history of Mexico, and despite the many challenges of the times Rafael Guízar never gave up his spiritual and pastoral devotions.

Rafael's parents supported his decision and soon the boy entered the seminary at Zamora, Michoacán. Rafael became a priest on June 6, 1901, at the age of 23, and soon embarked on one of his countless "apostolic missions," to serve many who lived the rural communities and across the countryside in central Mexico. Because he was from a family of means, Rafael used his own money to establish a school for poor girls and two colleges for boys, in addition to setting up the Congregation of Missionaries of Our Lady of Hope, a religious community, in 1903. The year 1910 saw the beginnings of the Mexican Revolution and the first of two major persecutions of the Catholic Church in early 20th Century Mexico. Guízar saw the need to minister to soldiers on both sides, especially on the battlefield to administer the Catholic sacraments such as confession and last rites. He was on the revolutionary government's blacklist, however, and had a bounty on his head. With his congregation wiped out and his public career gone, Father Rafael Guízar went underground, so to speak, and fled to the safety of Mexico City where he set up a printing press and began to publish evangelical materials. The government shut him down and he fled the city, accompanying factions of the revolutionary army in disguise – sometimes as a junk dealer, a doctor or a musician – but always ministering to the soldiers in secret and fulfilling his duties as a priest. With a price still on his head, he was captured in 1915 and sent to jail to await a firing squad. Guízar protested and claimed that they arrested the wrong man and that he really wasn't Father Rafael Guízar or a Catholic priest at all, but a poor traveling musician. One of the jailers gave him an accordion and told him to play. Father Rafael did just that and filled the jail with marvelous renditions of popular Mexican folk songs. Everyone was entertained and he soon had them convinced that they had arrested the wrong man. One of his captors was noted as saying, "Here's 25 pesos. Take the accordion and go." Little did they know that as a priest-in-training, the future saint was the head of a musical group he founded at the seminary called "Los Gallos Misticos," or in English, "The Mystical Roosters."

   As soon as he left the hands of the revolutionaries Guízar escaped to Texas and by 1916 he found his way to Guatemala where he stayed for 8 months. After Guatemala it was on to Cuba; he had a sister who had married well and was living a good life in Havana. Besides a brief stint in Colombia, he lived in Havana for 3 years. Everywhere he went, even if it was for a brief time, Guízar set up missions to help the poor and underserved. He was relentless in this regard and worked tirelessly to assist those in need. By late 1919 Guízar was named Bishop of Veracruz and was sent back to Mexico. By the time of his arrival on January 4, 1920, the state of Veracruz had suffered a terrible earthquake in which thousands of people were killed, especially in the interior of the state. Guízar forewent the pomp and circumstance of an official investiture and hit the ground running when he arrived at his new post. He immediately took a train to the interior, the areas most affected by the quake, to give assistance and solace to those in the direst need. The first years of his term as bishop were marked by his intense approach to evangelization and helping the rural areas of his jurisdiction. Guízar was often seen traveling by burro or on foot to get to the communities that needed him the most. His pastoral outreach was once again thwarted by the changing political situation in Mexico by 1926 with the outset of the Cristero Rebellion, that brutal internal conflict of the late 1920s which pitted rural Catholic lay people and clergymen against the forces of the anti-Catholic, anti-clerical central government headed by President Plutarco Calles. A few uprisings happened in 1926 and full-scale violence ensued by 1927, most notably in the countryside of the states of Zacatecas, Jalisco and Michoacán. By 1927 all priests were prohibited from celebrating the mass and ordered confined to their residences or to relocate to urban areas. Most clergy did not take part in violence, although many, like Bishop Guízar, defied the authorities and continued performing Catholic rites. Guízar's seminary was the only functioning training center for Catholic priests during the entire conflict and had over 300 young men enrolled. The Church hierarchy in Mexico tacitly supported the grassroots rebellion and the authorities in Rome condemned the Mexican government. By 1928, Dwight Whitney Morrow, the US Ambassador to Mexico at the time became involved and eventually helped broker a truce between government forces and the Cristeros. In the end, approximately a quarter million people died in the fighting. Because he was a controversial figure and once again wanted for his subversive activities, Bishop Guízar spent a little less than two years abroad for a second time, going back to Texas, Cuba, Colombia and Guatemala to check on the progress of the missions he had founded in those areas less than 10 years before. In 1929 he found himself back in Mexico and assumed his pre-Cristero activities

    The end of the Cristero Rebellion did not end the hard times for the Catholic Church in Mexico, nor did it make life easier for Bishop Guízar. To limit the power of the Church, Adalberto Tejada Olivares, governor of the State of Veracruz declared in 1931 that there would only be one priest for every 100,000 citizens. Once again, things were tense between government and religious authorities, and July 25, 1931, saw another tipping point, the murder of a 23-year-old priest, Angel Dario Acosta. On that July evening, government militiamen entered the Assumption Cathedral in the city of Veracruz and opened fire, killing Angel Acosta who had just baptized an infant. The incident so outraged Bishop Guízar that he ordered all churches throughout the state to be closed in protest. Feeling the political pressure of this move, Governor Tejada ordered Guízar to be shot on sight and offered a bounty on his head. The bishop's reaction was not to flee the country but to head directly to the governor's office and confront Tejada face-to-face. The bishop told the governor that he respected authority but wished that the governor would shoot him himself instead of having a poor parishioner kill him to collect the few pesos bounty. Impressed by Guízar's bravery and honor, Tejada rescinded the order and told the bishop he was free to go about his business. The governor also lifted all the restrictions he had placed on the church in Veracruz. After this, Bishop Guízar continued his missionary work and ministered to tens of thousands of people in need. The future saint had suffered for many years from a variety of health conditions, from tuberculosis to diabetes to circulation problems. His very busy schedule and his tireless dedication to his causes exacerbated his health issues. Knowing that his end was near and not wanting any trouble taken for elaborate funeral services, in his final days Guízar was quoted as saying, "I want to die like the poorest of the poor." He had a heart attack and passed away on June 6, 1938 at the age of 60.

    Twelve years after his death, the Archdioces of Veracruz decided to exhume the body of Rafael Guízar y Valencia and inter him inside the Xalapa Cathedral. When they opened the coffin, they saw that his body was still intact and incorrupt, even down to his bight blue eyes. While this is not a prerequisite for sainthood, it is considered by the Catholic Church to be a good sign, and Bishop Guízar was put on the track to sainthood, first declared a "servant of god," then "venerable." Pope John Paul II beatified him on January 29, 1995. After the beatification, church officials investigated two medical miracles attributed to Guízar's intercession. In one instance a woman named Cirana Rivera who was infertile due to a hereditary medical condition gave birth to a healthy boy after praying to the bishop. The other medical miracle also involved the birth of a baby.

Valentina Santiago was told by her doctor that her baby would be born with severe birth defects as evidenced by various ultrasound images. During her pregnancy Valentina went to the Xalapa cathedral daily and prayed to Rafael Guízar, and the baby was born without the defects as seen in the many ultrasounds. The humble bishop was canonized by Pope Benedict XVI on October 15, 2006, and now takes his rightful seat among Mexico's pantheon of saints.

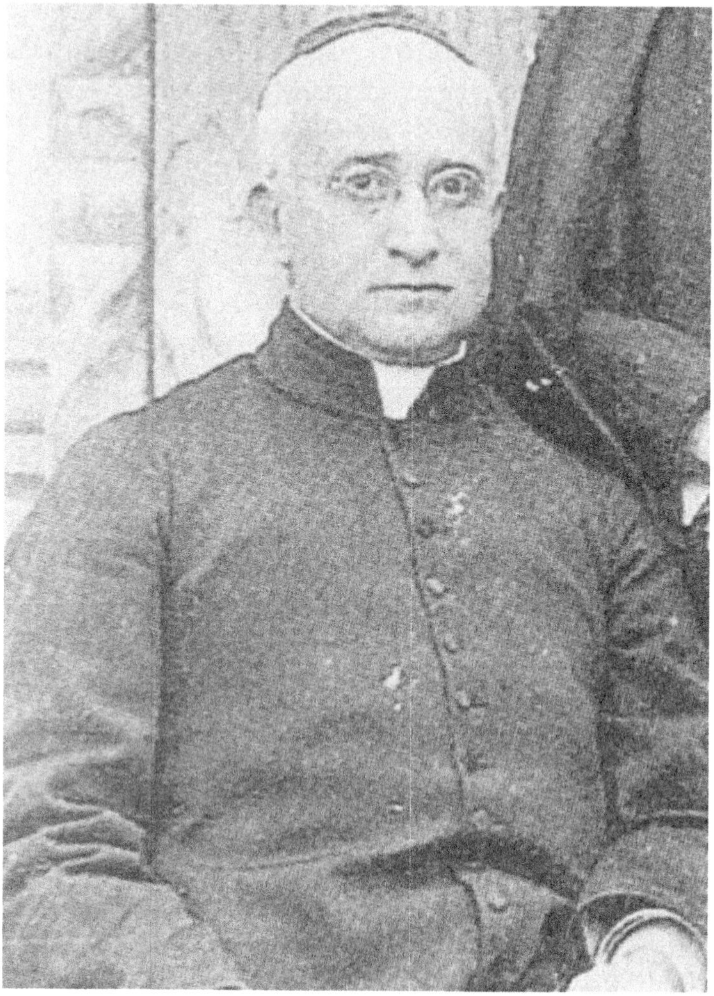

JOSÉ MARÍA DE YERMO Y PARRES
FROM PRIVILEGE TO SAINTHOOD

Born on November 10, 1851, to a wealthy family in Mexico City, the life José María de Yermo y Parres was marked by an unwavering dedication to social reform, particularly in the areas of education and charity. Throughout his life he served as a tireless advocate for the marginalized and neglected.

José María de Yermo y Parres was born into a privileged and devout Catholic family, which laid the foundation for his deep religious faith and social consclousness. After the untimely death of his mother, young José was sent to live with his aunt and grandmother. His upbringing instilled in him a strong sense of empathy and a genuine desire to help those in need. Early in his life, he displayed an aptitude for intellectual pursuits and a profound dedication to social justice.

At the age of 17, Yermo decided to pursue his religious vocation by entering a religious order called the Congregation of the Mission. After years of rigorous theological training and spiritual reflection, he made his vows to the order in 1868. Yermo's superiors decided to send him to the order's headquarters in Paris where he served until 1870. When he returned to Mexico, the young José Yermo had a crisis of faith and decided to leave religious life. By the end of the decade, he resolved his crisis and on August 24, 1879, he was ordained a priest. After his ordination, Yermo was assigned to two small rural churches where he witnessed immense poverty and misery. This affected him profoundly. So, Yermo's ministry from the very beginning was marked by a sincere commitment to the welfare of the less fortunate. By 1885, he organized "The Shelter of the Sacred Heart," a service organization to help the poorest of the poor and would serve as the the foundation for his later endeavors.

José María de Yermo y Parres's most enduring and impactful contribution was the establishment of the Congregation of the Servants of the Sacred Heart of Jesus and of the Poor, often referred to as the Yermo Sisters. In 1900, Yermo formally founded this religious congregation with the central mission of providing care and education to impoverished and vulnerable populations, particularly orphaned children.

Under Yermo's visionary leadership, the Yermo Sisters became widely recognized for their dedication to serving the poor and marginalized. They established orphanages, schools, and homes for those in need, providing not only education but also spiritual and emotional support to countless individuals. José María de Yermo y Parres's commitment to education was at the core of his mission. He fervently believed that access to quality education was fundamental for the development and upliftment of individuals and communities. Through the Yermo Sisters and the institutions they established, he worked tirelessly to ensure that underprivileged children had the opportunity to receive an education and build a brighter future. Yermo's vision of education transcended mere academic instruction; it encompassed the moral and spiritual development of students. His institutions sought to instill values, character, and a sense of purpose in the young minds they nurtured.

Yermo's philanthropic and social advocacy efforts extended beyond education. He founded homes for the elderly and cared for those who were sick and suffering. His approach was holistic, recognizing the importance of addressing not only the material needs but also the spiritual and emotional well-being of individuals in distress.

The Yermo Sisters, under his guidance, became known for their selfless and compassionate work among society's most vulnerable. Yermo's advocacy for the poor and marginalized was rooted in his strong Catholic faith and his unwavering belief in the dignity of every human being.

Yermo's path was not without its challenges. The social and political landscape of Mexico during his lifetime was marked by turbulence and change. The Mexican Revolution and its aftermath posed significant challenges to the work of the Yermo Sisters. Nevertheless, Yermo's resilience, unwavering commitment to his mission, and deep faith allowed him to overcome these obstacles.

José María de Yermo y Parres's contributions did not go unnoticed. His dedication to education, charity, and the well-being of the poor earned him the admiration of many, both within and outside the Catholic Church. His virtuous life and selfless service were officially recognized when he was beatified by Pope John Paul II on May 6, 1990. This was a significant step toward his eventual canonization as a saint. On May 21, 2000, Pope John Paul II canonized José María de Yermo y Parres as a saint of the Catholic Church. His canonization recognized the exemplary life of a man who dedicated himself to serving the less fortunate and upholding the values of compassion, education, and faith.

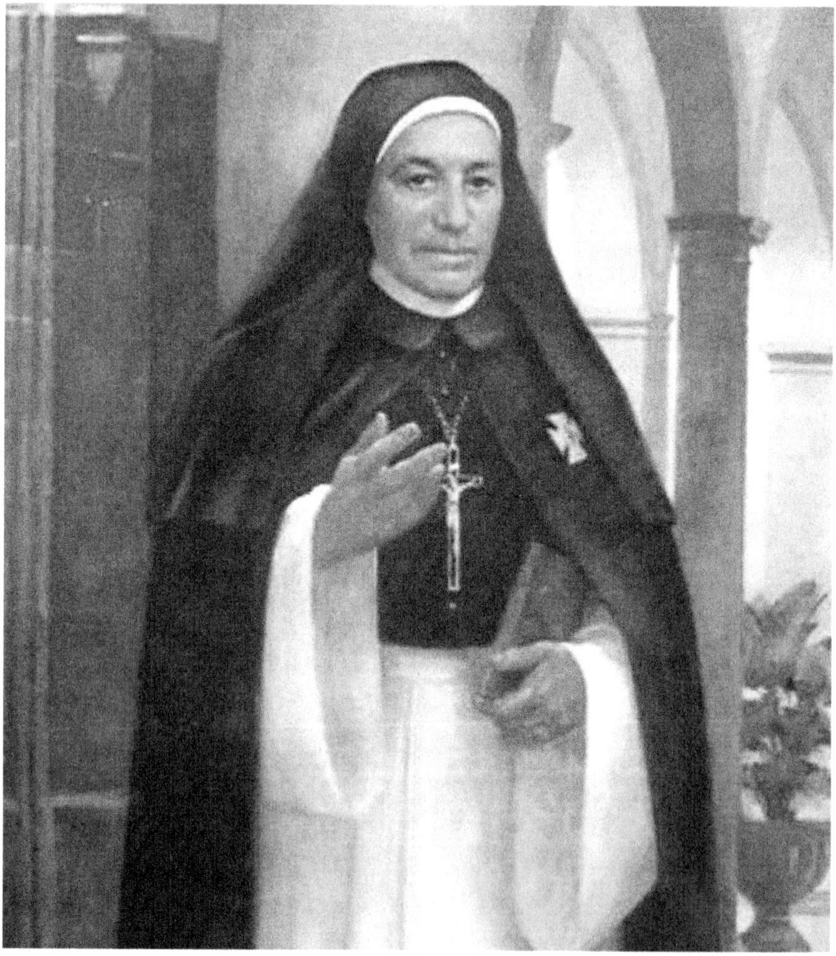

MARÍA NATIVIDAD VENEGAS DE LA TORRE
PATRONESS OF MEXICAN NURSES

María Natividad Venegas de la Torre was born on September 8, 1868, in Zapotlanejo, Jalisco, one of 12 children. Her parents were religious to such a degree that her father gave up his studies to become a lawyer because he claimed it conflicted with his faith. At 16 young María lost her mother, at 19 her father also died and so she went to live with an aunt. It was during this time when the idea of consecrating herself completely to Christ in a religious order began to take root in her. This decision she pondered for the next 18 years, when a course of spiritual exercises clarified her ideas.

She wanted to consecrate herself to God but not, as others had advised her, in a congregation of contemplative life. She preferred not to shut herself off from the world in a cloister, so she chose to join the "Daughters of the Sacred Heart", a community of pious women who had been running a small hospital for the poor in Guadalajara for more than twenty years. At the time María joined at the age of 37, it was not a real religious congregation, but a lay association recognized by the Church, which is waiting for its leader. María Natividad immersed herself in assisting the poor and sick for 16 years, accepting the various roles assigned to her up to that of Superior. A few months after her election, the diocesan bishop himself suggested that she write the Constitutions for an authentic religious community which could then be approved as an official Congregation.

In three years, she managed to make the Religious Congregation of the Daughters of the Sacred Heart take shape and was elected as Superior General of her new order on January 25, 1921. The congregation helped tens of thousands of sick and injured people and continued serving people throughout the Cristero Wars during which she opened her hospital to the differing factions of the conflict. While head of this order, many people regarded María as a saintly or holy figure, and some claimed her mere presence had a calming healing quality on her patients.

Since its original founding, the Daughters of the Sacred Heart has expanded their network of hospitals and clinics to take care of poor, sick, and elderly people in Guatemala, Honduras and, more recently, also in Africa. María, smiling and simple, led the new Congregation until 1954, when she passed the baton to the new superior, and retreated to a slower pace due to illness. She spent her last years amid great physical suffering, passing away peacefully at the age of ninety on July 30, 1959.

After proclaiming that María Natividad lived a life of "heroic virtue," Pope John Paul II beatified her on November 22, 1992, and made her Mexico's first female saint on May 21, 2000.

DON VASCO DE QUIROGA
BISHOP OF UTOPIA

Driving through the evergreen forests of the highlands of the Mexican state of Michocán the traveler will find on the map a curious place called Villa Escalante. Villa Escalante is the modern-day formal name for a town historically known as Santa Clara del Cobre. If you take the short bus ride from Morelia or Pátzcuaro to this place you will be greeted by the sounds of hammers on copper, the *ting* *ting* *ting* of craftsmen shaping newly forged pieces of red-orange metal into beautiful and functional works of folk art. Famous for its big copper *cazos* or cauldrons, the town is also known for a wide variety of things made from this ubiquitous metal, from jewelry to candleholders to fancy tableware and other utilitarian items. It seems like the whole town is engaged in some sort of copper craft production. Other towns in this part of Michoacán – the traditional homeland of the Tarascan or Purépecha people – specialize in certain crafts, too: In Paracho, guitars; in Tzintzuntzan, a certain type of pottery; and so on. This craft specialization is the legacy of a single person, a man named Vasco de Quiroga, who worked tirelessly well into his 90s to try right the wrongs of the people who came before him.

Vasco de Quiroga hailed from a minor noble family from the Kingdom of Castile, one of the Iberian kingdoms that eventually became the modern nation of Spain. He was born in the province of Ávila, in the village of Madrigal de las Altas Torres, the same place where Queen Isabella of Christopher Columbus fame was also born. There is some dispute as to what year Quiroga was born. At the time of his death in 1565 it was noted that he was 95 years old, so that would put his birth year as 1470. However, in 1538, in his own hand, Quiroga wrote that he was 60 years old. That would put his birth year as 1478. In any case, he was born into a society that was rapidly changing. As a teenager or young adult, Quiroga lived through the expulsion of the Muslims from Spain, the discoveries of Christopher Columbus and the formation of the Spanish Empire. Although Quiroga later became a bishop, his primary focus of study as a young man was law and he had no aspirations to become a priest or to serve in any sort of ecclesiastical capacity. Early on, Quiroga distinguished himself as a well-read and brilliant young man. After spending time working in the records office for the legal courts in the town of Badajoz near Spain's border with Portugal, Quiroga eventually became a judge in southern Spain only a few years after Islamic rule had ended in the area. By the early 1500s Spain had expanded into North Africa, capturing several Arabic towns on the coast. One of these was Oran, located in modern-day Algeria. Vasco de Quiroga served as a judge in Spanish-occupied Oran from 1520 to 1526. By 1528 he found himself back in Spain at the royal court where he moved among powerful and influential people. There he befriended the Cardinal of Toledo and also Juan Bernal Díaz who was a member of the Council of the Indies which oversaw Spain's overseas possessions. It was through his connections at court during this time that Vasco de Quiroga came to serve the Spanish king in the New World. By this time, he was already approaching 60 years old.

The Spanish colonies in Mexico, then called New Spain, had serious issues regarding governance at the time of Quiroga's dispatch to the New World. Before the viceroy system was set up, the Spanish overseas territories were governed by *audencias*. An *audencia* in Spain in its most traditional sense was strictly a court of justice. In the New World, *audencias* were established not only so that legal disputes did not have to be sent all the way back to Spain to be heard, but they also performed legislative and executive functions. *Audencias* consisted of a president and four judges called *oidores*. The first *audencia* in the New World was established at Santo Domingo on the island of Hispaniola in 1511. The first one to be established in New Spain, called the *Real Audencia de México,* was formed in 1528 and was headed by man named Nuño de Guzmán. Guzmán was a former bodyguard of King Charles V of Spain and founded the Mexican city of Guadalajara during this *audencia*. Guzmán was also known for his heavy-handed leadership style and ruled over New Spain with absolute authority. To cite an example of his brutality, Guzmán once had a Tarascan Indian king dragged behind a horse and burned at the stake in a quest for information about a gold treasure. To solidify his power, during the time of his presidency of the *audencia* Guzmán prohibited any direct written communication between Mexico and Spain. Horrified at what had been taking place under Guzmán's watch, the first Bishop of Mexico, Juan de Zumárraga, wrote a letter to the King of Spain that was encased in wax and put in a wooden cask that was smuggled on a ship headed for the mother country. When the Spanish king heard of Guzmán's atrocities, he was removed as the head of the *audencia* and a completely new *audencia* was formed in 1531. Vasco de Quiroga was part of the second *audencia*, serving as a judge.

One of the first things that Quiroga did when he arrived in New Spain was to establish a hospital with his own money located in the modern-day Santa Fé area of Mexico City. He called it a "hospital-pueblo" which not only provided medical care but offered food to the hungry, shelter to the homeless and work to those who wanted it. It also served as a church center where indigenous people converted to Christianity. The Hospital-Pueblo of Santa Fé was Quiroga's first attempt to put to practical use some of the principles of the European Enlightenment. Quiroga was very much influenced by the works of Sir Thomas More, the Lord Chancellor under England's King Henry VIII, and read Bishop Zumárraga's copy of More's 1516 book *Utopia* about a fictional perfect society existing on an island off the coast of South America. In More's *Utopia*, the government of the fictional island was a welfare state where private property was abolished and there existed community warehouses to supply goods. Everyone worked, but only 6 hours a day, and women had equal legal status with men. Hospitals were free and freedom of religion existed throughout Utopia, with most people either being monotheists or worshippers of the moon, the sun, the planets or ancestors. Slavery existed, but only as a form of punishment or a way to deal with foreigners. Quiroga was so taken by More's Utopia that he translated it into Spanish. A few years later he would apply some of More's philosophy on a larger scale when the political situation in New Spain changed again.

Vasco de Quiroga, who is celebrated today throughout the Mexican state of Michoacán, first arrived in that area in 1533 as a royal inspector right after the Chichimec Indians revolted. Quiroga was overcome with grief at what he had witnessed in Michoacán in the wake of the First Audencia under Nuño de Guzmán. After over a year of inspection, Quiroga was recalled to Mexico City and resumed his role as a judge under the Second Audencia. In 1535 Quiroga wrote a lengthy legal treatise arguing against the Spanish Crown's limited reversal of a 1530 law abolishing Indian slavery. This writing, called "*Información en Derecho*," also was the first written account of Quiroga's different approach for dealing with the Indians. He made the case that the rights of the indigenous should be respected and that instead of being so heavy handed with the Indians that they should be gathered together in towns to work in specific crafts and industries. In these controlled communities, the Indians could be better governed and guided. The way these towns would function would loosely be based on Thomas More's Utopia. The basic unit would be the family. 30 families would be grouped and overseen by someone holding the office of *jurado*, which corresponded to More's office of Syphogrant. Groups of 10 *jurados* would be governed by a *regidor*, which was equal to the Utopian office of Philarch. Above the *regidores* would be two *alcaldes menores* and one *alcalde mayor*, which corresponded to the idea of a Utopian prince in More's work. Quiroga added an extra layer to the Englishman's hierarchy, though; while all the aforementioned offices were to be held by the indigenous Tarascan Indians, on top of it all was a *corregidor*, a Spanish mayor of the town who answered to royal authority. Quiroga already had a literal and figurative "ear of the emperor" back in Spain and his plans were met with enthusiasm.

    As mentioned earlier, Vasco de Quiroga was not a priest. In 1538, however, he was "fast tracked" by the king of Spain and the pope himself and made Bishop of Michoacán, a newly established position. As bishop, Quiroga thus set out to implement Utopia. He set up the industry-specific towns, taught the Tarascans limited self-government and converted the remaining non-believing Indians to Christianity. Quiroga was also known as a "man of the people" in that he spent much time visiting the small towns and villages throughout his bishopric employing a gentle hands-on approach, even well into his 90s. The brutal days of Spanish rule under Nuño de Guzmán had been replaced by a peace and prosperity that was only a dream under the First Audencia. Quiroga went on to found another hospital-pueblo in Michoacán and the Colegio de San

Nicolás, which today is one of the oldest institutions of higher learning in the Americas. On his death, he bequeathed over 600 books from his personal collection to San Nicolás. The college and the fact that the Tarascan villages to this day still produce some of the most beautiful crafts in all of Mexico testify to Quiroga's effectiveness. To this day, the descendants of his flock endearingly refer to Quiroga as *Tata Vasco* or Father Vasco. Some people, though, look past the nearly mythical elements of the Quiroga story and have recently examined the kind octogenarian bishop more closely. Indigenous activists scorn the Tata Vasco legend and see the man as a tool of the Spanish Conquest and an instrument in the eradication of native cultures and languages. As a supposed follower of the Enlightenment, Quiroga did not guarantee freedom of religion in his newly formed communities. While he may have ended the bloodshed and the physical brutality inflicted on the Indians, Quiroga was part of a larger cultural genocide, critics will argue. Those who counter this critical view see a wise, older man faced with the dire situations of his times endeavoring to do the best with what he was given to deal with. Quiroga did not create the Conquest, only worked within the system to right some of the wrongs of the past and move forward with new tools into a new age. Whichever side one may be on, the contributions of Tata Vasco to the modern nation of Mexico are indisputable and enduring. Over 400 years later he remains a beloved figure and a champion of the common people of Mexico.

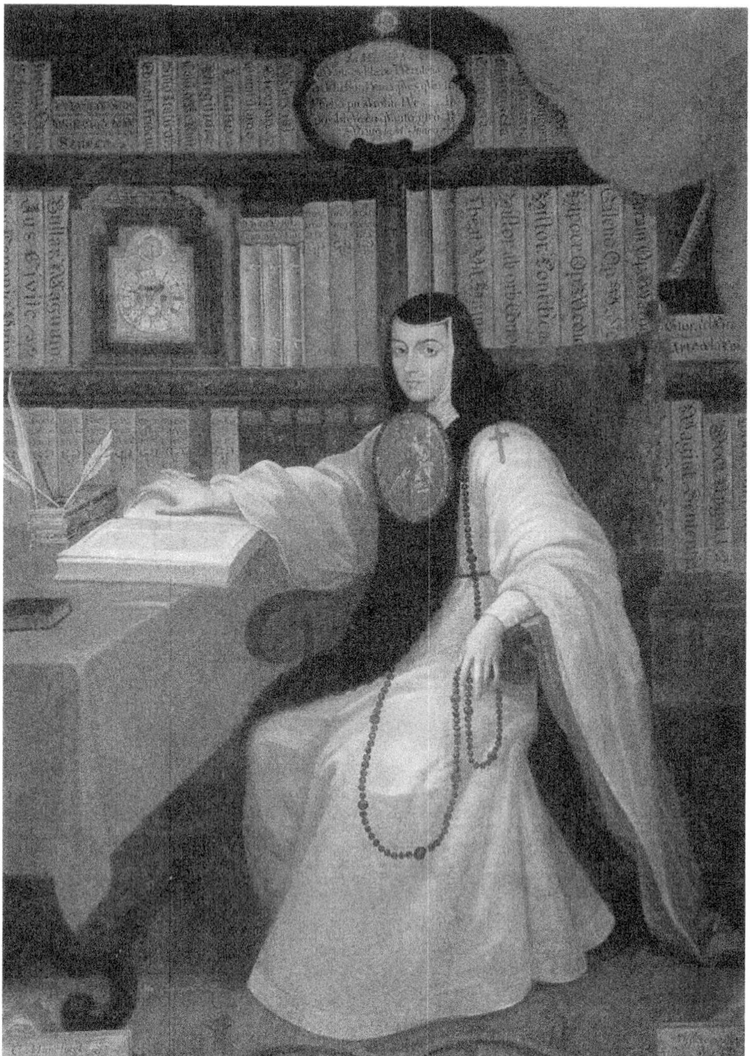

SOR JUANA INÉZ DE LA CRUZ
A MAGNIFICENT LIFE

"I was born where solar rays
stared down at me from overhead
not squint-eyed as in other climes."

So wrote the nun, Sor Juana Inés de la Cruz about her humble birth, in the small town of San Miguel Nepantla, in the fertile foothills of the Mexican volcano Popocatépetl. The person who would later become one of the most renown and controversial women in colonial Mexico was born on November 12, 1648, in this sunny place between Cuernavaca and Puebla in central New Spain. While lost to history for the better part of two hundred years, it was only in the 20th century that scholars and biographers began examining the life and times of this fascinating historical figure. One of the giants of Spanish literature of her time and read from Spain to India to the Philippines, many people do not know much about this woman other than wondering casually who is behind the face on the Mexican 200-peso note.

Juana Inés de Asbaje Ramírez de Santillana was born in colonial Mexico a full century after the Aztec Conquest. Juana's mother, Isabel Ramírez de Santillana, never married and had five other children from two different men. Although somewhat scandalous for 17th Century New Spain, Juana's mother made do as she was from a family of modest means. Young Juana's maternal grandfather, the Andalusia-born Pedro Ramírez de Santillana owned two profitable haciendas. Juana's mother, Isabel, managed the hacienda at Panoayán. Juana never knew her father, a Spanish military captain from the Basque region named Pedro Manuel de Asbaje. As Juana's father was from Spain and her mother was Spanish born in the New World, Juana was considered *criolla* in the social hierarchy of colonial Mexico.

As a young girl Juana spent a great deal of time in her grandfather's very extensive library. Her yearning for knowledge led her to follow her older sister to school to eavesdrop on lessons. By the age of three Juana could read Latin and by five she was able to understand the various ledgers and accounts connected with the finances of the hacienda. The budding poet wrote her first poem by the age of 8. In her grandfather's vast book collection Juana discovered a work on the grammar of Nahuatl, the native language of the Aztecs. Within a year, likely with some help of native speakers in her life, Juana mastered this indigenous language and would later even write poetry in it. Modern-day authors who want to classify Juana as "oppressed" or "marginalized" claim that she learned Nahuatl to get a better understanding of her indigenous roots. This is not true. As stated earlier, the Ramírez and Asbaje families were pure Spanish. Juana learned the Aztec language because it was widely used around her and depending on the viceroy in charge at any given time, Nahuatl was an official language of New Spain, alongside Spanish. Besides, in that massive library of her grandfather's there was most likely a book or two of poetry written in Nahuatl. Many do not realize that in Mexico there was a highly refined Aztec literary tradition that predated the Spanish and continued well after the Conquest. Juana was simply continuing the Nahuatl tradition and was adding work to it, respectfully paying homage to an ancient art form of the land to which she was born.

By the age of sixteen, Isabel Ramírez decided to send Juana to Mexico City. Juana wanted to go beyond the family library and receive a formal higher education which was not permitted for girls at the time. She even told her mother that she would cut her hair and dress as a boy just to get into school. Isabel Ramírez used some old family connections to get Juana a position as a lady-in-waiting at the viceregal court. She immediately came under the protection of the viceroy's wife, Leonor del Carretto, the daughter of the esteemed Italian Marquess of Grana and Knight of the Golden Fleece, Francesco del Carretto. Leonor and Juana became fast friends. The viceroy's wife was impressed with the teenager's broad and deep knowledge of many subjects. While at court, the young Juana dazzled courtesans with her plays and poetry. The viceroy at the time, Antonio Sebastián de Toledo, Marquess of Mancera, decided to put the girl to a test. He gathered a group of highly respected mathematicians, theologians, jurists and philosophers to ask Juana a series of questions. She solved every math problem correctly and answered every query to the experts' satisfaction. An observer of this literal inquisition remarked that seeing Juana match wits with this learned group was like watching "a royal galleon fending off a few canoes." By her late teens Juana caught the eye of many potential suitors of very high station in colonial society and her writings started to become popular among the educated class of New Spain. Some of what she wrote was considered controversial and way ahead of its time, especially her writings about sexist double standards and the unequal treatment of men and women. Given her outspoken observations, some consider Juana to be the New World's very first feminist.

Following are stanzas from Sor Juana's poem "You Foolish Men":

"You foolish men who lay
the guilt on women,
not seeing you're the cause
of the very thing you blame;
if you invite their disdain
with measureless desire
why wish they well behave
if you incite to ill.
You fight their stubbornness,
then, weightily,
you say it was their lightness
when it was your guile.
In all your crazy shows
you act just like a child
who plays the bogeyman
of which he's then afraid."

Juana's primary concern was learning, and since formal higher education and university life were off limits to her, she found refuge in the only other place available to her: The Church. There, she set out on a path to become a cloistered nun. In the year 1667 Juana de Asbaje entered the Convent of Saint Joseph, a community of discalced Carmelite nuns and stayed there for a few months. As the community had very strict rules, Juana transferred to another convent belonging the hermetical Order of Saint Jerome, also known as the Hieronymites. With their more relaxed rules, Juana was allowed to indulge in her intellectual curiosities, write and study for hours on end. It was there, after she took her vows, where she became Sor Juana Inés de la Cruz. While cloistered in the convent, she turned her cell into a library and a salon where she received intellectuals, nobles and other elites of New Spain. The viceroy and his wife continued their contact with Sor Juana and became her loyal patrons, helping her writings get broad exposure in Spain and throughout the Spanish Empire. She also had the unlimited financial support of María Luisa Manrique de Lara y Gonzaga, the daughter of a powerful Italian duke. Although Sor Juana couldn't leave the convent she had the best of all worlds: She had intense periods of solitude for writing, learning and contemplation, and because she had a degree of fame from her writings, she interacted with fascinating people who visited her and enriched her, causing her to grow even more intellectually.

Sor Juana wrote volumes, and her favorite form was poetry, specifically in *silvas* and *villancicos*. A *silva* is a poem using 7- and 11-syllable lines, most which rhyme, although there is no fixed order or rhyme, and there are no fixed number of lines. This poetry form is considered very aristocratic and for people of higher rank. These poems are often full of high emotion and detailed description. A *villancico* is a more common type of verse which traces its origins back to music from medieval dance forms in Spain and Portugal. This poetry includes a repeatable refrain in between stanzas. In Sor Juana's time, *villancicos* were mostly religious and recited or sung during saints' days or other church feasts. The only musical work of Sor Juana's to survive to the present day is a four-part *villancico* now in the archives in the Metropolitan Cathedral in Guatemala City. The name of the composition is *Madre, la de los primores*, or loosely translated into English, "Mother, the one of the most delicate." In addition to the massive amount of poetry she left behind, Sor Juana Inés de la Cruz composed many plays. Besides her many dramas, Sor Juana's notable comedies include, *Pawns of a House* and *Love is but a Labyrinth*. Critics consider *Pawns of a House* to be Sor Juana's greatest work. The story is a comedy of errors about two couples who are in love but cannot yet be together. It involves marital intrigue and explores complicated relationships all set to the background of the ever-evolving complex society of urban colonial Mexico. In addition to the poems, the plays and the music, Sor Juana also wrote essays on society and religion that sometimes caught the eyes of those in authority.

One private essay she wrote critiquing the sermon of a powerful Portuguese Jesuit got the famous nun into a bit of trouble when it was made public. The Bishop of Puebla at the time, Manuel Fernández de Santa Cruz, published Sor Juana's essay without her permission under a pseudonym, Sor Filotea. The essay was seen as a criticism of the hierarchical structure of the church. In a somewhat passive-aggressive move, after he published Sor Juana's essay under a fake name, the bishop published his critique of that essay. In this critique he said that the female writer, as a woman, should devote her life to prayer and service and should give up her writing. Sor Juana watched this play out and decided to write a public response called, *Reply to Sister Filotea*. In this response she defended a woman's right to an education and insisted that women be leaders in higher education, among other things. The response caught the attention of the Archbishop of Mexico and other higher-up church officials who then wished to censure Sor Juana. By 1693 the literary nun stopped writing as part of her penance to atone for her "waywardness." A document dating to 1694 describing Sor Juana's atonement is signed by the nun. She doesn't use her name, but writes, "*Yo, la Peor de todas,*" "I, the worst of all women." As part of her penance, she sold off all her books, said to have numbered over 4,000 volumes. She also had to get rid of all her scientific and musical instruments, all drawings, charts, and assorted papers, including over 100 unpublished works, most of which do not survive to this day. Stripped to nothing, Sor Juana was tasked with tending to the sick, specifically the most ill of her own order in the convent. A little over a year after she was forced to give up everything, on April 17, 1695, she was stricken with the plague and died. The poet and controversial thinker once known throughout the Spanish literary world had passed away in obscurity. Centuries later, scholars and literary critics are still trying to understand thoroughly this monumental intellectual and important underrated historical figure.

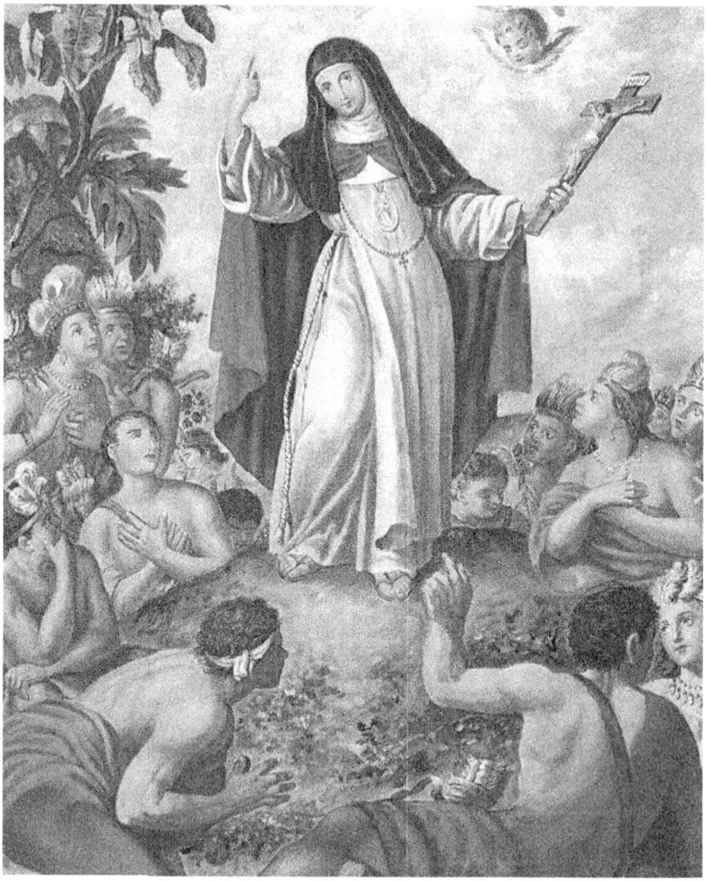

THE CASE OF THE BI-LOCATING NUN

The year was 1626 and the place was the northern fringes of the Spanish Empire in the New World. A group of several dozen Jumano Indians arrived at the mission of San Agustín de la Isleta located about 13 miles south of modern-day Albuquerque, New Mexico. Curiously, the Indians were carrying crosses and asked to speak with the *Custos,* or head, of the newly established Franciscan missions. The head of the missions was the middle-aged Portuguese friar Afonso de Benavides also known by his Spanish name, Alonso de Benavides. The *Custos* knew that the Indians before him were not from the local pueblos. The leader of the group described their long trek of hundreds of miles from the Big Bend area of Texas to the Isleta mission. When asked why they had traveled so far and why they were carrying the crosses, the leader explained that they had been instructed to do so by a young woman wearing a blue robe who had appeared to them several times over the past year. The "Lady in Blue" apparently instructed the Jumano group in the basics of Christianity and told them to seek out the help and protection of the missionaries. Benavides was impressed with the Indians' knowledge of Catholic rites and honored their request to be baptized. In 1629, Benavides dispatched a contingent of Franciscans led by Juan de Salas to minister to the Jumanos in their home territory. The friars established a temporary presence south of modern-day Amarillo, Texas. The Franciscans built a more permanent mission three years later in the year 1632 in a Jumano-controlled area south of modern-day San Angelo, Texas. These were the first missions established in Texas. Through their work at the missions and from their travels to Indian towns and encampments throughout the region, the Franciscans surmised that the Lady in Blue had appeared one hundred times or more to various groups across a vast geographical area, ranging from the modern states of Texas, New Mexico and Arizona in the US to the states of Chihuahua and Coahuila in Mexico. Dispatches from Spain to New Spain identified the Blue Lady as a cloistered Spanish nun by the name of María de Jesús de Ágreda who had apparently been ministering to the Jumano Indians for years without ever having left the confines of her abbey in Spain. How was this possible and who was this mysterious bi-locating nun? What role did she play in the evangelization of northern New Spain?

Sor María de Jesús de Ágreda was born in the province of Soria, Spain in April of 1602. Her birth name was María Coronel y de Arana, and she was one of 11 children of Francisco Coronel and Catalina de Arana, 4 of whom made it to adulthood. By the age of 4 María had shown great spiritual knowledge and was confirmed by the Church. According to biographers, the young María had ecstasies and visions throughout her early childhood and by the age of 12 she made the decision to become a nun. She opted to join the discalced Carmelite order in the town of Tarazona in neighboring Aragón. Before embarking on the journey to the Carmelite convent, María's mother had a vision that she would turn the family home into an abbey and she and her daughters would commit their lives to being nuns. María's father protested, claiming that Catalina becoming a nun would violate their marriage vows. It took Francisco Coronel three years to agree to his wife's plans. At that time, Francisco himself decided to live the life of a religious devotee. He entered a Franciscan friary as a lay brother in the town of Naida and left the house to his wife and daughters to turn it into a nunnery. Catalina and her daughters re-christened their old home the Monastery of the Immaculate Conception and invited nuns from other communities to come live with them and instruct them in the ways of ecclesiastical life. María was 16 at the time. Two years later, at the age of 18, María began her bi-location, appearing to the Jumano Indians of the northern reaches of New Spain without ever leaving Spain.

The Spanish explorer Álvar Núñez Cabeza de Vaca may have been the first to encounter the Jumanos in 1535 near modern-day Presido, Texas at the convergence of the Conchos River and the Rio Grande. For many years, the area was known by the Spanish as La Junta and was a gathering place of tribes from many indigenous nations. A later explorer, Antonio de Espejo, who was the first to use the term "Jumano," crossed paths with this group at La Junta during his 1582 journey of exploration to the northern parts of New Spain. Historians do not agree on whether the Jumanos were a sedentary people or if they were nomadic buffalo hunters and traders. Espejo would encounter the same type of people on his way north along the Pecos River almost to the modern-day Texas-New Mexico border. Some early accounts place the range of the Jumanos over a large geographical area, from the mid-Rio Grande valley of New Mexico through the plains of Kansas, Oklahoma and Texas, to the northern flatlands of the modern country of Mexico. The heart of their homeland seemed to have been the valleys of the Pecos and Conchos Rivers and both sides of the Rio Grande just north and west of the Big Bend area. The Jumanos had very little contact with the Spanish at the time of the alleged apparitions of Sister María. This is one reason why it was such a surprise to see the Jumanos' deep knowledge of the Catholic Faith at the time the group arrived at Isleta asking to be baptized. After the rapid formal Christian conversion of the tribe, the Jumanos allied with the Spanish to attack and defeat their enemies, the Apache and the Wichita. By the early 1700s, the Spanish had lost interest in the western part of Texas. To them, the Indians were Christianized and pacified, and the region has little economic value.

    Back in Spain, Sister María, experienced the visions and ecstasies that would seem to have confirmed her bilocation. Without any knowledge of northern New Spain, the nun was able to describe the people and terrain with a fair degree of accuracy. María's greatest instances of bilocation occurred between 1620 and 1623 during which time the young nun caught the attention of the office of the Holy Inquisition. Not only was Sister María to be examined for her supposed inexplicable visitations to the New World, but the inquisitors were also curious about the nun's ability to levitate, witnessed by dozens of people in and around her abbey in Spain. When quizzed about how she managed to accomplish the task of being in two places at the same time, the young nun replied, "I was transported by the aid of angels." Sister María had very powerful allies which helped smooth the process of her examination. Known throughout Spain as a venerated mystic, the humble nun was the long-distance spiritual advisor of King Phillip IV of Spain. The two exchanged over 600 letters, a valuable correspondence that still survives to this day. As part of Sister María's examination under the authority of the Office of the Holy Inquisition, letters were sent to the remote Franciscan outposts of

New Mexico asking for confirmation of María's ministry to the Jumanos. The letters were hand-delivered by the friar Esteban de Perea, who remained in the New World and is known today as "The Father of the New Mexican Church." The head of the Franciscans in New Mexico, Alonso de Benavides, received the letters from Perea just weeks after the group of Jumanos arrived at the Isleta mission asking to be baptized. Benavides wrote a reply to the inquisitors in Spain who were handling María's case. With the King of Spain behind her and solid confirmation from the "boots on the ground" in the New World, Sister María's case was closed. Her inquisitors not only exonerated her, they praised her. The nun continued to write letters to her king and penned voluminous amounts of material on religious matters. Her most famous work, spanning 6 volumes, was *Mistica Ciudad de Dios, la Vida de la Virgen María*, or in English, *The Mystical City of God, the Life of the Virgin Mary*. The book outlines the life of the Virgin Mary and gives meticulous details of the childhood of Jesus. She wrote the book in a semi-trance state, and some allege that she was in direct contact with the Virgin Mary herself to write the book. Sister María would write 13 other books before her death in 1665 at age 63.

Sister María's last appearance in the New World happened decades before her death. According to the legend told among the Jumanos, during her last visit the "Blue Lady" told these faraway people that her work was done, and the remaining unbaptized Jumanos needed to seek out the Franciscans and complete the conversion. After she disappeared, the hillside became covered in a blanket of bluebonnet flowers, as if to represent the never-ending presence of the "Blue Lady." It is ironic that the bluebonnet is the official state flower of Texas.

And what of the Jumanos? What happened to them? By the year 1750 they had ceased to appear in the historical record as a distinct people. Researchers believe that they were most likely absorbed into the surrounding tribes, becoming part of the various nearby Apache groups or blending in with the Caddo or Wichita people. Some believe that they became "detribalized" and either settled into the Spanish missions of central Texas or moved south into Mexico and became part of the *mestisaje* blend of modern Mexico. Others theorize that most of the Jumanos died from infectious diseases or were killed off in inter-tribal wars. According to Dan Flores who wrote an article for *The Journal of American History* in 1991, the Jumanos migrated north to the Black Hills region and became the Kiowa. In the 21st Century a group of some 300 people have emerged in west Texas who have been calling themselves the Apache-Jumano Tribe and are seeking official recognition from the federal government of the United States. The current tribal chieftain, Gabriel Carrasco, believes that there are up to 3,000 Apache-Jumanos living throughout the American Southwest and northern Mexico.

While fragments of the Jumanos are coalescing and seeking to reestablish their tribal identity in the 21st Century, there is a movement in Texas to make Sister María de Jesús de Ágreda a saint. Pope Clement X opened the path to sainthood by declaring Sister María "Venerable" less than ten years after her death. The pope declared her thus for her, "heroic life of virtue." The process for her beatification began in 1673 but has not yet been completed. In 1909 Church authorities opened Sister María's casket to find that her body was incorrupt. A reopening of the casket in 1989 reaffirmed this. In May of 2019 a group of 38 people from the San Angelo, Texas area went to Vatican City in Rome to try to re-open the case for sainthood for Sister María. If María de Jesús de Ágreda eventually becomes canonized, will Texas and northern Mexico claim her as one of theirs or will she be considered a Spanish saint? Perhaps both?

MEXICAN FOLK SAINTS, HEALERS AND MYSTICS

As a country steeped in a sense of deep religious faith, Mexico is home to many folk saints, holy ones and supernatural traditions that go counter to or run parallel with official Catholic Church doctrine. Some of this is based on aspects of indigenous cultures going back thousands of years, while some of it is very contemporary and has come about to meet the needs found in 21st Century Mexican society. As more people in modern Mexico see the Catholic Church as ineffective and outdated, the alternative religions and ideas continue to grow and gain strength. Desperate times may call for desperate measures, and the folk saints, healers and mystics are meeting a need in Mexico that the traditional church cannot or will not meet.

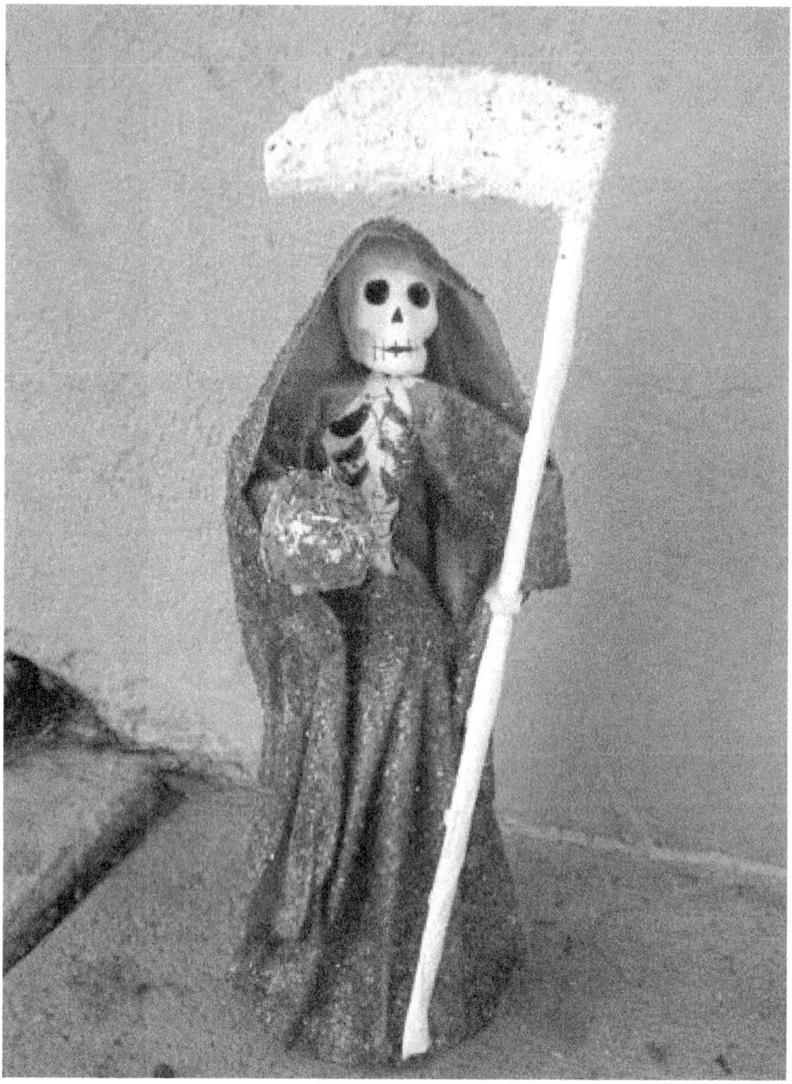

THE SANTA MUERTE: DEATH RESPECTED

She has many names including *La flaca* ("the skinny girl"), *La hermana blanca* or *la niña blanca* (the white sister or white girl), *La huesuda* (the bony one), *La madrina* ("the godmother") and *La niña bonita* ("the pretty girl"). Often, she is referred to in the superlative and is called *La Santisima Muerte*, or "The most holy death." With tens of millions of followers, the reach of the Santa Muerte extends across the border as well as her believers have increased in number in the United States over the years. So, who is this often hideous-looking saint? La Santa Muerte – or in English, Saint Death or Holy Death – is personified as a hooded and robed skeleton figure holding a scythe and a globe. She is often holding an old-fashioned scale or balance and is sometimes accompanied by an owl. Sometimes she is also holding an hourglass. Many of her depictions look like an illustration from a heavy metal band t-shirt, as her imagery closely parallels that of the Grim Reaper. She is dressed in different colors for different occasions and serves multiple purposes. Her veneration is looked down upon by the Catholic Church and has been called "demonic" and "anti-Christian," yet she is followed by millions, mostly the marginalized, the dispossessed and those who have given up all hope.

Anthropologists have called this type of veneration a "cult of crisis" in that it comes out of times of dire social and economic hardship. As economic times have worsened in Mexico and while violence has increased, we see an increase in people putting their faith in the skeleton saint.

No one knows exactly where this saint came from, although the imagery suggests that part of this phenomenon came from the Grim Reaper of European legends. The context – Mexico – suggests that part of the phenomenon came from the Aztec goddess Mictecacehuatl, or "Lady Death," the ruler of the underworld. Its modern usage and increase in popularity in these times also stem from modern circumstances. So, we have what the anthropologists call a syncretic belief system, one that blends two or more beliefs to come up with something different.

The reverence for the Santa Muerte began in the 1960s, but its rapid growth has occurred only in the beginnings of the 21st Century when her veneration became less secret and more overt. The main shrine to this folk saint only appeared in 2001 when a woman from the Tepito area of Mexico City named Enriqueta Romero decided to display publicly the 5-foot-tall statue of the Santa Muerte given to her by her son. Now, there are many similar shrines throughout Mexico, but this is the oldest and most attended. Every first of the month there is a special rosary said at the Romero shrine and people bring their statues and Santa Muerte articles to be blessed. As the Santa Muerte is not an officially recognized Catholic saint, she doesn't have a feast day on the Catholic calendar. Some people celebrate her day on the 15th of August, the 15th of September or November 1. The services performed at the Santa Muerte shrines, including masses and rosaries, are always done by lay people. Behind the Virgin of Guadalupe, the Santa Muerte is the second-most venerated religious icon in Mexico, surpassing St. Jude, the patron saint of the impossible, in the early 2000s.

So, what does the Santa Muerte do and who exactly are her followers? As mentioned before, she appeals mostly to the marginalized and the dispossessed. People who feel like the Catholic Church has forsaken them have been drawn to this folk saint. This includes the incarcerated, homosexuals, prostitutes, petty criminals, drug dealers and the chronically poor. She has also become the patron of people who work at night and who need protection during the dark hours like taxi drivers, bar workers and so on. She functions much like a regular Catholic saint in that you petition to her for help or give her thanks for favors or miracles granted. As she has wide appeal, the Santa Muerte serves many functions. People pray to her for matters concerning love, health, money, legal issues, and pretty much anything else you can think of. In a major departure from the other Catholic saints, the Santa Muerte is often called upon to work a curse upon an enemy or to exact revenge. Her main function, though, is to provide a smooth transition from this life to the next. Most devotees pray for an "easy death" in the face of an increasingly violent and desperate world. Just as with the Grim Reaper of Europe and the Aztec death goddess Mictecacehuatl, you need to respect death to ensure a pleasant death and you do this by giving offerings, praying and by lighting candles.

Lighting candles is an important feature of the veneration of the Santa Muerte. Different color candles are lit depending on the different requests of the devotee. Before being lit, the candles must be rubbed all over the person's body to ensure that the energy and intentions of the devotee are transferred to the candle. Blue is used for healing of the sick and for wisdom. Green is used for legal problems. Yellow or gold is used for money. White is for giving thanks. Red is for love. Multicolored is for everything. Black is for calming, but it is also used to counteract negative magic, for protection against enemies or to invoke a curse. Offerings left for the saint include cigarettes, alcohol, money and fruit, especially apples. Visitors to shrines often blow cigarette smoke in her face for luck.

The Catholic Church has a problem with the Santa Muerte for various reasons. On his last trip to Mexico, Pope Benedict XVI chastised followers of the Santa Muerte and claimed that the whole phenomenon was a cult. Some say that the Church is upset because it doesn't have control over the Santa Muerte movement or that it simply doesn't understand it. The Church however has said that praying to the Santa Muerte is counter to some of the basic teachings of Christianity. Christ came to the Earth to fulfill the promise of eternal life. Death equals sin and therefore praying to death is in direct opposition to turning to God through Jesus Christ for salvation. Death is a phase of life, not a person, and to have a good death the church says one must have a good life and observe the sacraments. The staunchly religious completely reject the Santa Muerte as the tool of Satan used to trick people into a false devotion. Just in the past 15 years, the Santa Muerte has become one of the most controversial topics in Mexico.

Can one be criticized for one's faith, even if it is in a skeleton-faced lady who grants curses? Is this just another example of an object of intention having a desired psychological effect or are there larger forces at work here connecting people in a roundabout way to the Divine?

JESUS MALVERDE

JESUS MALVERDE: ROGUE OR SAINT?

He is known by several nicknames: Mexico's Robin Hood, The Generous Bandit, The Angel of the Poor, The Drug Saint and The King of Sinaloa, but was he even real? And to whether he was real, does it matter? He has a following of hundreds of thousands of people in Mexico and the United States, mostly the dispossessed and the downtrodden, and to them he is very real. Who was this man?

There is very little in the historical record to support that Jesus Malverde even existed. The legend is supposedly based on a man named Jesus Juarez Mazo, who was from a small town outside the city of Culiacan, the capital of the great state of Sinaloa on the Pacific coast of Mexico. Mazo was born on December 24, 1870, and died on May 3, 1909, killed by the authorities for his banditry. He grew up extremely poor during a time of huge disparities in income in Mexico, and especially in Sinaloa. This was the age of the Porfiriato, the reign of the Mexican dictator Porfirio Díaz, and Sinaloa was ruled by an elite class of wealthy hacienda owners. Mazo's parents either died of a curable disease or because they were just poor, according to legend, and instead of struggling to earn a living with his menial labor jobs, the man later known as Malverde turned to a life of robbing from the rich. He is called El Bandido Generoso, the Generous Bandit, because he gave away most of what he stole from the wealthy *hacendados*.

In one of the more popular versions of the story, the wealthy governor of Sinaloa, Francisco Cañedo, challenged Jesus Malverde to steal the governor's sword out of his hacienda, and promised to grant him a pardon if he was successful. Malverde slipped in and out of the governor's home and left a note in place of the sword. Incensed, the governor went back on his word and had the police hunt down Malverde to face justice. According to popular lore, Jesus Malverde met his demise through hanging. He was hanged outside the courthouse in Culiacan and was denied a proper burial. He was just left to hang on the makeshift gallows the governor had set up. When his body fell to the ground, people placed stones and pebbles on top of it, in the sort of a fashion of a cairn, to give their popular bandit a more proper burial. Later, a shrine popped up on the spot, and we will get back to that later. I want to mention briefly an alternate ending to the Jesus Malverde story that I heard from an older lady on one of my many adventures in Mexico. She said that she was from Sinaloa, and she knew family members who were alive when Jesus Malverde was killed. He wasn't hanged, according to her, but shot by firing squad and left to lie in the dirt. A woman then ran up to his body and dug up some of the dirt that was soaked in his blood. Later that blood-soaked dirt was put into small bottles and shrines throughout northern Mexico grew around the veneration of these relics. Nowhere have I been able to verify this story in any printed material I have come across while researching this topic.

As mentioned before, there is little evidence that Jesus Malverde was even real. The dates and incidents of his life loosely coincide with the life of Jesus Juarez Mazo, but there is no confirmation that Mazo ever gave back to the poor or that he had the famous run-in with the Sinaloan governor. Researchers claim that the Jesus Malverde persona is based on an amalgamation of two other bandits from the state of Sinaloa popular around the same time. They were named Heraclio Bernal and Felipe Bachomo. These two were seen as heroes of their time because of their disdain for authority and for their elusiveness. The death of a real man, Mazo, though, seemed to be the starting point of the development of Jesus Malverde as a folk saint.

A shrine to Malverde sprang up near the courthouse where he was supposedly killed. For most of the 20th Century, this man was seen as a miracle worker of the common person, the poor, the lower classes. Jesus Malverde was a victim of society's injustices while he was alive, so as a poor person who is also a victim, he will listen to you. He will hear your prayers and deliver miracles to you. People have sought out his help mostly with issues regarding finances, employment, incarceration and other run-ins with the law and business problems. The devotee can petition Jesus Malverde for help, much like one would ask for a miracle from any Catholic Saint. The only difference here is that if the devotee fails to uphold his or her end of the bargain, the miracle petition turns into a curse.

What does the Catholic Church think of all of this? Simply put, it doesn't recognize him even though the common people treat Jesus Malverde as they would a catholic saint on par with Saint Jude or even the Virgin of Guadalupe. He even has a feast day, May 3rd, the day he was supposedly executed by the authorities. There are shrines all over northern Mexico to Jesus Malverde and people go to them as they would any other Catholic saint. In his 2012 visit to Mexico, Pope Benedict XVI admonished followers of folk saints like Jesus Malverde likening the phenomenon to a cult. Even with the pope coming to Mexico and shaking his finger at wayward parishioners, the adoration of Jesus Malverde has increased over time and sees no sign of stopping.

Long before the pope's visit, the popularity of this saint got a huge shot in the arm from the illegal drug trade. In the 1980s and 1990s the various cartels appropriated the Jesus Malverde phenomenon as part of a calculated PR strategy. See, Malverde was like them, fighting against authority and giving back to the community with their illicit earnings, building hospitals, schools and roads in poor and rural communities and providing employment when the government refused to help. The drug traffickers used their supposed devotion to the saint to also show that they, too, are common people, just like you and me. Many Jesus Malverde shrines throughout Mexico have been built by the *narcotraficantes* themselves.

The modern shrine to Jesus Malverde in Culiacán is across the train tracks from the original shrine that sprouted up right after the bandit's supposed 1909 death. The original shrine was demolished in the 1970s to make a parking lot to accommodate the ever-expanding government buildings surrounding the original courthouse. There was a story I stumbled across about how no one wanted to be the one to do the actual demolition of the shrine and that the bulldozer operator was drunk at the time of the demo to ease the pain of the thoughts of the sin he was committing. Eyewitnesses claim that when the bulldozer got to the cairn that covered the body of Jesus Malverde that the rocks were jumping out like popcorn popping out of a fire. Alas, no film footage exists.

The new shrine is modern and ample and has a main altar with a bust of the saint for adequate veneration. People come from all over Mexico to make this pilgrimage to ask Jesus Malverde for help. Alms are collected for local charities, and those articles left behind in thanks are given away to the poor. Every May 2nd there is a party at the shrine in the evening and in the morning of the 3rd, the day of Malverde's supposed execution, the main bust of the saint is taken out of the shrine, cleaned, and paraded around the neighborhood. Vendors sell food and the atmosphere is very festive, much like any Mexican fiesta to celebrate a saint, except the statue doesn't end up at a church and there is no mass. To those people who celebrate him and believe in him, there is no doubt that Jesus Malverde is the real deal.

So, what of the miracles ascribed to this folk saint? Are these manifestations of the power of focused intention in action? Is it mass psychosis? Wishful thinking? Perhaps these questions are best left to the researchers and the faithful.

TERESA URREA: MYSTIC, HEALER, REVOLUTIONARY

The year was 1889. The place was a *rancho* between the Yaqui and Mayo Rivers in the southern part of the Mexican state of Sonora outside the town of Cabora. Teresa Urrea, the 16-year-old daughter of ranch owner Tomás Urrea, was dead. Young Teresa had fallen ill two weeks before and no one knew what was wrong with her. The members of the household went about the sad task of preparing for the teenage girl's wake. On the day of the wake, while laid out in the coffin, Teresa gasped for air and sat up suddenly. The people in attendance were amazed and stories of the girl's resurrection spread quickly throughout southern Sonora and northern Sinaloa. Not known at the time, Teresa had spent the previous 14 days in a cataleptic state. Catalepsy is a nervous condition characterized by muscular rigidity and the body's inability to react to external stimuli. In a cataleptic condition, the body's involuntary functions such as breathing or heartbeat, also slow down dramatically. So, instead of being sick and then dying, Teresa's body seized up and her muscles couldn't move, thus giving the appearance of death. When she came to, Teresa said boldly that they should not get rid of the coffin because an indigenous girl who worked on the Urrea ranch named Huila would be dead soon. Huila died the next day. When asked how she could have known this, Teresa explained that while she was in the cataleptic state, she was receiving visions from angels, saints and the Virgin Mary herself. This very thoroughly witnessed series of events was the beginning of something that would change not only the life of Teresa Urrea but the history of northern Mexico.

Teresa Urrea was born in the small town of Ocoroni, Sinaloa, Mexico, on October 15, 1873. Her mother was a 14-year-old ranch hand named Cayetana Chávez from the small town of Tehueco, Sinaloa. Teresa's mother was indigenous, but sources are conflicted as to which indigenous group she belonged. Some claim Mayo, other sources say Yaqui, and still others say that she was from the same tribe that bore the name of the town where she was born: Tehueco. Teresa's father was Tomás Urrea, a wealthy rancher on whose lands Cayetana Chávez worked. Don Tomás did not recognize Teresa Urrea as his daughter until she was 16 years old in the year 1889. Before that, Teresa was raised mostly by her aunt and her mother alternating living between the towns of Cabora and nearby Aquihuiquichi. She lived among the Mayo and Yaqui people and could understand at least one indigenous language. As a young girl, when Teresa's body would freeze into one of its cataleptic states, she was seen in two different ways by those around who knew her: Either she needed to be committed to a hospital never to be seen again, or she was a special person given a special gift. Always after coming out of these prolonged seizures, young Teresa would claim that she had visions or that she received instructions from divine beings. The biographers and researchers are unsure what happened to Teresa's mother at around the age of thirty when Teresa was sixteen. Some say she died; some say she just left the Urrea *rancho*. In any event, because Teresa's mother was no longer in the picture, Tomás recognized Teresa as his and sent for her to come live with him in the main ranch house. It was a different life from the drafty and dusty shack she lived in with her aunt and mother. It took her some time to get used to the life of privilege that the social position of rancher's daughter afforded her. In the first few days of her life in the ranch house she made friends with the indigenous girl mentioned earlier, Huila. Huila was the daughter of a local healer, a *curandera*, and she had heard of Teresa's reputation of trances and mystical experiences. Huila thought that Teresa's gifts of vision and prophesy could be combined with healing, and so she taught Teresa about local native herbal and spiritual practices used to cure the sick. At the time of Huila's death Teresa had already had somewhat of a reputation for herbal healing and prophesy with the locals and the ranch workers. Teresa's remarkable "resurrection" only increased her legitimacy in the eyes of the true believers, and word of miracles associated with her spread across northern Mexico like wildfire.

    Within a few months of her famous 14-day cataleptic state, Teresa started drawing large crowds of people to the Urrea Ranch. She would lay her hands on people to diagnose unknown illnesses. Sometimes Teresa's healings included a combination of the laying on of her hands with rubbing the affected area with a mixture of earth and her own saliva. In certain rare cases Teresa would mix her own blood with dirt along with herbs, as she had learned from her friend Huila. A subtle scent of roses was said to emanate from Teresa, and some attempted to collect her sweat or tears to use as perfume. As Teresa considered her powers to be divine gifts, she did not charge for her treatments. Teresa Urrea's humility and her quiet but intense charisma eventually drew thousands to the Cabora ranch to be cured or simply just to witness a miracle.

Teresa had an uncanny natural ability to address masses of people. She traveled to nearby towns and other ranches to talk before large groups in the open air. Sometimes she shared her predictions and sometimes she shared her thoughts on social issues. Before a crowd of hundreds, she predicted a massive flood and declared which areas would be spared. A flood came, as she had foretold, with the areas left untouched by water just as she had described in her public prediction. In her speeches Teresa often spoke out against abuses of the Catholic Church and emphasized the individual's direct connection to the divine, casting away the need for clergy or any other intermediaries. As the church was aligned with the government at the time, some people saw Teresa's comments as borderline sedition. By the end of 1889, just months after her miraculous rise from the dead, Teresa was being called "La Santa de Cabora," or "The Saint of Cabora." Another name for her was "Santa Niña," or, "Holy girl." Also, by the end of the year 1889 Teresa Urrea was getting the attention of higher-up Mexican government officials after the national press began covering her activities, specifically the Mexico City newspaper *El Monitor Republicano*.

As Teresa Urrea's popularity as a folk saint grew throughout northern Mexico, entire towns began petitioning her for help. The village of Tomochic, Chihuahua called on Teresa after suffering from a long drought and experiencing socio-economic and political instability. On December 7, 1891, Teresa arrived at Tomochic, gave one of her inspiring speeches and then violence erupted between townsfolk and government officials. A second revolt on the day after Christmas caused 40 federal troops to be called to the area to quell the unrest. Teresa fled the town to escape possible arrest, but by then the national government, under the leadership of Mexican president Porfirio Díaz saw the folk saint as a rabble rouser and a threat to law and order. A well-organized group of Mayo people invoked the name of Santa Teresa Urrea during an attack on the town of Navojoa, Sonora on May 15, 1892. The insurgents took the plaza and killed several military officers to protest the discrimination and exploitation they suffered at the hands of the government and the landowners. As they claimed that Teresa Urrea was responsible for stirring up the discontent of the indigenous people of the region, The Díaz government called for Teresa Urrea's arrest and exile.

    On May 19, 1892, Santa Teresa was apprehended and, without trial, was exiled to the United States, where she initially resided in Nogales, Arizona, in a house provided by her followers. There, as in all the places where she lived, Teresa continued to cure many people for free, especially Mexicans and Mexican Americans. Even in exile, she continued to influence her people. In November of 1895 Teresa relocated to Solomonville, Arizona. In this small mining town, there lived two other high-profile Mexican exiles who were banished by the government of Porfirio Díaz, Lauro Aguirre and Flores Chapa. The two started a Spanish-language newspaper called El Independiente which actively called for the overthrow of the Díaz regime. Teresa Urrea helped with the newspaper and although her feet were now firmly planted in the United States, in 1896 she was again associated with another rebellion in Sonora. On August 12, Yaqui fighters stormed the Customs House in Nogales, on the Mexican side of the border to protest abuses by the government. During the attack, the indigenous attackers were heard shouting: "Long live the Saint of Cabora!" In addition, photos of her were found among the belongings of the Yaquis killed in the attack. Some fighters wore her photo over their hearts for added protection. The association of this event with Teresa significantly increased her image as a revolutionary. In the minds of some US and Mexican citizens the idea prevailed that a woman who was worshiped by people like the Yaquis, and who apparently exercised mystical control over this uncontrollable group, must be a witch. Although Teresa used her powers for the "sacred" purpose of healing, it was considered that she applied them to charm the feared Yaquis into destroying the established social order and attacking the good citizens of both the US and Mexico. Consequently, some called Teresa Urrea the Nogales Witch. In 1896, Teresa moved again, and this time relocated to El Paso, Texas. It was here where Lauro Aguirre also moved his newspaper *El Independiente*. In the following years, the Mexican government tried to blame Teresa for many other minor uprisings and skirmishes fought by the indigenous and dispossessed mestizos against the ruling authorities. A *New York Times* article attributed over 1,000 deaths on the border and beyond to Teresa's influence. Although Teresa made a public statement denouncing all violence in the *El Paso Herald*, in January of 1897 under direct orders from President Porfirio Díaz the Mexican government tried to kill her. She went into hiding.

In the year 1900, at the age of 27 Teresa Urrea married a man named Lupe Rodriguez who was a Yaqui miner. The press would later claim that Teresa's marriage was a trick arranged by the Mexican government after word got out that her new husband tried to force her on a train that would take her back into Mexico. The marriage dissolved and the Santa de Cabora moved to California to help a sick boy who had meningitis. While in San Francisco Teresa contracted with a pharmaceutical company to go on a lengthy public tour as a healer. The tour never failed to draw large crowds, but the pace was demanding and there were logistical complications with traveling and setting up events that Teresa couldn't tolerate. She eventually fell in love with her translator and bore him a daughter in 1902. They moved to Los Angeles where she continued her advocacy for social causes alongside her healing. In 1904 Teresa and her American husband had another child and bought a house after relocating to Ventura, California. The miraculous healer, sadly, died of tuberculosis at the age of 32. She was buried in Clifton, Arizona and her devotion continued long after her death. Scholars have yet to assess the full impact that this woman had on the cultural and political landscape of northern Mexico and the southwestern US during very troubled times.

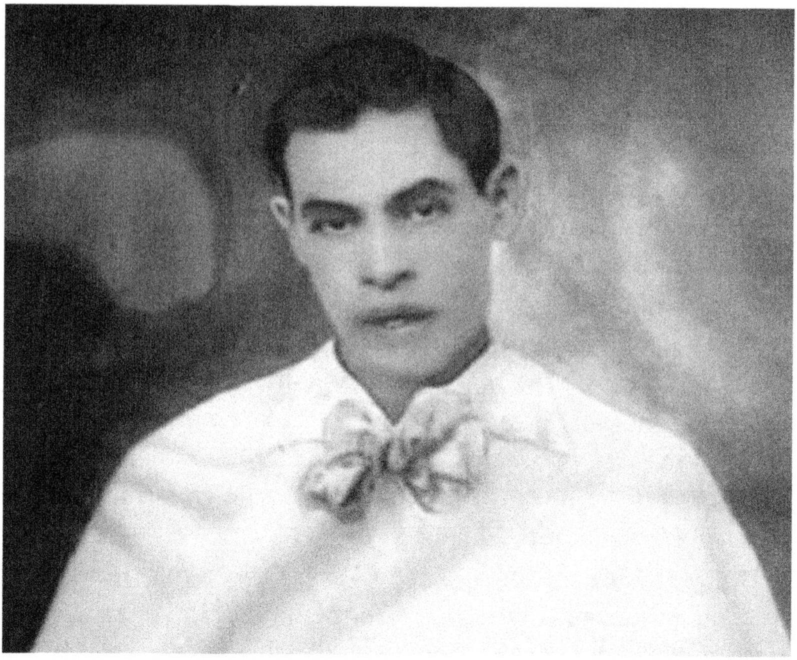

EL NIÑO FIDENCIO: MIRACULOUS HEALER OR FAKE?

The date was February 8, 1928. The official presidential train carrying Plutarco Elías Calles, the first popularly elected president of Mexico, slowed down before making its final stop in the dusty desert town of Espinazo, Nuevo Leon. As the train slowed, the Mexican president was taken aback by the massive shantytown that had sprung up on the outskirts of a town of normally a hundred or so people. The shantytown had already gotten a nickname: *El Campo del Dolor*, or in English, "The Camp of Pain." People living in these makeshift shelters, some constructed out of twigs gathered from the nearby desert, had come to this inhospitable place for the same reason as the regal-looking President Calles: they were hoping for a miracle, a cure, maybe just some hope, from a notorious local faith healer named El Niño Fidencio. Few people knew that the Mexican president was suffering from a mysterious skin condition, later described as a form of nodular leprosy, and while no doctors in Mexico City could seem to help Calles, the president decided to make an official visit to this small northern town to seek a miracle cure from this young man who had started to become so famous throughout Mexico and the rest of the world. The Niño Fidencio received the most powerful man in the country as he would have received any humble villager who had made the journey in hopes of a cure. After several faith healing sessions with Fidencio, including a 6-hour honey bath, President Calles' skin condition disappeared, and he returned in robust health to his life back in the nation's capital. The Niño Fidencio's fate as a miracle worker was now sealed.

Born on November 13, 1898, in Valle de las Cuevas near the town of Iramuco, Guanajuato, José de Jesús Fidencio Constantino Síntora would later grow up to be the most famous *curandero*, or folk healer, in the history of Mexico. At the age of 8 young Fidencio had already begun to show his knack for healing. When his mother broke her arm, the young boy set the broken bone with sticks and the healing root of a night-blooming cactus. When asked how he knew what to do, Fidencio had no idea where he had learned that technique. Fidencio was semi-literate as he left school at the age of

10 to work. In 1909, at the age of 11, he and his older brother Joaquín left for the Yucatán to work on a maguey plantation. He was away from home for about 2 years. When he returned to Iramuco, he promptly left the town for the city of Morelia with the family of his friend, Enrique López de la Fuente. Fidencio, now 13, found work in the home of a wealthy family as a kitchen boy. Enrique, who was 2 years older than Fidencio, soon left Morelia to fight in the Mexican Revolution up north. Fidencio would also leave to head up north, but not as a fighter. By 1915 it is reported that he was living near his sister Antonia who was working on a hacienda in Nuevo Leon. Also, by 1915, after his duties in the revolution ended, Fidencio's friend Enrique got a job on a sprawling ranch just outside of the town of Espinazo owned by a wealthy German named Teodoro von Wernich. When Fidencio heard of his friend's arrival in the same area, he asked for work at the same ranch and was immediately put to use in the kitchen and doing household chores. By that time, at the very end of his adolescence, is when Fidencio got the nickname "El Niño" because his voice had not grown deeper, he was not able to grow a beard and he had a soft-looking face. The name, El Niño Fidencio, would stay with him until his death and beyond.

    It was there at the von Wernich ranch where Fidencio honed his healing abilities. In his spare time, he would wander the desert and commune with nature, observing animals and their interactions with the plants. He also sat with and learned from a local indigenous woman, a *curandera*, who taught him more about native plant remedies. Fidencio was a quick study and soon became known locally as a healer, practicing his type of folk medicine in his off hours. The owner of the ranch, Teodoro von Wernich, eventually made Fidencio the unofficial medical doctor of his various properties tending to both humans and animals. As Fidencio's regional notoriety grew, his childhood friend, Enrique, tried to control him, seeing Fidencio as a possible money-making machine. Fidencio was never into the money aspect of what he was doing, however, and saw his life on earth as a one of service to God through healing the sick. In his 20s Fidencio claimed to have had several supernatural visions and visitations, sometimes slipping into trancelike states to connect with an unseen spirit world. In one vision he was visited by a bearded man who showed him previously unknown secrets of desert plants that went beyond what the indigenous *curandera* had taught him. It was during this vision, sometime in 1927 that Fidencio believed he was given his mission on earth to heal and perform miracles, using a combination of plant-based remedies and his own techniques involving energies and a special connection to the Holy Spirit. To compound this, locals also believed that Fidencio was the fulfillment of a prophecy of a desert hermit who lived in the mid-1800s, a folk healer named Tatita Santo. Santo claimed that a great redeemer would arrive in Espinazo and would appear underneath the large pepper tree that grew in the center of town. The event that really propelled the Niño Fidencio's healing career happened in late 1927. His employer, Teodoro von Wernich, was suffering from a sore on his leg that would not heal. He had been to many doctors, but no one could cure him. Fidencio made a paste out of desert plants, applied the paste to the affected area, bandaged the leg and von Wernich's wound miraculously healed. Von Wernich was so impressed that he placed an ad in a major newspaper in Mexico City celebrating the healing powers of his young employee. It was after this ad ran in the capital city's newspaper when the floodgates opened, and people began arriving at Espinazo by the thousands. The shantytown around Espinazo grew as multitudes of people – suffering from all kinds of afflictions from tuberculosis to insanity – waited weeks or even months to be seen by the Niño Fidencio. The town soon got a post office and a telegraph station to accommodate the increase in population. Trains arrived with more frequency. During 1928 and 1929 reporters representing newspapers throughout Mexico came to Espinazo to write stories about this miracle worker. Through all of this, Fidencio maintained his humble demeanor, never demanding money or special treatment, and could be seen walking about the dusty streets of the town barefoot, dressed as a simple pilgrim. To many, Fidencio was a living, breathing saint.

Not all the attention Fidencio received was positive. As he was not an officially ordained member of the clergy, the Catholic Church had a problem with Fidencio's healing ministry. The fact that tens of thousands of sick people were congregated in the shantytown on the outskirts of town drew concern from governmental health authorities. The possibility of contagion was very high. Indeed, many people did die in the Campo del Dolor as the wait was long for a cure or because they were already in the terminal stages of their ailments when they arrived at Espinazo. Several times Fidencio was called before the health authorities and each time he was allowed to continue with what he was doing with no changes made. A charge of practicing medicine without a license, for example, was dismissed because Fidencio never used packaged medicines, only local plants and his own faith-based techniques.

And what were some of these techniques? Although sometimes it appeared that the Niño Fidencio would go into a trance before curing someone, he always denied that he was part of the spiritist movement that was popular in the late 19th and early 20th Centuries that relied on trance mediumship to connect with the spirit world for healing. To many outsiders and non-believers his healing techniques were more theatrical and shocking than clinically serious. To make the mute talk, for example, sometimes he scared them with a chained-up mountain lion. He often performed healing sessions while swinging on a swing with his patient on his lap because he believed that when one was not connected to the earth, one was also not connected to earthly sin and the mundane. Fidencio performed many operations, and he operated on people using no more than a shard of broken glass. All his operations, from removing tumors to extracting bad teeth, were performed without anesthetic and were reported to be completely painless. Sometimes Fidencio would climb the large pepper tree in the middle of town and throw fruit into the crowd of the faithful that had gathered around him. Anyone who was hit with an apple or an orange was immediately pronounced blessed and was surely on his or her way to recovery. Fidencio once made a paralyzed girl walk by throwing candy at her to encourage her to get up to gather it (and it worked). It is unknown what his actual success rate was, but the number of people who claimed to have been healed by the Niño Fidencio run into the tens of thousands. He continued to see hundreds of people per week up until his death on October 19, 1938, at the age of 40. It is said that he died of exhaustion and that his charge on earth to heal all the people he could was too much for him in the end.

The legacy of El Niño Fidencio lives on. On his deathbed he predicted that his spirit would live on in other mediums once his physical body passed away. Immediately after his death, people began to channel the spirit of the Niño Fidencio and claimed to heal by using his energies. The most famous among them was a woman named Cipriana Zapata, more commonly known as Panita, who founded the Independent Fidencista Movement which has spread throughout Mexico and to parts of the United States. These Fidencio-inspired mediums are called *materias* and there are several of them who operate in the town of Espinazo to this day, sometimes concurrently, which may seem baffling, as it is a mystery how the spirit of the Niño can occupy several mediums at once. On and around every October 19th, on the anniversary of Fidencio's death, the town of Espinazo has a fiesta which can draw up to 40,000 people. As there are very little accommodations in such a small town, many faithful people just camp out, and the outskirts of the town are reminiscent of the famous shantytown of the sick and hopeful that existed in the 1920sand 1930s. There are many focal points during the annual fiesta. There is the shrine devoted to Fidencio that contains his tomb and personal effects. Dedicated pilgrims crawl on their knees or get down on the floor and roll up to the main altar of the shrine. People often faint in the shrine's presence and slip into trances. It is believed that during the fainting spell the consciousness leaves the body so that the person can be taken over by the spirit of the Niño Fidencio. Outside the shrine is what is called the *charquito*, a pond of sulphurous mud imbued with special healing properties. Those looking for relief from an affliction or malady are dunked three times in the black pond. Another place in the town of special reverence is the remains of the famous pepper tree found in the prophecy of the desert hermit and used by Fidencio as a place from which to conduct mass healings and blessings. The tree died many years ago from of a frost, but the trunk and some of the branches remain, cordoned off by a fence. Another main focal point of the modern-day Fidencio pilgrimage is the Cerro de la Campana, a bell-shaped hill outside of town studded with white crosses and small shrines. Here, mediums channel the Niño Fidencio and other spirits and offer healings, blessings and advice. While the fiesta lasts for days, on the exact date of Fidencio's death, no mediums are allowed to channel Fidencio's spirit, as it is understood that on that day Fidencio's spirit is everywhere.

The Niño Fidencio story has lived on for many decades after the death of this mysterious folk saint, but some people remained unconvinced of this man's power to do anything. Debunkers and disbelievers claim that Fidencio's success rate was not that great and that many people left Espinazo disappointed and uncured. The death rate in the shantytown was high and the town had to open two new cemeteries to accommodate the deceased. Some point to a very political motivation for the popularity of this supposedly miraculous healer. Plutarco Calles, the president with the alleged skin condition who visited the Niño Fidencio was a declared atheist who enacted laws to break the power of the Catholic Church. Calles' anticlerical laws were responsible for the Cristero War, a bloody conflict from 1926 to 1929 that claimed over 100,000 lives and pitted government forces against pro-Catholic Church fighters. Was President Calles' visit to the Niño Fidencio, and the massive attention Fidencio received from the press at the time, part of a plan to create an independent spiritual movement to further dilute the power of the Catholic Church in Mexico? Was Calles really in need of a legitimate healing? That may never be known. What is known for certain is that what happened in that dusty town in the early part of the 20th Century still reverberates to this day and has believers and non-believers completely mystified.

PACHITA:
PSYCHIC SURGEON, MEDIUM AND MYSTIC

In the Colonia Roma Norte neighborhood in Mexico City, across the street from the wooded and shady Plaza Rio de Janeiro stands a somewhat spooky-looking red brick building built in 1908. While the sign in the front of the building says "Edificio Rio de Janeiro," the locals call this place something else: *La Casa de las Brujas,* or in English, "The House of Witches." It is so named not just because of its spooky appearance. Visitors to the building and passersby have reported strange phenomena in and around the building. Apparitions of various forms have been sighted there and a strange energy field enveloping the building has been reported throughout the years, especially since the late 1970s. It is perhaps not just a coincidence that for many years the beautiful building in this somewhat upscale Mexico City neighborhood was home to one of Mexico's most famous psychics and mystical healers, a woman known to all as Pachita. Pachita died there on April 29, 1979. To this day some claim to see her stout figure standing in one of the windows looking across the wooded plaza with a stern expression on her face.

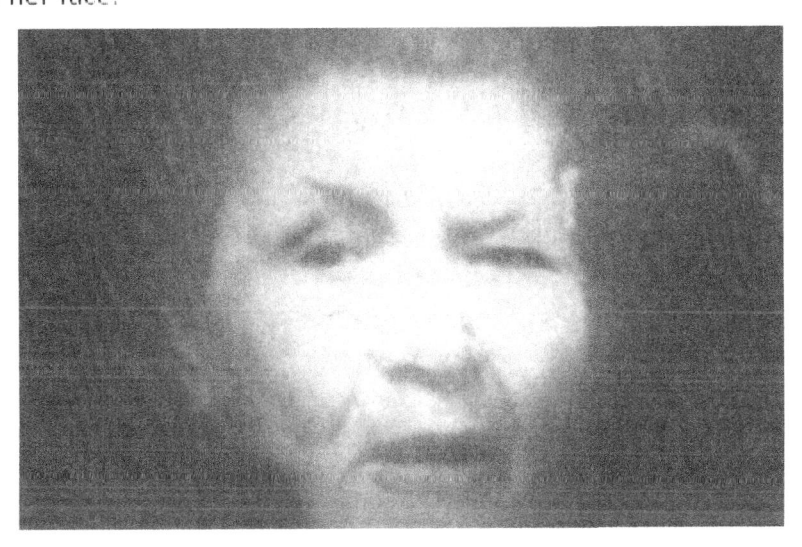

Pachita was born Bárbara Guerrero in the town of Parral in the Mexican state of Chihuahua in about the year 1900. As a little girl she began to hear voices and by the age of ten she was already demonstrating the ability to heal people. As a girl, she would slip into trances and claim that her body was being taken over by an entity she called, "El Hermanito," or in English, "The Little Brother." She would later identify El Hermanito as Cuauhtémoc, the last emperor of the Aztecs and nephew of Montezuma. While in her trance state Pachita could heal people, she could see the future and she would often speak languages unknown to her. By the time she was a young adult Pachita left rural Chihuahua and headed for the big city. She established herself in the building later known as the Casa de las Brujas on the tree-lined Plaza de Rio de Janeiro Street where she lived and had a small consultation office. It did not take Pachita much time to cultivate a loyal following from all socioeconomic classes and backgrounds including some high-ranking members of Mexico's political and social elite who would visit her secretly.

Before her healings and procedures with people Pachita had a specific routine to prepare herself. She would sit in a chair in front of an altar in her consultation room and then would close her eyes and breathe softly until she heard a soft buzzing in her ears. According to Pachita the buzzing indicated that a shift in her state was about to occur, as if she was about to fall into a big hole into another form of consciousness or another dimension of consciousness. She would then "let herself go" and perform whatever healing was necessary as directed by forces outside of her control.

Pachita was most known for her psychic surgery. Very rarely seen outside the Philippines where it has been an accepted practice to many since the 1950s, this is Wikipedia's description of the procedure:

"Without the use of a surgical instrument, a practitioner will press the tips of his/her fingers against the patient's skin in the area to be treated. The practitioner's hands appear to penetrate into the patient's body painlessly and blood seems to flow. The practitioner will then show organic matter or foreign objects apparently removed from the patient's body, clean the area, and then end the procedure with the patient's skin showing no wounds or scars."

Pachita did not use her bare hands when practicing her craft, rather, her go-to tool for her operations was an old hunting knife with its handle fixed up with successive layers of duct tape. She would perform her surgeries swiftly and efficiently, often operating on several people at a time and always with one or two assistants helping her. Procedures were done under dim lights, preferably in candlelight, as Pachita claimed that bright lights harmed organs. Witnesses claimed that she could conjure new organs out of thin air and even with her crude tool, no one suffered from infections or bad side effects from the lack of the use of antiseptics or even anesthesia. As Pachita was the only one in Mexico performing psychic surgeries, she drew a lot of attention to herself from Mexicans and from people overseas. People came to the Casa de las Brujas from all over the world to witness, marvel or debunk.

One such investigator was Dr. Andrija Puharich, an American paranormal investigator whose claim to fame was bringing psychic Yuri Geller from Israel to the United States and thus making Geller a worldwide sensation. Dr. Puharich visited Pachita in January of 1978 with a small group of investigators to study her methods in depth. By the time of this visit Pachita was close to 80 years old and still doing 8 to 10 consultations or healings per day. Here is Dr. Puharich's testimony of his experiences:

"I decided to undergo instant surgery myself before allowing any of my own patients to be operated on by Pachita. For two years I had been suffering the gradual onset of spongy bone growth in both ears, causing progressive loss of hearing. The operation was to correct this.

I was not hypnotized before the operation, nor was any medication given. I lay down on the table, and some cotton pads were placed around the ear to absorb bleeding. Three witnesses were present, one of whom took photographs. Holding the knife in her right hand, Pachita quickly inserted 3 inches of the knife blade into the right ear canal; the forefinger of her left hand guided the blade in. The pain was acute; yet I did not scream, or try to avoid the knife, even though it felt as if the tip of the blade had penetrated the eardrum. After holding the knife in the ear canal for about forty seconds, Pachita withdrew it, and the pain ceased immediately. The left ear was operated on in a similar way; this time the pain was even greater – close to my breaking point. As soon as the knife was withdrawn however the pain stopped.

The surgery had taken three minutes; no sterile procedure was used, and Pachita's bare hands were covered with blood from previous operations.

After the operation there was only minimal bleeding. But a new complication appeared. My head was ringing with loud noises – so loud that I could not hear what people were saying to me. I was given a tincture and told to put one drop in each ear daily; the noises decreased gradually, and by the eighth day after the operation had ceased altogether. In fact, my hearing was now so acute that I suffered painfully from hyperacusis (which is the abnormally increased power of hearing); this condition lasted for about two weeks. One month after the operation my hearing was completely back to normal. After this experience I felt completely confident in Pachita's treatment, and able to recommend her instant surgery to patients."

While known for these unconventional surgeries, Pachita also performed other sorts of consultations for her clients, often in her famous trance states. Many of her treatments used the patient's own belief systems for help in their healing. Those who had strong faith in the Catholic religion, for example, were given specific prayers to say or offerings to make to specific saints. Pachita was said to use her gifts of ESP to act as a sort of psychotherapist to help her clients work through emotional issues or medical conditions that were based on emotional issues. She was also well-versed in the use of Mexican herbs after studying healing methods used by indigenous healers throughout the country. Because of her vast knowledge of Native American herbal medicine, Pachita was often classified as a shaman. In fact, Mexican author Jacobo Grinberg Zylberbaum included her in his multiple book series on Mexico's famous indigenous healers called *Chamanes de México*, or in English, *Shamans of Mexico*.

Dr. Grinberg, in addition to being a prolific author, was one of Mexico's most controversial neuroscientists. Meeting Pachita to write his book series on Mexican indigenous folk healing totally changed his views on medicine, biology, healing and psychology. Grinberg, a professor at the National Autonomous

University of Mexico, also known as UNAM, had professional interest in and was widely published in the fields of the physiology of learning and memory, physiological psychology and visual perception. Dr. Grinberg spent several months studying Pachita, traveling with her and meeting with her patients. The UNAM professor was convinced that what Pachita had managed to do was somehow combine two different types of realities or fields to heal her patients. Grinberg theorized that the brain creates and emanates what he called a "neuronal field", almost like a personal Wi-Fi signal that interacts with the broader and larger "Source Field," or what he called a "pre-space structure." This Source Field or pre-space structure is a field that all time, space, energy, matter, consciousness and biological life emanates from. In Grinberg's own words, these are the rather technical conclusions he came to about the interaction of the two fields from observing the elderly Mexican healer:

"The pre-space structure is a holographic, non-local lattice that has . . . the attribute of consciousness. The neuronal field [created by the brain] distorts this lattice and activates a partial interpretation of it that is perceived as an image. Only when the brain-mind system is free from interpretations, do the neuronal field and the pre-space structure become identical. In this situation, the perception of reality is unitary, without ego and with a lack of any duality. In this situation, pure consciousness and a feeling of an all-embracing unity and luminosity is [sic] perceived. All the systems that spiritual leaders have developed . . . have had the goal of arriving at this direct perception of the pure pre-space structure. . . . The science of consciousness that I would like to develop is a science that will try to understand, study and research the above-mentioned ideas."

Jacobo Grinberg embarked on a series of experiments to test out his theories on the "Mind/Source" interface that continued after Pachita's death and involved other human subjects. In 1994 Grinberg published his findings in the prestigious peer-reviewed scientific journal *Physics Essays* in an article titled "The Einstein-Podolsky-Rosen Paradox in the Brain; The Transferred Potential." Soon after the article was published Dr. Jacobo Grinberg

Zylberbaum disappeared, and no one has seen or heard from him since.

Although considered by many throughout Mexico as a folk saint, Pachita is not without her detractors, even to this day. Critics range from those who see her as being merely misguided but with good intentions, to being an outright fraudster and hoaxer. One American paranormal researcher, Johanna Michaelsen, even claimed that Pachita was harnessing unseen demonic forces in her healings. The treatment that Pachita was most known for, psychic surgery, has been branded as a medical fraud by most legitimate medical authorities worldwide. The miraculous cures experienced by Pachita's many thousands of patients may simply be chalked up to the placebo effect, according to skeptics. Others, although wary of her genuine healing talents, recognize Pachita's ability to harness the mind-body connection in healing through her use of talk therapy and basic psychoanalysis during her consultations. Whether a fake or a gifted healer, Pachita continues to inspire wonder and controversy to this day.

JUAN SOLDADO: FOLK SAINT OF MIGRANTS AND THE WRONGLY ACCUSED

The place is Tijuana, near Mexico's border with the United States. The time is the present day. In the morning hours Virginia begins setting up her stand in front of Panteón Numero Uno. Also known as the old Puerta Blanca Cemetery because of the white arch at its entrance, the *panteón* is located on Avenida Venustiano Carranza in a residential neighborhood and receives hundreds of visitors per day. Besides the occasional breaks for family functions and holidays, for over 40 years Virginia has been a loyal sentinel manning her post: a small curio stand right outside the white arch of the graveyard. Besides the usual rosaries and standard religious icons, Virginia specializes in items featuring the image of a young man in a green shirt and green hat. Some of her most popular items are plaster-cast busts of this person, some of them painted with overarching eyebrows and pink lips, appearing almost comical. A keychain with this young man's face will set a person

back 18 pesos, about as much as a small bag of street churros available at a neighboring food vendor. The image found on many items in Virginia's stand is that of Juan Soldado, who in life was known as Juan Castillo Morales. Virginia and other devotees often refer to him affectionately as "Juanito," "Little Juan," or "*El*

Soldadito," "the little soldier." Panteón Numero Uno contains both the place of death and the grave of Juan Soldado, marked by two separate shrines. The cemetery is an unlikely site of devotion for tens of thousands of people dating back to the late 1930s. What draws people to this place and who was Juan Soldado?

Tijuana in the early 1900s was a much different place from what it is today. At the turn of the century, it was a sleepy border town with a population of only a few hundred people. The Mexican state of Baja California was still a territory then, and as it is now, Tijuana was more tied to the United States than it was to the central authority in faraway Mexico City. Tijuana started to boom in the 1920s with the enactment of the 18th Amendment to the US Constitution which prohibited the manufacture, transportation, and sale of alcoholic beverages. Americans crossed the border to drink and engage in other illicit activities and the town grew to accommodate the Americans' vices. The crown jewel of the Tijuana gambling and bar scene was the opulent Agua Caliente Casino and Hotel which opened in 1928. It had a championship golf course, a racetrack, tennis courts, spas, various entertainment venues and even its own private airstrip to fly in Hollywood elites and European royalty. American actress Rita Hayworth was discovered at the Agua Caliente, performing in a stage show. The operation was so lavish and impressive that American mobster Bugsy Siegal used it as an inspiration for his own operation in Las Vegas and thus it served as the impetus for the development of the Las Vegas Strip. One of the partners in the resort was Abelardo Rodriguez, the Military Commander and Governor of the Baja California Territory and future president of Mexico. The Agua Caliente employed thousands of Mexicans until two things happened: 1. The Twenty-First Amendment to the US Constitution ended Prohibition in 1933, and 2. The President of Mexico, Lázaro Cárdenas, made gambling illegal in all Mexican states and territories in 1935. The casinos and card rooms and many of the bars closed by the late 1930s, including the Agua Caliente, causing labor unrest in Tijuana due to the resulting high unemployment. Once a destination for people from all over Mexico looking for work and new opportunities, the city fell on dark times with much civil strife because of the catastrophic changes to the economy. The Mexican president made sure that there was a strong military presence in Tijuana to quell any popular uprisings. Among the members of the army stationed at this unruly border town was a young private named Juan Castillo Morales, the future Juan Soldado, or Juan the Soldier.

Historians, folklorists and devotees know little about the early life of Juan Castillo Morales. Some believe that he was born in 1914 and some think he was 20 years old at the time of his death, making his birth year 1918. Most researchers agree that he was born in the state of Jalisco, in west-central Mexico. Castillo seemed to be nothing other than an ordinary soldier until the events of February 1938. On February 13th an 8-year-old girl named Olga Camacho Martínez disappeared on her way to the store. Her mother called the police to affect a search, but by sundown the police came up empty-handed. Accounts vary widely as to what happened next. Some say that the strangled and violated body of Olga Camacho was discovered near Tijuana's military barracks. Juan Soldado's superior officer, Jesse Cardoza, asked Juan to retrieve the body. People who witnessed Juan gather up the body accused him of being the little girl's murderer. In some stories Cardoza is the one responsible to what happened to Olga. In other stories it was another high-ranking official. In whatever version, Juan Castillo Morales ends up being framed for a crime he didn't commit. Whether innocent or guilty, the angry Tijuana citizenry, already in a state of stress due to the socio-economic situation in the town, focused their anger and frustrations on the young army private from Jalisco. The father of the murdered little girl belonged to one of the major labor unions in Tijuana and some thought that Olga's murder was instigated by government forces which opposed the power of the local labor unions. A mob comprised of labor unionists, communists, anarchists and anyone else who took issue with the territorial government and the Mexican military gathered outside the police station where Juan Soldado was being held in temporary custody pending military trial. The mob grew over the course of two days and eventually set fire to the police station and Tijuana's City Hall and prevented firefighters from putting out the blazes. A state of anarchy existed in Tijuana and the local authorities transferred power over to the Mexican army. The military clamped down, jailed or shot some of the protestors, but had a tenuous hold over the town. The military leaders figured that the only way to placate the mobs was for them to sacrifice Juan Soldado, no matter if he was innocent or guilty. After a farcical military trial, Juan Castillo Morales was court-martialed and scheduled to be executed. To the angry mobs, this could not happen fast enough. While transporting their prisoner, some military officials encouraged Juan to flee, and he did. The whole point of this was for them to shoot Juan in the back as he ran away. Shooting him while he supposedly was trying to escape ended any sort of delay that arranging for a formal firing squad would have entailed. Instead of dragging the situation out for even one more day, the situation ended in an instant. With the death of Juan Castillo Morales, the mobs went home.

Many people saw through the miscarriage of justice and believed the whole time that someone either higher up in the military or in the territorial government killed the little girl and framed the young private. Out of respect for the young soldier, people started to pile rocks on the spot where Juan Castillo fell from his bullet wounds. The military, not wanting a martyr on their hands, cleaned away the stone pile and washed away any remaining blood that was still on the pavement. The day after they did this, according to many eyewitnesses, the blood returned to the pavement. The military scrubbed it down again, and the blood appeared the next day as before. As word spread throughout Tijuana of the returning blood, many people began to visit the site of the impromptu execution. The curious also began visiting the grave of Juan Castillo had claimed to experience many supernatural occurrences in the cemetery near the young soldier's final resting place. Dozens of people claimed to see blood ooze from Juan's crypt, while others claimed to hear ghostly proclamations of innocence and other assorted wailings. Several witnesses even claimed to see a ghostly honor guard marching in the cemetery. As stories spread throughout Tijuana of the otherworldly happenings surrounding this young man's death and gravesite, popular opinion shifted, and many people started to believe that Juan Soldado had died an innocent man.

To many believers, if a person is killed for a crime he did not commit, he will enjoy a position in heaven closer to God. Many people started to go to the Puerta Blanca Cemetery not just in hopes of experiencing something supernatural, but to ask the spirit of Juan Soldado to help them with desperate conditions and situations. As more and more people visited the *panteón* asking for assistance or begging for a miracle, it slowly transformed into a place of pilgrimage. Two small shrines spontaneously grew, one around Juan Soldado's final resting place and one around the site of his execution. As is typical for shrines in Mexico, these are full of small offerings, candles, flowers and ex voto plaques from devotees. The ex votos are written testimonies for prayers answered sometimes accompanied by a descriptive picture. A small metal strongbox sits in the middle of the graveside shrine to accept small monetary donations for the upkeep of the two shrines. The shrine gets no financial assistance or help of any kind from the Catholic Church because the Church does not recognize Juan Soldado as a saint.

    Why do people visit the shrines and what miracles do they ask from this reluctant folk saint? As with other folk saints throughout Mexico, like the Santa Muerte or Jesus Malverde, people go to Juan Soldado when traditional Catholic saints no longer work for them. Many people petition Juanito when their situations are hopeless. Generally, though, people pray to him when a relative is incarcerated or for safe crossing into the United States for themselves or someone they know. In the more than seven decades of the Juan Soldado phenomenon El Soldadito has been credited with curing illnesses, resolving financial problems, interceding in matters of love and helping people with overcoming serious addiction. He even has a special feast day, just like a fully recognized Catholic saint, and that day is June 24th. While some people come to this small cemetery from all over Mexico, Juan Soldado is more of a regional saint, drawing most of his devotion from the people of northern Mexico and the US state of California. As long as the comfort and miracles continue, Juan Soldado will soldier on.

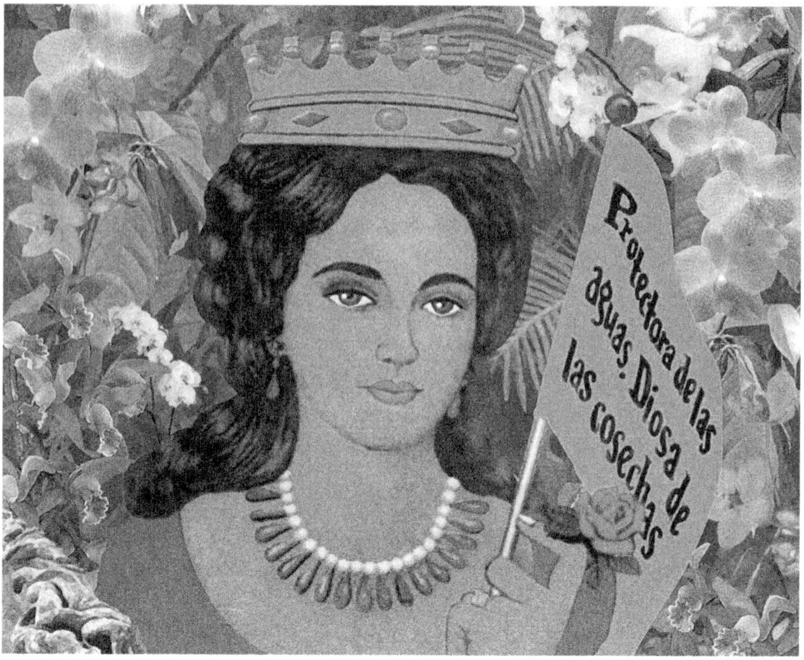
Protectora de las aguas. Diosa de las cosechas

MARÍA LIONZA:
MEXICO'S IMPORTED INDIGENOUS SAINT

In March of 2023 a monsignor in Mexico City issued a colorful flyer that soon had widespread distribution on the internet. The flyer was called "*Los Santos que no son santos*," or in English, "The saints that are not saints" and it warned "good Catholics" not to get caught up in idolatry or "false veneration." The full-color flyer had images familiar to most Mexicans. Number one on the forbidden list was Jesus Malverde. Beside him was the Niño Fidencio. The third one on the list was the famous folk saint of Tijuana, Juan Soldado. Alongside the martyr from Tijuana on this flyer of forbidden saints was none other than the Santa Muerte or Santisima Muerte, also known as the Niña Blanca. Below Jesus Malverde was a somewhat unfamiliar image. The image is that of a voluptuous woman in a red cape. She has long black hair and is wearing a golden crown. She holds a cornucopia or horn of plenty full of tropical fruits. She is María Lionza and is relatively new among the pantheon of Mexico's forbidden folk saints not recognized by the Catholic Church. She is said to represent love, peace, harmony, kindness, happiness, and abundance. Icons and statues dedicated to María Lionza have been popping up in the urban areas of Mexico just in the past 5 years or so and devotion to her is on the rise.

The title of this chapter is "María Lionza: Mexico's Imported Indigenous Folk Saint," which begs this question: How can an indigenous saint be imported? The answer is that María Lionza was an indigenous woman who lived in Venezuela and her veneration began there. The 2020 Mexican census showed that Venezuelans made up the third largest immigrant group in Mexico behind Guatemalans and people from the United States. Statistics show that legal immigrants from Venezuela and their descendants number over 50,000 in Mexico. Demographers estimate that there could be over 10,000 more Venezuelans living in Mexico illegally with most of the immigration – both legal and illegal – happening within the last 15 years. The 60,000+ Venezuelans have brought their culture with them and that includes aspects of their folk religious beliefs. As culture is shared, some people in their new land have shown interest in this intriguing and powerful saint called María Lionza, and her following is growing in Mexico among non-Venezuelans. So, who is María Lionza and what is her story?

    Like so many belief systems, or stories within those systems, there is more than one narrative of María Lionza's origins. In the most popular story, she is the daughter of an indigenous chief who ruled in what is now the state of Yaracuy in the central-western region of Venezuela. At birth, María Lionza's name was Yara, and when she was old enough to live on her own, her father sent her to live on Sorte Mountain until he was able to find a suitable husband for her. While drinking from a mountain stream, María Lionza was attacked by a gigantic anaconda that swallowed her whole. In this version of the story, she was still alive inside the huge serpent, and she asked the mountain for help. The spirits of the mountain freed her from the snake, but María disintegrated and thus became part of Sorte Mountain. This is why the mountain today is a pilgrimage spot for those believing in María Lionza, people who call themselves the "*lionceros*." This first version of the origins of this folk saint has a slight variation: Instead of dissolving into the mountain, the mountain spirits made the anaconda explode and its remains rained down on the land, thus explaining the region's torrential rainstorms. The second version of the María Lionza origin story has her as the daughter of a powerful indigenous chief and a European woman who was either captured by the natives or was shipwrecked. María's mother died in childbirth. The European woman was very fair, and this is why María Lionza is often depicted as having lighter skin and light eyes mixed with some indigenous features. In this origin story, María went to Sorte Mountain as a young girl and at the side of a mountain stream, instead of being attacked by a snake, she saw her reflection in the water for the first time. When she saw that her eyes were green and so much different from the rest of her people, she realized that she was unique and decided to ask the mountain to help her become a shamanic leader. In either story, María Lionza worked many miracles during her long life and after death she became more powerful, and people began to worship her. In early Spanish colonial days, her indigenous name of Yara transformed into "Santa

María de la Onza," or, loosely translated into English, "Saint Mary of the Wildcat." For hundreds of years the Catholic Church looked the other way as a region of Venezuela had their old feminine spirit Yara take on aspects of the Virgin Mary. As a *santo* closely associated with nature and often depicted among wild animals, the forest wildcat, known in South America as "*la onza*" became part of her name. Over time, "La Onza" contracted to one word, "Lionza," and so she became known as Santa María Lionza.

Over the centuries that she has been venerated, this localized indigenous mountain spirit grew more popular throughout Venezuela and merged with elements of Catholicism and west African religions brought to the Americas by enslaved people. By the late 1800s, the followers of María Lionza also adopted elements of European and North American spiritism, as this tradition began to move into the urban areas and started to permeate higher socio-economic classes. The religious traditions surrounding the adoration of María Lionza are now a mishmash of various beliefs, customs and cultural perspectives. Scholars refer to this as syncretism.

In the Universe over which María Lionza presides as "*La Reina*," or "The Queen," she is one of what the Venezuelans call the "*Tres Potencias*," or "Three Powerful Ones." By her side, but having less power, are two formidable and influential spirits called Guaicaipuro and Negro Felipe who are both based on historical figures. Guaicaipuro is the spirit of a 16th Century leader of the Teques and Caracas tribes. He led a coalition of indigenous people which revolted against the Spanish, but he was ultimately killed by conquistador Francisco de Infante in the year 1568. The other *potencia* seen on María Lionza's side, Negro Felipe, is based on a combination of real-life men of African descent. He is said to be a blend of two people: Pedro Camejo, known to history as "Primero Negro" and a man named Negro Miguel. Camejo was a slave who earned his freedom by fighting with Simón Bolívar during Venezuela's war of independence. Negro Miguel is often called Rey Miguel, or King Miguel. He led the first successful slave revolt in Venezuela's history and ruled a small independent kingdom in the wilds of Venezuela called Buria from 1552 to 1555. As warrior spirits, both Negro Felipe and Guaicaipuro are thought to give balance to María Lionza's femininity while also providing a sense of what modern people would call "equity" by representing different races. In this different take on the Trinity, it is clear that María Lionza is the one who is the most powerful and most revered of the Tres Potencias and Negro Felipe and Guaicaipuro are seen as strong supporters. María Lionza and the other *potencias* preside over different "courts" or groupings of saints and spirits. This is where the María Lionza devotion shows its Afro-Venezuelan roots as is very similar to other syncretic or blended African-based spiritual movements found in the Americas such as Santería, Candomblé and Macumba. Some of the most popular groupings or "courts" of saints include indigenous, African, freedom fighters and Viking. In the María Lionza system of beliefs even the spirit of Eric the Red, the Viking who discovered Greenland, can be called upon to help in this world. These courts of *santos* are populated by a wide number of people who were once alive from a drug cartel leader who was seen as a Robin Hood figure to some of Venezuela's ex-presidents. Although prayers and offerings can be made to the spirits in the courts, everything flows up through María Lionza.

María Lionza's official feast day is October 12th. On that day, people make pilgrimages to Sorte Mountain in Venezuela, and in recent years, many Mexican devotees have been making this annual pilgrimage. People had been going to the mountain for centuries to show respect to the folk saint or to tap into her power but in the early 20th Century a man named Lino Valles built the first roads to the mountain. Today, Valles is seen as the first apostle of María Lionza. He has his own statues and rituals dedicated to him in the context of this folk religion. Along the pilgrimage route are what are called *perfumerias*, little esoteric shops that sell spiritual supplies to the *lionceros*. As an aside, some of the articles at these shops can now be found at *botanicas* in some major Mexican cities. On the mountain, many ceremonies take place conducted by *materias*, or mediums, who channel spirits. *Materias* are exclusively men. After dark and by candlelight, the public gathers around as the mediums take on the spirit of an old Norse warrior or an African chief. The *materias* also conduct ceremonies to bless or cleanse participants which may include spraying them with alcoholic beverages from their mouths or asking them to lie in a circle of candles while they chant unintelligible prayers. While some of these rites may seem like "black magic" or may be called "satanic" by outsiders, followers will be quick to say that María Lionza represents love, abundance, balance and hope for a brighter future. There is no evil connected with her.

The devotion to María Lionza has increased exponentially over the years. As seen in devotions to other folk saints, people will turn to the unconventional when they feel like traditional institutions have failed them. In Venezuela, the government is seen as a failure and the Catholic Church is doing little to relieve the misery of millions of people. The Venezuelans in Mexico have transplanted their powerful symbol of love and hope into new soil, and in this new country the devotion to María Lionza is growing. Sometime in 2024 a pilgrimage site to this imported indigenous folk saint is planned for someplace in the mountains outside Mexico City which will serve as a proxy for Sorte Mountain in Venezuela, the original home of the young indigenous woman named Yara who became a saint. Perhaps in 10 years' time, or maybe sooner, María Lionza will occupy a very prominent position among Mexico's pantheon of alternative religions.

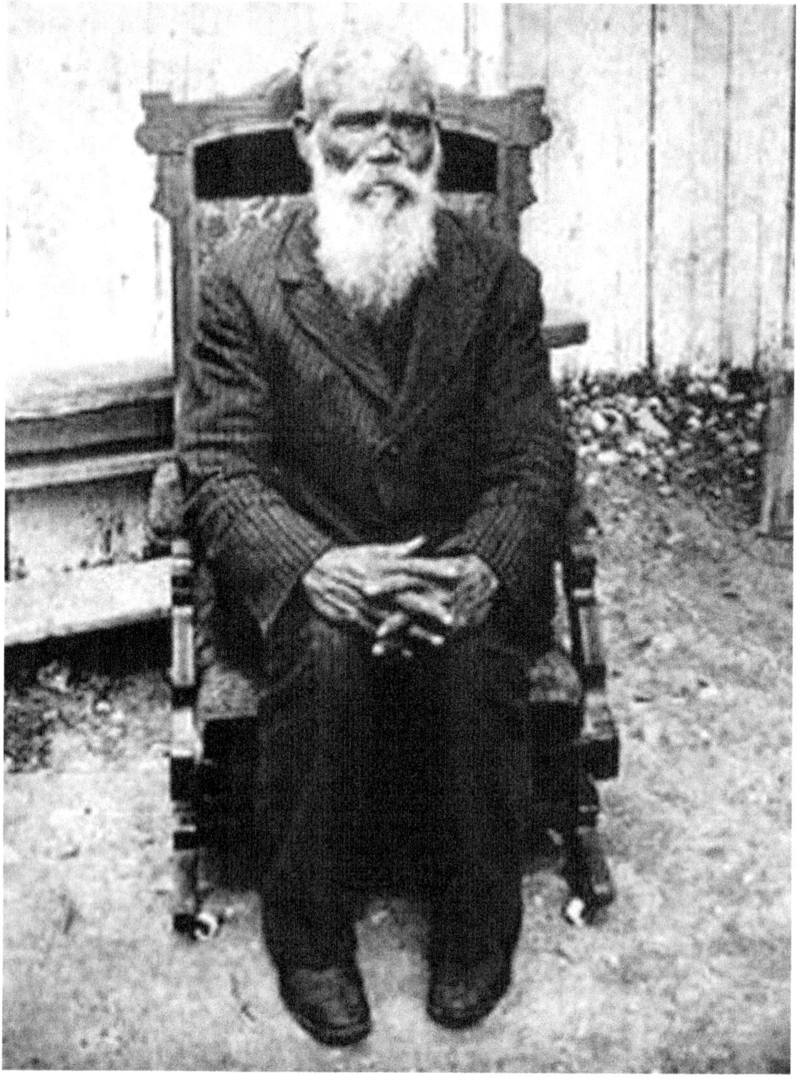

DON PEDRITO JARAMILLO: HEALER, CLAIRVOYANT, FOLK SAINT

About 70 miles north of Mexico's border with the United States in the dusty Texas town of Falfurrias, there is a shrine to a very interesting man who spent half of his life there ministering to sick and troubled Mexicans and Mexican Americans. Sometimes referred to as a clairvoyant, a folk healer and even a magician, the man's name was Pedro Jaramillo and is more affectionately known as Don Pedrito. The shrine, built near Don Pedrito's grave, exists because even more than a century after the man's death, devotees still believe that he has the power to cure or to just make things in life better.

Pedro Jaramillo was born near Guadalajara, Jalisco in 1829. His family were poor shepherds, and when he was a young man tending to sheep, Don Pedrito crashed into a tree branch while riding a horse. The blow knocked him unconscious, and he broke his nose, tearing the flesh down to the bone. When he regained consciousness, he had the urge to stick his face in the cool mud of a nearby creek for relief. He did this for three days. After those three days, although he was left with a visible scar on his nose for the rest of his life, Don Pedrito was completely healed and claimed that he heard the voice of God telling him that he would be a great healer. There is not much documentation on Don Pedrito's early years as a *curandero*, or folk healer, in Mexico, but he must have spent a great deal of time honing his craft and learning from other natural and spiritual healers. There are volumes written on the folk medicine of the Mexican *curandero* who used herbs, barks, teas and mineral concoctions to cure the physically sick or to affect other positive changes in people or animals. This folk healing is a blend of Catholicism, indigenous herbal medicine and in some instances, modern-day spiritism. In Don Pedrito's case, he emphasized the use of water in healings, and stressed over and over the need for faith in a higher power in the healing process. Perhaps because his nose took three days to heal, the number three was important in Don Pedrito's prescriptions, as was the number nine. Although some of his remedies could be quite complex, some of his advice to patients and clients included drinking more water, eating more vegetables, and taking baths at designated times. While in Mexico, he worked many day labor jobs until he could live off donations from people who came to see him for his special gifts. Throughout his life, Pedro Jaramillo never charged for his consultations or treatments.

In 1881, Don Pedrito crossed over to the US and established himself in Brooks County, Texas, settling on the banks of the Los Olmos Creek, where he lived in a small adobe home and established a small rancho where he raised livestock and grew beans and corn. The land was donated to the *curandero* by a local man named Antonio Hinojosa Pérez. By the time he arrived in Texas, Don Pedrito's reputation had already preceded him, and the locals welcomed such an esteemed individual. Oftentimes there would be a hundred or so people sitting in the shade of the creek-side trees outside of Don Pedrito's small hut, waiting to be seen. Visitors marveled at the curandero's ability to know things about them that he couldn't possibly have known, so in addition to being known as someone who could cure most anything, Don Pedrito was known as a kind of psychic. This inspired awe and sometimes fear in people. All the while, Pedro Jaramillo emphasized that it was not he who was doing any sort of healing or prognosticating, but that the power flowed from God through him. Although he never charged for his services, his patients and clients rewarded him with gifts of money or other tangible goods. Don Pedrito always shared the wealth and was often seen buying food for needy families or helping people out of bad financial situations. He often gave away the remedies he prescribed for free.

In October 1971, American author H.C. Arbuckle traveled to south Texas hoping to meet anyone who had known Don Pedrito. The author interviewed an 85-year-old man named José Lozano who would visit the curandero with members of his family when he was a boy in the early years of the 20th Century. Here is the interview which gives a wonderful first-hand account of what Pedro Jaramillo was really like:

"Mi tío was the mail carrier from Los Olmos to Concepción and made the route daily. He rode a horse part of the time and walked part of the time, for it was sandy land and very hard on both horse and man to make the long, long trip. It is *muy lejos* from Los Olmos

over to Concepción, very far, maybe even five or six miles."
Buenos, pues, my uncle was such a drunkard that one day he was so *borrachón con mescal y tequila* that he fell off his horse and left the mail right there in the middle of the road, made it back to town on the horse, and finally came home to sleep it off. *Mi tío* knew that if he kept this up he would surely lose his job and he decided to see Don Pedrito for a *remedio* to cure him of his *borracho*."
Entonces se va por Los Olmos, *muy lejos*, maybe even five or six miles away. The great man was at home and, when *mi tío* went to his house, hat in hand, to consult him, Don Pedrito greeted him with these words: '*Hijo*, you are the *borracho* that carries the mail from Los Olmost to Concepción and you want a *remedio* to cure you of this problem. Is this not why you have come?'"
My uncle fell to his knees, for how could Don Pedrito know this? Did he not live... at least five miles away? Surely, *sin duda*, Don Pedrito was anointed of God and a truly wise man, if not a *mágico* himself." This then is what the wise Don Pedrito said: '*Acerquita a su casa, hay una laguna*' (or in English, 'Really close to your house is a lake'). My uncle thought, 'How does Don Pedrito know of that little lake near my house? I live *muy lejos*, maybe even five or six miles away!' The great man continued, 'In the morning, take a bath in the lake; on the third day take another bath, and three days after that, another bath. With faith! Without faith, nothing will help you, but *con fé*, you will be cured.'"
The very next morning, *mi tío* took the first bath, clothes and all, in the *laguna*; the third morning after that, he took the second bath; and the final third morning, the third bath. All this he did *con fé*, (with faith), knowing that he would be cured."
And as sure as I am sitting right here and now in my house, *mi tío* never to his dying day after that took anything stronger than coffee or tea. He never touched a drop of any pulque, mescal, tequila, wine or even beer. I know this to be a fact, for I was there, and I know what I know. And I know that it was the faith, in Don Pedrito, in El Señor Dios, and in their combined powers, that cured my uncle."

In 1894, by popular demand, Pedro Jaramillo made a medical mission trip to San Antonio. It was then when he began to show up on the radar of the professional medical establishment. The American doctors in San Antonio labeled the Mexican healer a dangerous quack, perhaps out of jealousy of Don Pedrito's popularity and his track record of providing miracle cures. Seven years after this visit to San Antonio, the American Medical Association and the US Postal Service sued Jaramillo in federal court claiming he was offering fake cures and was using the US Mail to commit fraud. The case was dropped because his lawyer, a famous south Texas politician and attorney named José Tomás Canales, argued that Don Pedrito never charged for his cures and treatments. Canales was a big fan because the *curandero* healed his sick mother a few years before when modern medicine had failed her.

    Don Pedrito Jaramillo died on July 3, 1907, at the age of 88. He had never married but he had adopted two sons soon after arriving in the States. When they cleaned out the famous *curandero's* modest adobe hut after he died, they found a hoard of over 10,000 silver fifty-cent pieces along with thousands of letters from people asking for help or sending their sincere thanks for healings performed.

    The shrine that exists on Jaramillo's property is maintained by the descendants of his neighbors who keep his memory alive. This pilgrimage site attracts people from both sides of the border. Since his death, Don Pedrito has grown into a folk saint in his own right with people leaving petitions in the form of written letters accompanied by candles and other offerings, hoping for healings, family harmony or assistance with financial matters. The devotion to this Mexican icon has increased over the years and so have the mystery and powers ascribed to him. Legends and stories have emerged since his death that defy belief and are impossible to verify and add to the *curandero*'s mythos. His memory has even succumbed to 21st Century "wokeness" and cultural revisionism. On Don Pedrito's Wikipedia page and in subsequent blogs that repeat and copy things endlessly, the folk healer is described as having indigenous parents from the Tarascan or Purépecha tribe, even going so far as to cite a source that does not even contain this information. One look at Don Pedrito's photos where he is sporting a long, white, Santa Claus beard dispel these bad attempts at cultural revisionism. No native Tarascan looks like this and the Purépecha territory was nowhere near Guadalajara where Don Pedrito's family was from. Given more time as a folk saint, Don Pedrito's devotion will most likely grow and may change into something else entirely. Such is the nature of grassroots belief and the mortal intersection with the supernatural and divine.

OTHER RELIGIOUS CURIOSITIES

Besides saints, religious healers, and manifestations of the Virgin Mary or Jesus, Mexico is home to other religious curiosities that draw in the faithful. Following are some examples.

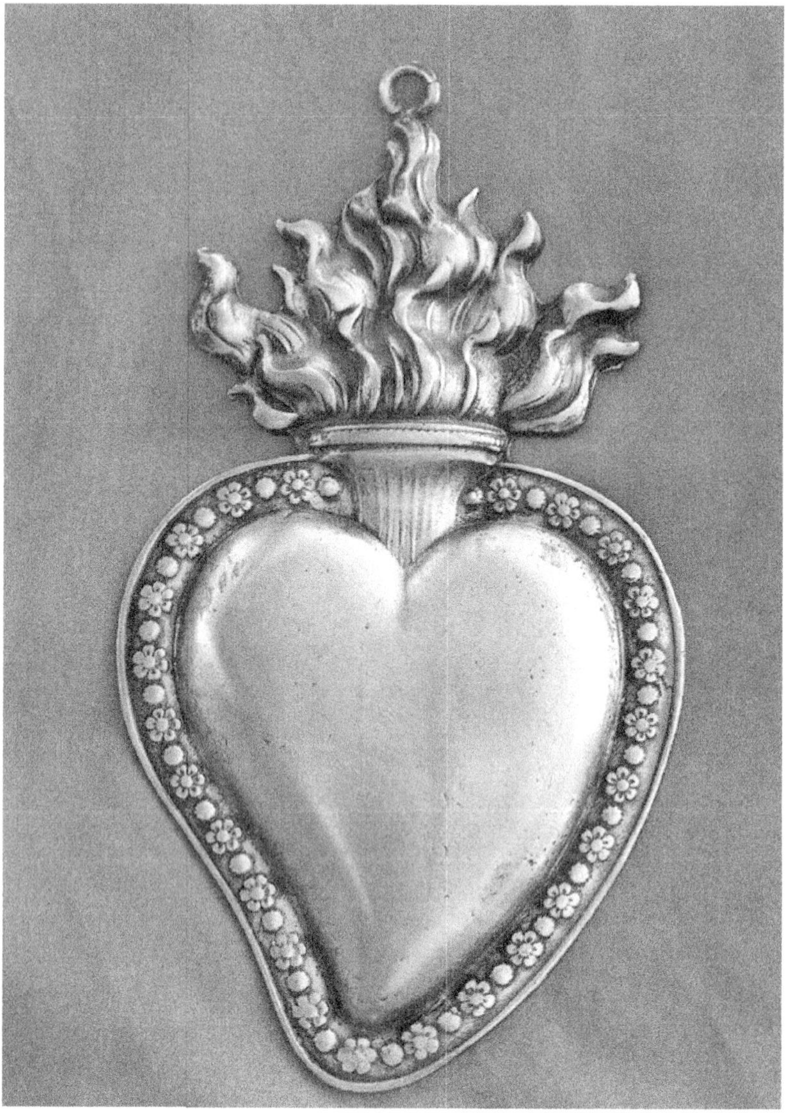

THE MAGIC OF MILAGROS

What are milagros?

They are small metal charms (the larger ones are called *ex votos*) in the form of body parts, animals, etc.

How are milagros used?

The traditional way to use Milagros goes back centuries. If a faithful person has something in his or her life that seems insurmountable, he or she may "make a deal" with a saint or a virgin and ask for help. If the miracle is granted, the faithful person will follow through on his or her end of the bargain, and that may include a trip to a shrine to leave something there as a physical representation of thanks. People who have a little more money may commission a painting called an ex voto, which is usually on wood or tin, which illustrates the miracle that occurred, or the favor granted. Those who can afford to part with only a few pesos will buy the metal charms that come in the shape of body parts, people, animals, plants and a wide array of inanimate objects. The milagros usually come in shapes specific to the miracle. For example, if someone wishes to give thanks for the healing of a broken arm, the devotee will purchase an arm milagro and leave it in the shrine. For a cow that recovered from illness, a cow milagro is used, and so on. The milagros are very literal and there are no special meanings for the individual pieces other than what is visually evident. Inside the shrine the milagros are usually left in a designated sacred space. This could either be a room off to the side, a wall or separate chapel. Often these sacred spaces need to be "cleaned out" and the contents are usually sold by the parish to raise money for the poor. Many works of devotional art, and older or more interesting milagros end up in secondary craft markets because of this practice. Many of the little milagros for sale in the stalls outside the shrines have been used multiple times. People believe the multiple uses of these objects only give them more power.

This traditional use of votive offerings similar to milagros dates back thousands of years to Ancient Greece. When the Roman Empire took over the Greek world, the Romans adopted the practice of leaving small gifts of thanks for the gods made out of clay, wood or metal in a symbolic form appropriate to the miracle that occurred. The Roman practice of votive offerings continued after Christianity was adopted throughout the Roman World and continued to live on in Catholic Europe for many centuries after the fall of the Roman Empire (today they are still used in parts of Spain, Portugal, France, Italy and southern Germany). As Christianity spread to the New World, milagros found new territory on which to flourish and in modern-day Latin America they are used most widely in Mexico. Today, many of the traditional shapes – arms, legs, eyes – share religious store shelf space with more modern milagros such as airplanes, cars and even computers. There is a milagro for pretty much everything, except for money, because it's frowned upon to pray for increased wealth. To get around this, many people in Mexico use the corn milagro to symbolize abundance and prosperity and use the charm accordingly.

    In an era of international trade and increased ethnic awareness in the States, milagros have become popular among Americans. Many people in the US use these small devotional objects as good luck charms much like a rabbit's foot or a four-leaf clover. Milagros adorn charm bracelets and other pieces of folk art jewelry. Milagros are often found nailed on to crosses or covering other wooden objects like saint statues or shoes, in a purely decorative fashion. Many people who have some degree of belief that the milagros may help them, carry them or have them in their homes in *anticipation* of a miracle or to hope for something and not to offer thanks. They are used to focus intention or even to draw on positive energies. To traditionalists, this may seem like the opposite of the milagros' intended use, but cultural elements always seem to adapt to new conditions when integrated into a new culture. Artists and jewelry makers have popped up on sites like etsy.com with creations like "healing charm necklaces" incorporating Mexican milagros. Creations are often elaborate and can sell for hundreds of dollars even though the cost of milagros at their manufacturing source in Mexico is often less than a nickel per piece. It's amazing how something so small can mean so much to people who value its use.

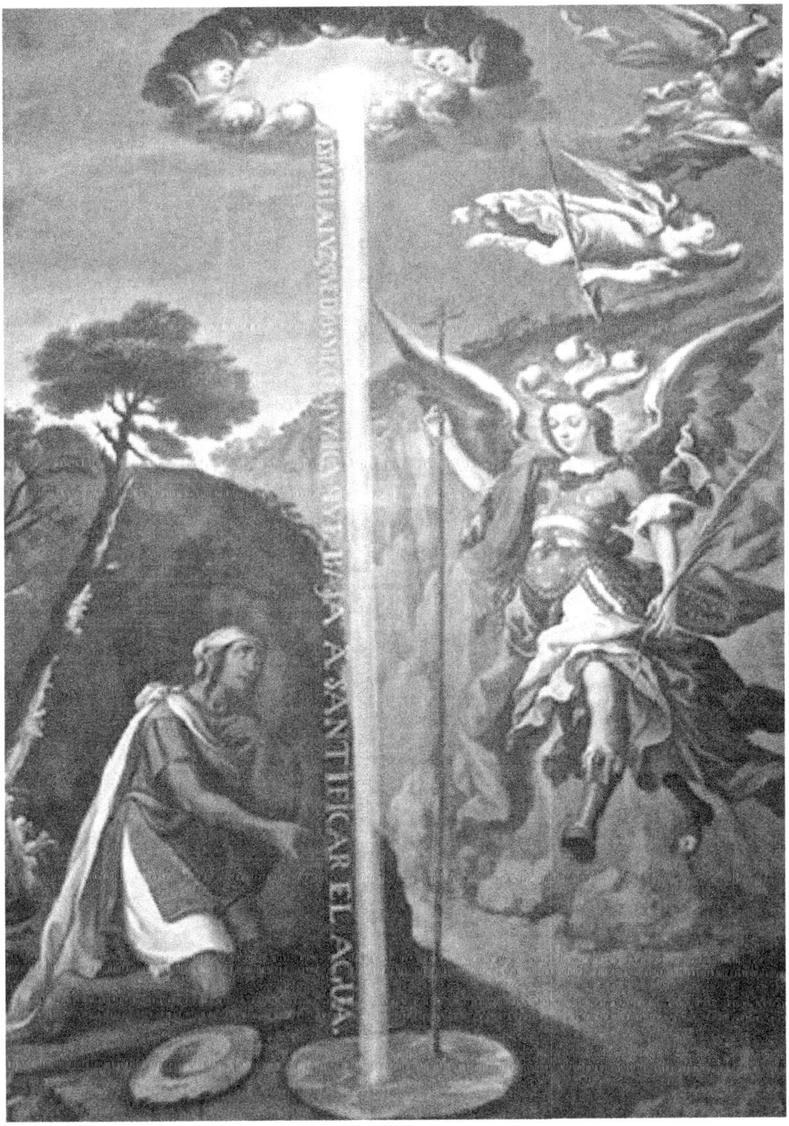
A SANTIFICAR EL AGUA.

ARCHANGEL MICHAEL AND THE WELL OF MIRACLES

The date was April 25, 1631, and the place was San Bernabé de Capula, Tlaxcala. The countryside was overrun with pestilence and to combat the plague the church fathers and civic leaders ordered a Procession of the Greater Litanies to beseech God's mercy. That procession took place on El Día de San Marcos, or the feast day on the Catholic calendar devoted to Saint Mark. In that procession was a 17-year-old indigenous boy named Diego de San Lazaro. Diego walked with the group – the whole town was present – until time itself seemed to slow down and the boy found himself in what would be described today as an alternate reality. He was present and animate but yet everything around him had frozen into a haze. Then, the heavens opened and in front of him above his eye level bursts of light and color soon gave way to a familiar image of the Archangel Saint Michael, the Supreme Commander of Heavenly Hosts, wielding a sword and clad in protective armor. The angel spoke to the young Diego:

"Know, my son, I am Saint Michael the Archangel and I have come to tell you that it is the Will of God and Mine that you tell the inhabitants of this town and its surroundings that in a valley between two mountain ridges you will find a miraculous source of water that will heal all diseases. It is under a large rock. Do not doubt what I tell you and do not neglect what I have sent you to do."

In a swirl of light and color, like the closing of a portal to another dimension, Saint Michael disappeared, and the procession resumed its normal pace in normal time. Diego asked other people around him if they experienced what he had seen and they all said, "no." After the ceremonies ended, the young man asked his neighbors and got the same response: no one saw the battle-ready archangel appearing so magnificently above the pious people. Diego dismissed the event as being something from his imagination. Perhaps the stress of the plague combined with the religious fervor of the ceremony had played tricks on his mind.

This was not the end of it, however. A few days later, the Supreme Commander of Heavenly Hosts reappeared to young Diego and this time he was not pleased. Saint Michael declared in a thundering voice:

"Why did you doubt what I have told you? Because you have not done as I commanded, you too, will now be stricken with the plague now afflicting your people."

The archangel disappeared once again in a tempest of color and light, and within moments Diego started feeling ill. Within just a few days his condition worsened. After a few weeks, his family was certain that Diego was going to die as he had been wracked by fever and had wasted away to almost nothing. Priests were called in to administer last rites to the nearly dead boy. It was then that the archangel appeared again, in front of many witnesses. Saint Michael grabbed young Diego by the hand, made him stand up and then the two of them disappeared in the usual intense swirl of light and color.

In a time immediately after these apparitions, the stories of these visitations were written down and were later compiled in a book authored by a Jesuit father named Francisco de Florencia and published in Puebla in 1898. From this book, we have a description of what happened after Diego returned home when he appeared out of nowhere into the same room where he had disappeared.

He announced to everyone:

"Saint Michael transported me to the place he had told me about before. With Saint Michael going before me through the night, everything was illuminated as the great prince passed, as if it were midday. Rocks and branches split apart as he passed, clearing a path for us. As we reached a certain spot, I saw Saint Michael holding a golden staff topped with a cross. 'From the place I touch with this staff will flow the miraculous spring I told you about during the procession. Make it clear to everyone that the illness you have suffered is a fruit of your disobedience.'

"Having said this, a great whirlwind rushed in amid the din of screams, wailing and moaning, as if a great crowd were being driven from the place. I shook with fear. It appeared the entire mountain ridge would tumble down on top of me during the turmoil.

"'Do not fear,' said my heavenly protector, 'these are the sounds made by the demons, thine enemies, because they know the great benefits that through my intercession the faithful will receive in this place from Our Lord. Many, seeing the marvels worked here, will convert and do penance for their sins, and all will give thanks to God for His mercies. Those who approach with lively faith and sorrow for their faults will, with the water from this spring, obtain relief in their labors and needs, and find a comfort in these waters for the sick on the point of death.'

"This being said, I saw a brilliant light descend from heaven, piercing the ground at the site of the spring. Saint Michael then said, 'This light that you have seen descend from heaven is the virtue God in His Divine Providence gives in this spring for the health and relief of the sick and needy. Make this known at once to everyone. That they may believe your testimony, I promise to work a great prodigy through you.' With that, Saint Michael disappeared, and I found myself here once again, completely restored."

Diego's family was amazed that the boy had returned completely healed of his sickness. They called in the head of the Franciscans to hear his story and then Diego was taken to the capital, Tlaxcala City, to have an audience with the governor. When Diego related his story to Tlaxcala's governor, the esteemed government official did not believe it, and his stated reason for this was that the Archangel Michael would never have chosen a poor Indian boy to be his messenger. Diego and the priests returned to San Bernabé de Capula. Now home, the boy gathered family members to go and carry out the wishes of the angel. Diego led his group to the place of the spring, in the valley between mountain ridges. There was a large boulder there on top of where the spring should have been just as Saint Michael had stated, and it weighed about half a ton. Several strong men tried to move the gigantic rock but couldn't. Diego said a small prayer to Saint Michael and tried moving the rock himself. He pushed the heavy boulder as if it were made of papier-mâché. Water then bubbled up from the earth where the rock once rested just as the archangel had predicted.

Word spread about the miraculous spring and people began going to the newly formed well to drink from the water, hoping for healings. The first to be healed was a little girl, and her family and neighbors saw it as a miracle. When Diego asked the girl's parents to share their testimony with religious and government officials, they were reluctant to do so, thinking that they would somehow be reprimanded or would face the agents of the Holy Inquisition. A few days after the girl's recovery, another person who drank from the well was also healed, and this person was reluctant to make the healing public for the same reasons stated by the parents of the cured little girl. Diego wanted to end the terrible plague and make the miraculous well known to all, but no one was cooperating. He turned again to the Prince of the Heavenly Armies, Saint Michael the Archangel.

When the angel heard Diego's prayers, he once again appeared before the boy in his characteristic vortex of lights and colors. Saint Michael spoke and said this:

"Why do you act cowardly, and are negligent in what two times now I have commanded you? Do you want to be punished once again for your disobedience? Arise, and have diligence in making known what I have commanded."

Diego was at an impasse. Desperate, he filled a jug of water from the Well of Miracles and walked some twenty miles all the way to the city of Puebla to see the archbishop there. After saying a small prayer to Saint Michael, Diego was led through the offices of the archbishop and was granted an audience with His Excellency to relate the stories of the angel's many appearances and the divine properties of the well. The archbishop gave the boy the benefit of the doubt and ordered the jug of water to be sent to the local hospital. There, people drank from the jug. One by one, all who sipped the water were miraculously healed of whatever ailment afflicted them. The archbishop then sent investigators to San Bernabé de Capula to test the water and to take down testimonies of healings and other miracles. In the ecclesiastical reports at the time, not only was it recorded that the plague was subsiding in the area, but the devotion to the Archangel Michael had increased dramatically. Some also claimed that there was a beautiful fragrance surrounding the well that would send people into a mild form of religious ecstasy. With the archbishop of Puebla satisfied as to the well's divine properties, he ordered a small chapel built on the site which was christened San Miguel del Milagro, or Saint Michael of the Miracle. Since the 1630s, the numbers of pilgrims to this sacred spot have steadily increased and the chapel has been enlarged or rebuilt a handful of times to accommodate the many devotees coming in search of miracles. The shrine sees its biggest influx of visitors on two days of the year: April 25, which is the day of the first appearance of Saint Michael to the young Diego, and on September 29th which is the official feast day of the Archangel Saint Michael. People still drink the waters from the well in hopes of physical cures or to assist in life's many battles. For the most part, Saint Michael does not disappoint the true believer.

THE MIRACULOUS HEALING WATERS OF TLACOTE

In May of 1991 on a ranch outside the town of Tlacote in the Mexican state of Querétaro, a sick dog took a drink from a small puddle near a well. Ranch owner Jesús Chahín Limón did not expect the dog to live much longer, but within days of drinking the water the dog had as much vibrancy and energy as it had had in its youth. The rancher, not believing what he himself had witnessed decided to experiment with the well water. He had people with illnesses come to the ranch and drink the water and those people reported seemingly miraculous results. The word got out and within months there were lines to receive the water with people coming from all over the world looking for cures for everything from migraine headaches to diabetes, from high cholesterol to even cancer and AIDS. Señor Chahín had inherited the property from his parents and lived a comfortable life on the ranch. Because of this he felt no need to charge people for the water, although he did seek to limit the amount individuals could take away, more from time and traffic concerns than anything. With help from the town, Chahín developed systems to handle the thousands of people who would come to his property per day to seek out a miracle. A triage system developed, with those with serious conditions shuffled into a shorter and faster line. It was reported that money came from the national and state governments to pay for the huge steel water containers to house the well water after a local priest sent some of the Tlacote water to an army hospital and cured 600 people. As with many shrines in Mexico, small enterprises in the town popped up to serve the multitudes of people. Townsfolk sold food, plastic jugs, mementoes and so on. Porters earned the equivalent of a few cents for hauling water for people too infirmed to wait in line or too debilitated to carry the water back to their cars themselves. Chahín never made one centavo on this whole phenomenon.

While the well attracted many people who ascribed religious or spiritual properties to the water, and many members of the clergy – from nuns and priests and even a Catholic bishop – praised the water for its divine aspects, Chahín never claimed that there was anything supernatural behind the cures and relief supposedly attributed to what was coming out of the well on his property. He was quoted as saying in a *Washington Post* article from January 1992: "The water weighs less than H2O. It is a mystery for science why it weighs less." After testing it, local health officials declared the water safe to drink and stated that it conformed to health and safety standards comparable to well water throughout the state of Querétaro. They could find no other special properties to the water in spite of the rancher's claims that it is somehow lighter than average. The Autonomous University of Querétaro performed a series of scientific tests on the water and also found nothing unusual about it; no strange chemical properties, nothing special at all. No amount of scientific tests would seem to stop the deluge of people from inundating the small town of Tlacote, however.

A UK nurse named Gill Fry employed by the organization Share International visited Tlacote in July of 1992 during the height of the water pilgrimages and kept a diary of her experiences. The September issue of the *Share International Journal* published Nurse Fry's account. Here is what she had to report in her own words:

"As a professional nurse, I was fascinated by reports of Tlacote water having healed so many ailments, including diabetes, epilepsy, arthritis, cancer and even AIDS. Having worked with patients for 10 years who have suffered the pain and anguish of such diseases, the idea of finding a cure, or partial cure, was indescribably exciting.

"It was thus that I set out, in July this year, on a quest to Mexico to collect the miracle water from Tlacote. From what I had read, I was expecting some hardship, at the very least to wait in line for three or four days and nights, in near tropical temperatures, and took with me a comprehensive survival kit (mosquito net, sunscreens, bedding, etc) and arrived prepared for any eventuality! I had also read that each person's water ration was generally three litres, and brought along several plastic containers. In the event, my expectations could not have been more wrong. A wonderfully kind colleague of Benjamin Creme in Mexico City took charge of me, drove me to Tlacote and, speaking the local language (which I do not), overcame each barrier and problem. Every door seemed wide open. My three-day stint turned into a mere three-hour wait; my water ration increased from three to 38 litres; and more wonderful still, I witnessed the most extraordinary photograph possibly in existence, which confirmed everything I had believed in for the last six years.

"Since May 1991 three million people have been to Tlacote, and at least six million people have drunk the water. The ranch owner, Mr. Chahín, keeps the registration files of every visitor, some of whom have travelled from as far as Europe and Russia. Many Mexican government officials, politicians, and artists have been seen waiting in the queue, which varies in size from 5,000 to 10,000 daily. The ranch is very clean, and the buildings brightly painted. Huge, lush trees provide the crowd with welcome shade from the scorching sun. I had imagined a dry, desert scene with chaotic, endless lines of exhausted people, but found everything very well organized, with the queue moving quickly and efficiently. After registering, Mrs. Chahin, the rancher's wife and resident doctor, checks each visitor's medical certificate and decides on an appropriate quota and dosage, prescribing the water orally, or externally as eyedrops, or enemas or direct application to the skin for skin cancer, eczema, etc. It must be an exhausting job answering a deluge of questions from thousands of people every day, yet she performs her task with endless patience and kindness, offering her advice freely. None of the ranch hands receives any money for this service, and they work from 9.30 to 15.30 hours every day. Mr. Chahin has never charged for the water, but considering the time and effort involved, to my mind a voluntary donation scheme could provide extra support and may sometime be introduced.

"After the doctor's consultation, one stands in line to receive the water. Huge stainless-steel tanks, which the government assisted in providing, pump the water to the plastic taps from the deep artesian well that, we are told, will never run dry. Having thought about this moment for months, I felt great elation as I watched my containers being filled. All my hopes were coming to pass and I had been given more water than I had ever dreamt possible. Thanking the ranch workers and tightening the lids further, I briefly pondered on the practicalities of carrying 38 litres of water, and the daunting thought of customs! (Curiously, in the event, nobody at customs asked a single question about the weight or contents of my overloaded bags, overflowing with miracle water.) Such worries were quickly dispelled as I was handed a cup of the water. It tasted wonderful, slightly sweet, pure and light. By the end of the day I had been given three cupfuls and some days later realized my mistake! I was to suffer a gastric upset for a week. The water is totally clean and pure, but very potent. The dosage needed is very small indeed. A couple of teaspoonfuls would have been plenty for me.

"I was shown around Mr. Chahin's office which had two long walls stacked with visitors files, and shelves covered with water-testing apparatus. Just as I was leaving, I was shown a framed photograph with the most extraordinary history and phenomenal implications. A man who had drunk the water, and had been healed, took numerous photographs of the ranch. On returning home, he had one frame left on his film. Anxious to finish and develop the film, he took a photograph of his new television set. The television was not on; the screen was blank. To his astonishment, after the film was developed, the last shot showed the television screen with a face upon it: the face of Christ with a crown of thorns on His head. I felt myself shiver as I looked at the powerful image. With limited time, I quickly took several photographs, hoping I could capture the rather faint impression, with the complications of bright sunlight and a reflecting glass covering. Fortunately, the photographs I took seem even stronger than the original, and the face is clearly visible.

"Travelling home with my exciting news, dragging my bags full of water, I felt triply blessed – my wait in line had been so short; I had been given gallons of water; and I had witnessed the most tangible evidence of God's presence."

In the early 1990s rumors circulated that Magic Johnson's HIV went undetectable after multiple visits to the Tlacote miracle well. While Jesús Chahín never met Magic Johnson personally, he did tell the *Washington Post*, "I did see a couple of tall black men one day." He did admit to seeing other celebrities who came seeking cures from his miraculous well. Among them were Spanish-language singers José José, Juan Gabriel and Julio Iglesias. High-ranking members of President Salinas' government also visited Tlacote seeking cures. Celebrities were often given special access and special privileges.

Perhaps a bit weary from the crowds, Chahín closed his ranch to the public for two weeks during Easter of 1993. After he reopened his ranch, Chahín saw a marked decrease in the crowds. Within a few years the people seeking a cure from the miraculous water dwindled to a small trickle.

In January 2015, Mexican newspaper *El Universal* went to Tlacote to see the current state of the town and to investigate what happened to Jesús Chahín and his special well. What they found was shocking. Chahín had passed away in 2004, ironically, from an aggressive form of cancer. His widow sold the property and the new owners, the Cosío family, had no plans to open up their property to the public ever again. The town of Tlacote, according to the newspaper, seemed like a ghost town, with many abandoned buildings and other dilapidated structures. After the boom ended in the mid-1990s, the town's economy ruined, many people left Tlacote to find work in the capital city of Querétaro or in other larger Mexican cities. And irony of ironies, during the *El Universal* investigation into the town in early 2015 they found that Tlacote had been without municipal water service for several months, the main water sources having all been exhausted, with only a scant few, deeper, private wells giving water. The town that was once known internationally for its water was effectively all dried up.

And what of the magic and miracles supposedly experienced at this place in the early 1990s? Thousands of people claimed cures of terminal illnesses. Many more claimed that the water helped them with minor conditions even though there was no scientific basis for any of these claims. Do we have on our hands genuine examples of the true power of belief and the mind's important role in the healing process or did those making the pilgrimage to Tlacote experience true miracles?

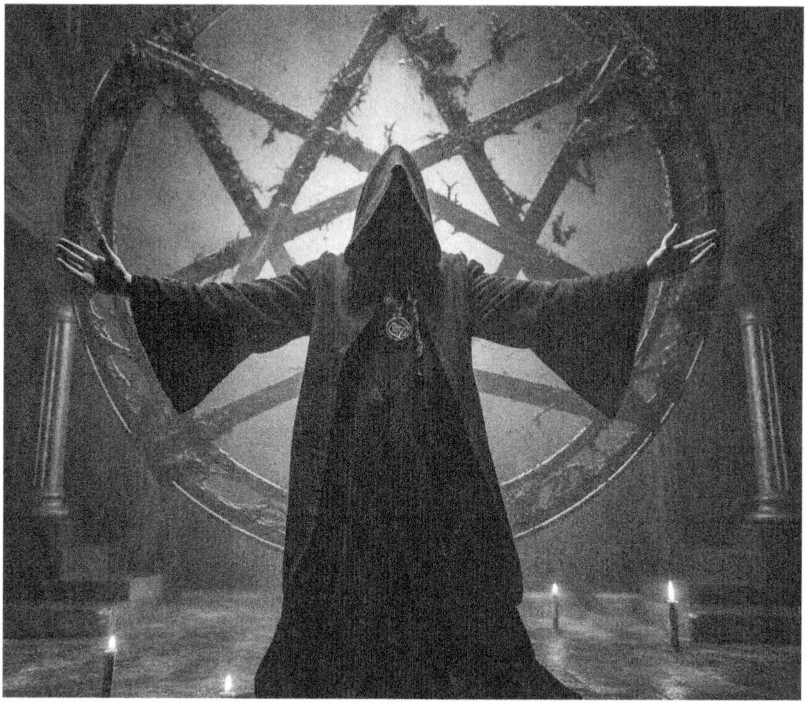

THE SORCERERS OF CATEMACO

    The town of Catemaco in the Mexican state of Veracruz is located at a crossroads of geography, time and space. The name of this lakeside jungle town of 35,000 people comes from the language of the ancient Aztecs, Nahuatl, and roughly means, "The Place of the Burning House." Long cut off from the rest of Mexico, the railroad first came here in 1912 and roads connecting it with the rest of the state of Veracruz only in the 1950s. Catemaco's remoteness and its seemingly indifferent attitude toward the outside world allowed for the development of a unique ambience in the town. From pre-Hispanic times, from probably before the Aztecs gave the region its name, the area has been known as a place of magic and sorcery. The arrival of successive waves of people to the area has added to the magical nature of Catemaco. While still mostly indigenous in the century or so after the Spanish Conquest, the area began to receive escaped slaves, and along with them, their African beliefs systems and cultures. When European civilization caught up with Catemaco, the Spanish introduced Catholicism to a population that was a blend of several native groups and various African nationalities. The already-established class of *chamanes* or sorcerers in the town incorporated Catholic saints and rituals into their magical practices. In addition to the more occult and spiritual aspects of the town, the area has long been a center for herbalism, as many different plants with curative properties grow abundantly in the jungles surrounding the town of Catemaco. Cures combining different plants and plant extracts have provided relief for hundreds of different ailments, and the indigenous medicinal plant wisdom runs deep. Over the years, the herbalist traditions have melded with the overlapping spiritual belief systems found here. Centuries later the blend of traditions is often hard to trace, but most recognize that what is happening in Catemaco is very powerful and unique to the region.

    The locals have realized this, too. In 1970, the *Brujo Mayor*, or Head Sorcerer, of Catemaco, a man named Gonzalo Aguirre, decided to get together with the rest of the spiritual and magical practitioners in the town to put together the first witch's conference. Aguirre inherited the position from a man named Manuel Utrera, who served as the town's head *brujo* for many decades and had his own ideas of uniting the various magical practitioners of the area, but never acted on those ideas. While the whole modern concept of a "witch" has been traditionally female, the majority of the *Maestros en ciencias ocultas* , or "Masters in Occult Sciences," of Catemaco, are men. This may be a result of the heavy influence of the indigenous and African cultures on the area's magical and occult traditions, which favored men as spiritual leaders and healers. The Aztecs had nearly 40 types of formal classifications for sorcerers and specialists of various magical arts, and all the roles were filled by men. The tradition of the African village "witch doctor" was also a traditionally male role. So, Catemaco now has institutionalized a "brotherhood" of male witches called the *Trece Brujos*, or Thirteen Sorcerers. Without being too tripped up on trying to define the nuances existing among the titles of the various people involved, the terms used to describe the various practitioners in Catemaco are numerous. Some prefer the English equivalent of "witch," "sorcerer," "warlock," "shaman," or "healer." The most commonly used Spanish word is *brujo* which translates to "male witch," in English. As previously mentioned, since 1970, the sorcerers of all different kinds have gotten together to have an annual conference. The original name of the gathering was *El Congreso Nacional de Brujos de Catemaco*, or in English, The National Congress of Sorcerers of Catemaco. Even into the 21st Century, the Catholic Church has always been against any gatherings of witches. Because of harsh criticism from local and regional Catholic Church officials and the bad PR that went along with it, the town's coven of 13 decided to change the name of the gathering in 2008. The newly rebranded annual festival is now known as *Fiesta de Ritos, Ceremonias y Artesanías Mágicas*, or in English, the Festival of Magical Rites, Ceremonies and Handcrafts. It now attracts hundreds of witches, sorcerers, *curanderos*, psychics, healers, fortune tellers and many charlatans. Even groups of Central European gypsies, known also as the Rom, come to Catemaco for the festival. Thousands of tourists also participate, and mostly come from other parts of Mexico, although outsiders are arriving in greater numbers with each passing year.

The annual celebration always takes place over the course of 3 days starting at the stroke of midnight on the last Friday of March. The *brujos* chose that time of year, the early spring, because it corresponded with many renewal and rebirth rituals that had been practiced and celebrated in different forms in the area for hundreds or possibly thousands of years. The witch fiesta always kicks off with a black mass on the shores of Lake Catemaco. The mass includes a public burning of a 10-foot star, usually 6-pointed. The burning of the star, according to the current Brujo Mayor of the town, Jaime Bervon Azamar, is so that, "both the good and evil gates will open." During the festival, Bervon states, both black and white magic are performed, and the rituals can take on many forms. Bervon started as a sorcerer's apprentice at age 13 and specializes in exorcisms and what are termed *limpias* or spiritual cleansings to rid a client of bad vibrations or to restore one's aura to a higher frequency. A standard Catemaco *limpia* involves a chicken egg, sprigs of rosemary combined with a fragrant local jungle plant, candles, a glass of water and either incense or perfume. To start, the practitioner will whisper several prayers to the Catholic saints while he lights the candles and prepares the bundles of herbs. He then rubs the client's body with the plant bundle, continuing the prayer whispers. After finishing the plant rub-down, the sorcerer takes the intact egg and gently rubs it over the person's body much as he does with the bundle of herbs. After rubbing down the person's body with the egg, he then cracks the egg into a glass of water. This is the divinatory part of the *limpia*. The *brujo* will examine the contents of the glass, and by looking at the patterns of the cracked egg in water he will give the client advice about the future or will suggest different courses of action that he or she will need to take. In that glass the person performing the *limpia* can also see the spiritual causes of the troubles that his client may be having and will make suggestions or prescribe herbal remedies to get the person back into balance. A traditional Catemaco *limpia* usually ends with the spraying of perfume or the lighting of a sweet incense to mark a new and clean beginning for the client. A kind of mass *limpia* occurs during the first Friday of the annual Catemaco fiesta at a place called Nanciyaga. Nanciyaga is a clearing in the jungle surrounded by rows of stone seats, like bleachers in a miniature sports stadium, where shamans light pots of sweet herb bundles and chant prayers for a reverent audience. No archaeological investigations have ever been done at the Nanciyaga site, but locals state that the location has been a place of ritual and worship since pre-Conquest times.

In an online interview, Mexican author and witchcraft expert José Gil Olmos offered his opinions of the Catemaco witch festival. Olmos is an investigative journalist for the Mexico-City-based news magazine *Proceso* and the author of the acclaimed two-part book *Los Brujos del Poder*, or in English, "The Witches of Power." Olmos states with some disappointment, "The congress has become a tourist event, and the mayor usually throws a few nighttime shows in the program so that people can dance and get drunk. So, if you go looking for a surprising sorcerers' congress, you end up attending a show." He also said, "A lot of the witches are con artists, so you have to ask around for the real ones." Later in the interview, Olmos countered his disappointment by affirming, "The first night is special. That's when both black magic and white magic rituals take place and, considering Catemaco is a beautiful place, it is worthwhile visiting."

The surrounding mountainous jungle area is indeed beautiful, and the Mexican government has set aside thousands of acres for the Los Tuxtlas Biosphere Reserve to protect the incredible variety of plant and animal life in and around the Lake Catemaco area. Curiously, part of the reserve is the tiny Isla de los Changos in the center of the lake. The island is so named because it is overrun by a colony of stump-tailed monkeys imported from Thailand in 1974. The alien monkeys are not the only strange creatures in the region according to the locals. Catemaco residents believe that the surrounding jungle is home to chaneques, a mythical race of mischievous elves. They also believe that the dense forests serve as perfect hiding places for naguales, the animal forms of sorcerers who have decided to shape-shift. Some of the natural formations in the surrounding areas are also considered sacred places. These places include the mountain called Mono Blanco and a natural grotto in the middle of the jungle full of evil spirits appropriately called The Devil's Cave. It was on Mono Blanco where the former head sorcerer of Catemaco, Gonzalo Aguirre, supposedly met Satan himself and made several deals with him. So, the rumor goes.

For those wishing for a perhaps more authentic spiritual experience with the sorcerers of Catemaco, locals recommend visiting the town in the off season, and not during festival time. Many *brujos* have set up offices like medical clinics complete with waiting and examination rooms. Some list their specializations on their storefronts and their business cards. One can see a general practitioner, more commonly known as a *Maestro en ciencias ocultas*, or "Master in Occult Sciences." A popular specialist in Catemaco is a *Yorbatero*, or one who practices a certain type of ritualistic massage. Another one is called a *Huesero*, who works with a client's skeletal system much as a chiropractor would in Western medicine. The specialties are as diverse as human ailments and concerns. If services of practitioners are too costly, amulet shops in the town also serve people looking for that special charm that will do the trick. Most people who go to Catemaco to visit the sorcerers are looking for guidance and reassurance. Those who visit to partake in the so-called "black magic," usually wish to curse or destroy their enemies. One of the governors of Veracruz, Fidel Herrera Beltrán, proposed setting up a national school of witchcraft in the town, but it never got off the ground because of too much opposition from both the Catholic Church and the general public. Nevertheless, there is something for everyone in Catemaco and the town boasts of hosting many celebrities and politicians. The current president of Mexico, Andrés Manuel López Obrador, was said to have been a frequent visitor of certain high-ranking *brujos* in the town. Although it is unknown if he is still in contact with any of the sorcerers of Catemaco, it is said that the president may have used them in his inauguration ceremonies at the Zocalo in Mexico City on December 1, 2018, witnessed by millions. Perhaps the power of the sorcerers of Catemaco is more far-reaching than anyone could imagine. For now, they remain a focus of curiosity and the standard bearers of a long and complicated tradition.

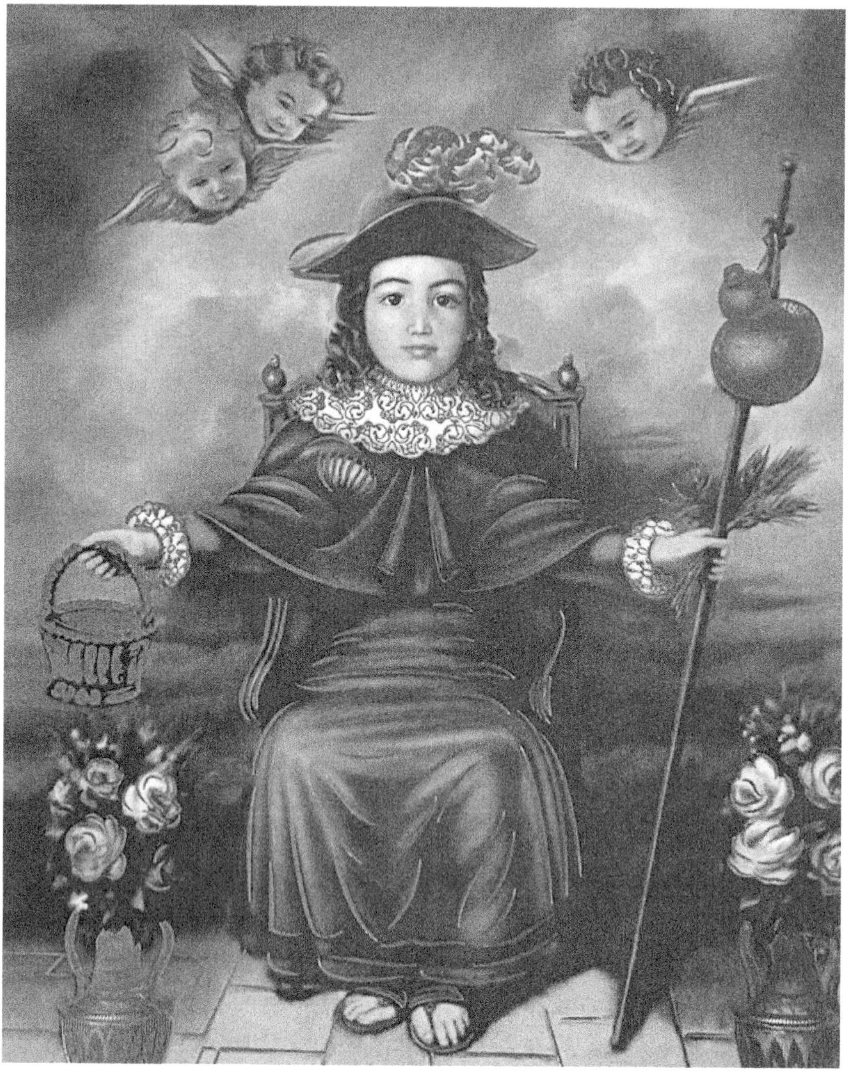

A FEMALE PRISONER MEETS
THE BABY JESUS

A woman who lived in a small town in Michoacán became jealous of another woman in her neighborhood because she was flirting with her boyfriend. This woman, in a fit of jealousy, stabbed her rival in the heart. She had no regrets for what she did and was eventually sentenced to life at a prison in the town of Quiroga. At the Quiroga prison she was assigned to a small cell, a permanent solitary confinement. This woman nearly went crazy in her solitude and tried to pass her time by making up stories in her head, imagining happy scenes of life outside the prison walls. Whatever she dreamed up, however, was always ruined by memories of the insane screams of her victim whom she killed in a fit of passion. Whenever that happened, she surrendered herself to the Santo Niño de Atocha, the Baby Jesus dressed as a traveler who is so familiar to many Mexicans.

After three years in prison the woman's health started to fade. She was not only tormented by the memories of the horrible act she committed, but she was also suffering from the poor quality of food that they dished up in that dank prison. One day, when she was feeling particularly low, she sat in the corner of her cell and stared blankly at the bars that stood between her and a cloudless sky. Suddenly, she noticed a smiling little boy in the opposite corner of her cell. The woman thought she was hallucinating and imagining the whole scene.

"How did you get into my cell?" she asked the little boy.

"I slipped in when the guards opened the door," he replied. "I'm so small they didn't even see me."

The little boy then opened a basket he was carrying and offered the woman food. Even though the food was the freshest she had seen in years she was more interested in the company and wanted to talk more with the ruddy-cheeked boy. He insisted she eat first, and she did. When she was finished with her meal she looked up and the little boy was gone. The woman was drowsy from the food and went to sleep. When she woke up, it was morning, and the little boy was standing over her. He took some food from his basket and gave it to the woman. After the woman finished eating the little boy told her that he would return once more and then he vanished. The woman had more questions for him, but he disappeared in the middle of one of her sentences. She continued to question her own sanity because she didn't believe that any of this was real.

Later that night, tired, the woman curled up on the floor and was about to fall asleep. In the corner of the cell the little boy appeared again in a glowing orb of light. The boy told the woman to follow him, and he began to burn a hole in the wall as he walked closer to it. As he kept walking, the hole turned into a tunnel. She followed him until she was outside, on the other side of the walls of the prison, in complete freedom. The little boy told her to look up in the sky and follow a bright star. She walked all night and did not realize that she had been traveling hundreds of miles following that star. When the sun came up, she found herself in the town of Plateros in the state of Zacatecas. When the church bells rang, she walked over to the beautiful sanctuary dedicated to the Santo Niño and fell to her knees when she saw the little boy that had appeared to her in her cell now in the form of a venerated statue.

SAINT ANTHONY AND THE HANDICAPPED BOY

In a small town in central Mexico there lived a teenage boy who was born without the ability to walk. His family could not afford a wheelchair, so he got around the best he could by using crutches. He dreamed of dancing with the pretty girls in town and riding fast horses. He had faith that one day San Antonio – Saint Anthony – would heal him and prayed daily for the saint's intercession. As time went by, the boy began to have doubts and then those doubts grew into a deep depression. That depression soon turned into a special anger directed toward the saint. "How long do I have to wait to be healed?" The young man repeated to himself. "You owe me and if I ever meet you, you will pay dearly." His rage continued to swell inside him.

The boy had a cousin who was very religious and one day offered to take him to the shrine of Saint Anthony in Puebla in his carriage. The young man agreed to go, although he was still very angry with the saint whom he thought had done nothing for him. Maybe his disappointment and rage would finally end if he confronted the saint in person and took out his frustrations directly on the statue. He concealed his anger and his ill intent by engaging in trite conversation with his cousin during the journey. Along the pilgrimage route they encountered many people. One of them was a priest walking alone. The teenager's cousin offered the priest a ride and he accepted. The padre began talking about how he found out that before he was born his own father had sold his soul to the devil. As a young man the priest befriended a bandit who was friends with the devil who promised to get the contract that the priest's father had signed. This story of redemption and hope made the disabled young man think twice about his own situation. He thought that maybe he should give Saint Anthony another chance. After a few more days on the road, the young man's anger swelled up inside him again, however. By the time they arrived at the *santuario*, the boy was angrier than ever. After his cousin helped him to the altar, the teenager started screaming at the statue of Saint Anthony to the shock of everyone there. "I'm tired of not being able to walk," the boy exclaimed. "I've prayed and prayed to you for many years, and you've done nothing for me! I hate you!" At that point, the boy pulled out a sizable rock from his pocket and threw it at the saint. To the boy's surprise, when he looked up, San Antonio had caught the rock and was about to throw it back at the angry and frightened boy. The boy was so scared that he got up and ran out of the church faster than a jackrabbit. When he was outside, the boy realized that he had used his own legs to run away from the rock-throwing saint. He turned around, walked back into the shrine and asked San Antonio to forgive him for his lack of faith.

THE RISE IN EXORCISMS IN MEXICO

Soothing mariachi music filled the air as crowds gathered outside the Colegio Miraflores in the city of León in the Mexican state of Guanajuato. It was right after sunset on Sunday, March 25, 2012. The people and music coaxed out of his guest quarters Pope Benedict XVI who was wrapping up his first visit to Mexico. The 84-year-old German-born pontiff made his appearance to the delight of a cheering crowd on his last night visiting the nation of nearly 100,000,000 Roman Catholics. A teenage girl presented His Holiness with a highly ornate sombrero which he wore as he was given a microphone. Benedict stated that in all his official trips he had never been received with such enthusiasm and love as he had experienced there and, "Now I can say that Mexico will always remain in my heart." The next day the pope was on a plane bound for Havana, Cuba, and while his visit to Mexico was full of much joy and celebration, the pontiff had a lot on his mind regarding the second most populous Catholic country in the world. He had gone to Mexico under troubling circumstances. Chief among the pope's concerns was the rise in the cult of the Holy Death – or in Spanish, "Santa Muerte" – which seemed to be experiencing exponential growth in Mexico along with other religious practices that stray away from the Catholic Church orthodoxy. The stories that Pope Benedict had heard about the increasing power of the Holy Death devotion along with the rise in satanic ritual abuse reported throughout Mexico were some of the real reasons why he visited that country. He was concerned that the Catholic Church was losing its grip on the Mexican people, and he wanted to know why. In the wake of the Pope's visit, the Church would come up with a strategy to solidify its base and try to expel the evil forces that it saw as a threat to its hegemony. The following year, in April of 2013, the President of the Pontifical Council for Culture of the Vatican, Italian Cardinal Gianfranco Ravasi, visited Mexico with the intent in conferring the first "Atrium of the Gentiles" outside of Europe. This meeting was intended to bring together believers and non-believers to talk about the spiritual destiny of Mexico. While open to dialogue to try to figure out what was going on, the cardinal reaffirmed the Catholic Church's position on the more "demonic" styles of worship going on in Mexico, calling the increasingly popular adoration of the Santa Muerte, "A dark, hellish cult of denial" and that "the greatness of culture and of the true religion is just to celebrate life, and this is exactly the opposite."

Indeed, it is very difficult to travel around Mexico these days without seeing the image of the Santa Muerte in various places, from store windows to bus stations, and for more information on the Santa Muerte phenomenon please see Mexico Unexplained episode number 9. It's estimated that some 10 million people worship the bejeweled, dressed up grim-reaper-looking skeleton known as the Santa Muerte and the phenomenon has nothing to do with the Mexican holiday Day of the Dead, or Día de los Muertos, which is a celebration of those who have passed and is a harmonious blend of Catholicism and ancient pre-Christian traditions. For more information about Day of the Dead in Mexico, please see Mexico Unexplained episode number 5. The Santa Muerte "death cult" is only part of what the Catholic Church sees as a larger problem, however, and the increase in the following of this folk saint and others appears to be a symptom of an underlying moral decay in Mexico and an increase in power by unseen, darker forces which have attempted to gain dominion over all of humanity since the beginning of time. To counter this view, others say that threats of drug violence, dire economic conditions and a breakup of the traditional social framework has led to tens of millions of people in Mexico living lives in despair. The seemingly empowering death cults give these marginalized Mexicans hope and fill the needs not being met by either the family, the Catholic Church or the Mexican government.

To combat what it believes to be the growing forces of evil in Mexico, the Catholic Church has either deployed or created a vast number of exorcists to deal with what it sees as an abrupt increase in literal demonic possession throughout the country. In fact there are more exorcists currently in Mexico than in any other country on earth. So, what exactly is an exorcism? According to the Catholic Encyclopedia found at New Advent dot org:

"Exorcism is (1) the act of driving out, or warding off, demons, or evil spirits, from persons, places, or things, which are believed to be possessed or infested by them, or are liable to become victims or instruments of their malice; (2) the means employed for this purpose, especially the solemn and authoritative adjuration of the demon, in the name of God, or any of the higher power in which he is subject."

The Catholic Church regards demonic possession as incredibly rare and before the 1970s when popular media such as movies and television brought demonic possession and exorcism into the mainstream, there were very few members of the clergy who were trained in this practice. In 1999 the Vatican issued revised rules for conducting exorcisms as it noticed the increase in interest in the ritual. First, a victim must be examined thoroughly by doctors and psychologists to rule out any mental or physical illnesses or evidence of substance abuse. From paragraph 1673 of the Catechism of the Catholic Church:

"Exorcism is directed at the expulsion of demons or to the liberation from demonic possession through the spiritual authority which Jesus entrusted to his Church. Illness, especially psychological illness, is a very different matter; treating this is the concern of medical science. Therefore, before an exorcism is performed, it is important to ascertain that one is dealing with the presence of the Evil One, and not an illness."

The case is escalated to ecclesiastical authorities if medical or basic spiritual help is not effective. Individuals who are demonically possessed may exhibit the following signs:

1. The loss of personality; for example, flying into tantrums or fits of rage
2. A change in the person's voice
3. Unnatural body postures or contorted facial features
4. Unnatural physical strength
5. Levitation of the person or nearby objects
6. Intense aversion or hatred toward religious objects

7. Coldness in the room
8. Understanding or speaking another language previously unknown to the possessed
9. Biting or cutting of the skin
10. Prediction of future events and knowledge of things unseen
11. Intense bodily pain or other physical ailments not explicable by science
12. The hearing of voices or receipt of other supernatural messages

The above is not an exhaustive list.

The exorcist approaches the demon-possessed with a sense of humility. The Church believes that Christ acts through the exorcist to cast out the demon. Standard prayers are used along with oils, incense and candles. The approach an exorcist takes is usually situational. Often, the victim of the possession is physically restrained so as not to cause harm to himself or herself, or to those in his or her surroundings. It may take many attempts for the exorcist to be successful, and sessions may stretch over months or years. Many people in Mexico believe that those who are possessed have a "spiritual inheritance" that gets passed down for 4 generations if the demons are not taken care of and expelled. This is not formal Church dogma, however.

On May 20, 2015, the Archbishop Emeritus of Guadalajara, Cardinal Juan Sandoval Íñiguez, along with the Archbishop Jesús Carlos Cabrero of San Luis Potosí and world-renown Spanish demonologist and exorcist Father José Antonio Fortea, gathered together with several Mexican exorcists from around the country to perform a mass exorcism in the Metropolitan Cathedral of San Luís Potosí. Called a *Magno Exorcismo* the complex ritual was not publicized beforehand so as not to draw attention to the rite. The participants gathered in the cathedral behind locked doors and began chanting and praying according to a proscribed ritual, including calling on the four directions – north, south, east and west – in the names of specific saints. An important part of the mass exorcism was the call to close The Door of the Abyss. One of the participants hit the floor of the cathedral with a large hammer and called upon the Virgin Mary to close the gates of hell to keep the Devil from escaping. Did the mass exorcism work? Is Mexico now free of demons? As with exorcisms on an individual, the Spanish demonologist who participated in the *Magno Exorcismo* told reporters that the ritual must be performed many times over the course of several years to make sure it is effective. If the Santa Muerte cult is any indication, the mass exorcism had very little effect, as the numbers of devotees in this folk saint, along with the reported number of exorcisms, have only increased since the event at the San Luís Potosí cathedral.

If the Santa Muerte devotion and satanic rituals are just symptoms of the increase of demonic influences in Mexico, then what do people believe is the cause for the increase in demonic activity in Mexico that would warrant these exorcisms? One of the most seasoned exorcists in Mexico, 80-year-old Father Francisco Lopez Sedano of the Parish of the Holy Cross in Mexico City, who has performed over 6,000 exorcisms in his 40-year career has some explanations. Father Lopez is the National Coordinator Emeritus of Exorcism for the Archdiocese of Mexico and has devoted his life to this subject. He has repeatedly stated that the Devil enters a person's body because the person has allowed him access. In other words, the victim has in some way let his or her spiritual guard down to permit the possession. The Devil's whole objective is to create a barrier between God and the individual human. Many people in Mexico believe that people are more easily possessed nowadays because there are just more demonic entities existing among humans on the earthly plane. The faithful cite the 2007 law that legalized abortion in Mexico City that intensified demonic activity throughout the country. With every baby aborted, so the folk wisdom goes, a new demon gets released upon the earth. The demons look for people to torment and to inhabit, and the same folk wisdom states that there are several ways which a demon can access a possible victim of possession. Many occult practices or even simple good luck rituals are said to make a person vulnerable. A séance a use of a Ouija Board or other "spirit board" to call on ghosts or spirits, even if used in good fun, may be exposing the participants to potential harm. The use of tarot cards has also been cited as possibly dangerous. There are many games that have popped up in Mexico because of the internet that have been causing concern among church officials because they are attractive to children, notable among them are the Charlie Charlie Challenge and the *Bellena Azul* or Blue Whale game. Children are more susceptible to these bad influences nowadays than in any other time in Mexican history, a church official stated. This is because of the breakdown of the traditional family and the fact that many children now come from a home where the mother is working and thus many children are left with a lot of unsupervised time. Charlie Charlie is a game of divination in which two pencils are put on a piece of paper in the shape of a cross and in each corresponding quadrant created by the pencils are the words "*sí*" or "*no*". A ghost called "Charlie" is invoked and participants ask the spirit yes or no questions, watching the pencils for movement. The Blue Whale game consists of a few dozen tasks of increasing complexity agreed to by participants beforehand with the last task usually involving suicide or murder. The very act of engaging in these games, demonologist believe, are incredibly dangerous, and participation in them may even open up portals to Hell. Other things that increase a person's vulnerability to evil forces according to Mexican believers include things as seemingly innocent as the practice of yoga and even the seemingly magic spell that Disney movies have over children. The extremely faithful would caution us to put away the yoga mat and turn off "Beauty and the Beast." In a country so haunted by evil and so overrun by demons, apparently one can't be careful enough.

BIBLIOGRAPHY

Arbuckle, H. C. "Don José and Don Pedrito." *Southwest Review*, vol. 59, no. 2, 1974, pp. 189–94.

Bierhorst, John. *Latin American Folktales: Stories from Hispanic and Indian Traditions*. New York: Pantheon, 2003.

Broussard, Ben. "San Miguel del Milagro: The Apparition of Saint Michael in Mexico." In, *Crusade*, January/February 2016, pp. 9-12.

Campos, Anthony John. *Mexican Folk Tales*. Tucson: The University of Arizona Press, 1977.

Castillo, Ana. *Goddess of the Americas: Writings on the Virgin of Guadalupe*. New York: Riverhead Books, 1993.

"Catholic Heroes... Mother María Guadalupe García Zavala," by Carole Breslin, in *The Wanderer,* 21 June 2016.

Chávez, Eduardo. *Our Lady of Guadalupe and Saint Juan Diego: The Historical Evidence*. Lanham, MD: Rowman and Littlefield, 2006.
Chesnut, R. Andrew. *Devoted to Death: Santa Muerte, the Skeleton Saint*. Oxford: Oxford University Press, 2012.

Cody, Edward. "Faithful Seek Miracles in Light Water." In *The Washington Post*, 27 Jan 1992, p. A10.

Comack, Marilyn, ed. *Saints and Their Cults in the Atlantic World*. Columbia, SC: University of South Carolina Press, 2007.

Conover, Cornelius and Cory Conover. "Saintly Biography and the Cult of San Felipe de Jesus in Mexico City, 1597-1697." In *The Americas*, vol. 67, no. 4 (April 2011), pp. 441-466.

Corbeaux, Lazarus. *Santa Muerte Rituals*. CreateSpace, 2015.

Egan, Martha. *Milagros: Votive Offerings of the Americas*. Santa Fe: Museum of New Mexico Press, 1991.

Fedewa, Marilyn H. "Jumano Native Americans Still Revere Lady in Blue," in *Tradición*, Winter 2008, pp. 19-20.

Ferguson, Wes. "How Curandero Don Pedro Jaramillo Became a South Texas Folk Saint." In *Texas Highways*, 27 August 2020.

Florencia, Francisco de. *Narración de la maravillosa aparición que hizo el Arcángel San Miguel a Diego Lázaro de San Francisco*. Puebla: Church documents, 1898.

Flores, Francisco. "El 'milagro' de Tlacote, la doble paradoja," In *El Universal*, 12 Jan 2015.

Griffith, James S. *Folk Saints of the Borderlands: Victims, Bandits and Healers*. Tucson: Rio Nuevo Publishers, 2003.

Huesca, Patricia. "Virgen en barrio de Monterrey 'llora' ante tragedias; el Vatican esperará 60 años para dar su veredicto." *La Crónica*, 26 Jul 2004.

Janvier, Thomas A. *Legends of the City of Mexico*. New York: Harper and Brothers Publishers, 1910.

Kosloski, Philip. "The Bi-locating Nun Who May Have Evangelized America," in *Aleteia*, 15 Aug 20.

Kurillo, Max and Erline Tuttle. *The Old Missions of Baja and Alta California, 1697-1834*. New York, M&E Books, 2014.

"La historia del niño Dios más grande del mundo puesto en Zacatecas," In *Milenio*, 21 Nov. 2019.

"Mass Exorcism Performed at Mexican Church." BBC: 26 Nov. 2013.

Miranda, Carolina. "At Los Angels Toppling of Junipero Serra Statue, Activists Want Full Story Told." *Los Angeles Times*, 20 Jun 2020.

Perdigon Castaneda, Judith Katia. "Una relación simbiotica entre La Santa Muerte y El Santo Niño de las Suertes." In, *LaminaR*, vol. 6, no. 1, June 2008.

Richards, Irmagarde. *California Yesterdays*. Sacramento: Harr Wagner Publishing Company, 1957.

Sachina, Manjuamud. "Conoce aquí la verdadera historia del Niño Dios Gigante de Zacatecas," In *El Sol de Zacatecas*, 21 Nov. 2019

Santo Toribio Romo: del sueño a la gloria. Dir. Moisés Cruz Jáuregui. Cuevas de Arena Films, 2012. Film.

Vanderwood, Paul J., *Juan Soldado: Rapist, Murderer, Martyr, Saint*. Durham, North Carolina: Duke University Press 2004.

Varner, Gary. *María Lionza: An Indigenous Goddess of Venezuela*. Lulu.com, 2007.

Zavaleta, Antonio Noé. *El Niño Fidencio and the Fidencistas: Folk Religion in the US-Mexican Borderland*. Authorhouse, 2016.

INDEX

A

Abab Xilotl, Antonio, 45
Acapulco, 43, 120
Acosta, Angel Dario, 161
Actopan, 104
Acxotécatl, 150
Africa, 167, 169
Africans, 94, 222, 223, 224, 249, 250
Ágreda, María de Jesús de, 180, 181, 184
Agua Caliente Casino, 215
Aguascalientes, 87, 88, 90
Aguilar, Erasmo, 90
Aguirre, Gonzalo, 249, 253
AIDS, 243, 244
Alanís, Pedro, 75, 78
Alaska, 155
Albuquerque, 180
Alcedo y Bejarano, Antonio de, 61
Altar of Forgiveness, 32, 34
Amarillo, Texas, 180
American Southwest, 28, 124, 184
Antes, Ana Lucía, 7
Antwerp, 31
Apache Tribe, 182, 184
Aquihuiquichi, 197
Aragón, Spain, 148, 181
Arizona, 180, 199, 266
arthritis, 244
Asbaje, Juana de. *See* Cruz, Juana Inés de la
Asbaje, Pedro Manuel de, 174
Assumption of the Virgin Mary, 46
Atemajac, 14
Atotonilco, 104
Atotonilco el Chico, 104
Atrium of the Gentiles, 260
Augustinians, 41
Australia, 19, 22
Autonomous University of Querétaro, 244
Aztec, 3, 5
Aztec Empire, 13, 25, 82, 85, 88, 94, 141, 147

B

Bachomo, Felipe, 193
Badajoz, Spain, 169
Baja California, 155, 215
Basilica of the Virgin of San Juan de Los Lagos, 9, 10
Basilica to Our Lord of Mercy, 53
Basque, 174
Belgium, 23, 31
Benavides, Afonso de, 180
Benedict XVI, 133, 134, 162, 190, 194, 260
Bernal, Heraclio, 193
Bervon Azamar, Jaime, 251
bi-location, 181
Black Christ, 59, 60, 61, 63, 82, 83, 84, 85, 93, 95, 96
Blue Whale game, 265
Bolívar, Simón, 222
Bolivia, 19, 22
Bosco, John (Saint), 20
Breed, London, 152
Broken Christ, 87, 89, 90
Brujo Mayor, 249, 251
buffalo hunters, 182

C

Cabeza de Vaca, Álvar Núñez, 181
Cabora, 196, 198
Cabrero, Jesús Carlos, 263
Cabrini, Frances, 125
Cage, Nicholas, 74
Cajon del Muerto, 89
California, 127, 152, 154, 155, 156, 157, 200, 219, 267, 268
Calles Law, 126
Calles, Plutarco, 126, 137, 160, 202, 207
Camacho Martínez, Olga, 216
Camino Real, 153
Campeche, 93, 95, 96
Canales, José Tomás, 229
cancer, 243, 244, 245, 247
Candlemas, 28, 41, 68, 77
Candomblé, 223
Cañedo, Francisco, 192

273

Cano de Coca Gaitán, Juan, 94
Caracas Tribe, 222
Cárdenas, Lázaro, 215
Cardoza, Jesse, 216
Carmel, California, 156
Carmelite Order, 181
Carrasco, Ermilia "Mila", 19, 23
Carretto, Leonor del, 175
Casa de las Brujas, 208, 209, 210
Castile, 168
Castillo Morales, Juan. See Juan Soldado
catalepsy, 196
Catemaco, 249, 251, 252, 253
Cave of Ostoc Teotl, 82
Celestial Lady, 47
Cerro de la Campana, 207
Chacaltianguis, 62
Chahín Limón, Jesús, 243
Chalma, 61, 62, 81, 82, 83, 84, 85
chaneques, 252
Charles III, 83, 154
Charles IV, 61
Charlie Charlie Challenge, 265
Charlie's Angels, 49
Chichimeca, 88
Chignahuapan, 49, 90
Chihuahua, 180, 198, 209
Chucky (doll), 74
Chumash Tribe, 152
Cihualpilli Tzapotzinco, 13
Clement X, 184
Clifton, Arizona, 201
Coahuila, 180
Coanos, 54
Cochabamba, Bolivia, 19, 22, 23
Colegio de San Nicolás, 172
Collins, Phil, 74
Columbus, Christopher, 168
Conchos River, 181
Congregation of Missionaries of Our Lady of Hope, 158
Congregation of the Daughters of the Sacred Heart, 166
Congregation of the Mission, 163
Convent of San Bernardo, 65
Cotija, 131, 158
COVID-19, 73
Coyolxauhqui, 8
Cristero Rebellion. See Cristero War
Cristero War, 59, 126, 127, 137, 207
Cristo del la Concordia, 22

Croix, Carlos Francisco de, 154
Cruz, Juana Inés de la, 174, 177, 178
Cuernavaca, 174

D

Dance of the Concheros, 105
Day of the Cross, 63
Day of the Dead, 261
de las Casas, Felipe, 118, 119, 120, 122
Devil's Cave, 253
diabetes, 161, 243, 244
Díaz, Porfirio, 192, 199, 200
Diocletian, 98
discalced clergy, 14, 119, 120, 177, 181
Disney, 265
Dominicans, 41, 149
Don Pedrito. See Jaramillo, Pedro
Donnie, Juan, 61
Durango, 98

E

Easter, 63, 82, 84, 88, 247
Eastern Orthodox Church, 20
Ecuador, 61
El Arenal, 104, 106
El Hermanito, 209
El Soldadito. See Juan Soldado
Enlightenment, Age of, 170, 172
epilepsy, 244
Epiphany, 71, 72
Eric the Red, 223
Espejo, Antonio de, 181
Espinazo, 202, 203, 204, 205, 206, 207
Espinoza, Luis Eugenio, 23
ex voto painting, 10
exorcism, 262, 264, 268
Extranormal (TV show), 58

F

Feast of the Presentation. See Candelmas
Federal District, 65, 140
Felipe de Jesús. See de las Casas, Felipe
Fidencista Movement, 206
Flanders, 31, 149
Flores, Trinidad, 130
Flower Wars, 147
Francis (Pope), 133, 134, 146, 157

Francis of Assissi, 153
Franciscans, 41, 54, 58, 118, 119, 121, 122, 141, 149, 153, 155, 180, 183, 240
Fry, Gill, 244

G

Gallardo, Juana, 75
Gálvez, José de, 155
Garcés, Julián, 148
Geller, Yuri, 210
Genovesi, Juan Antonio, 47
Germany, 72, 235
Gil de Leyva, 110
Godzilla, 74
Golden Gate Park, 152
Gómez de Cervantes, Nicolás Carlos, 15
González González, José Francisco, 93
González, Miguel Angel, 53
Graziano, Frank, 9
Greater Litanies, 238
Greece, 138, 234
Greenland, 223
Grim Reaper, 68, 188, 190
Grinberg Zylberbaum, Jacobo, 212, 213
Guachinango, Jalisco, 26, 27
Guadalajara, 8, 13, 15, 16, 17, 25, 27, 54, 56, 57, 75, 112, 125, 134, 137, 166, 169, 226, 230, 263
Guaicaipuro, 222
Guanajuato, 47, 78, 202, 260
Guatemala, 61, 159, 167, 177
Guerrero, 42
Guerrero, Barbara. *See* Pachita
Guinness Book of World Records, 72
Guízar y Valencia, Rafael, 158, 161
Guzmán, Nuño de, 13, 14, 25, 54, 169, 171, 172

H

Hacienda de Garabato, 88
Haro Campos, Manuel, 71
Havana, Cuba, 260
Hayworth, Rita, 215
Henry VIII, 170
Hidalgo, Miguel, 89
Hideyoshi, Toyotomi, 120, 121
Hieronymites. *See* Order of Saint Jerome

Híjar, Juan Fernández de, 25
Hollywood, 49, 215
Holy Inquisition, 154, 182, 241
Honduras, 167
Huila, 196, 197, 198
Hurricane Patricia, 17

I

Iberian Peninsula, 31
Illescas Pichardo, Idelfonso, 49
Información en Derecho, 171
Iramuco, 202
Isabella (Queen), 168
Isla de los Changos, 252
Isla del Santuario del Cristo Roto, 87
Italian-Americans, 125

J

Jalisco, 7, 16, 25, 28, 53, 54, 55, 75, 112, 124, 125, 126, 134, 137, 160, 166, 216, 226
Japan, 19, 120, 121, 122
Jaramillo, Pedro, 226, 227, 229, 267
Jesuits, 47, 82, 146, 154, 178, 239
Jesus, 1, 16, 20, 22, 28, 37, 47, 49, 51, 53, 55, 56, 57, 61, 62, 65, 66, 67, 68, 71, 72, 73, 77, 78, 81, 83, 87, 89, 90, 94, 101, 102, 106, 110, 112, 113, 142, 158, 163, 183, 190, 192, 193, 194, 195, 218, 220, 232, 256, 262, 266
Jesús María, Bartolomé de, 83
Jiquilpan, 131
John Paul II, 21, 124, 138, 140, 144, 146, 162, 165, 167
Johnson, Magic, 247
José José, 247
Juan Diego, 3, 4, 5
Juan Soldado, 214, 216, 218, 220, 268
Juarez Mazo, Jesus, 192, 193
Jumano Tribe, 180, 181, 184, 267

K

Kansas, 182
Kiowa Tribe, 184
Ku Klux Klan, 127
Kumeyaay Tribe, 156

L

La Chaparrita, 28
La Generala, 16
La Junta, 181
La Milagrosa, 15
La Pacificadora, 15
La Peregrina, 28
La Reforma. *See* Reform Laws
Lady in Blue, 180, 267
Lake Chapala, 54, 130
Lara y Gonzaga, María Luisa Manrique de, 177
Las Vegas, 215
Latin, 8, 9, 49, 53, 63, 71, 90, 96, 100, 124, 146, 174, 235, 266
Lent, 105, 107
Leo XIII, 20, 47
León, 47, 78, 260
Let's Go North! (stage play), 125
levitation, 182
limpia, 108, 251
Lizana y Beaumont, Francisco Javier de, 65
López Obrador, Andrés Manuel, 253
Lopez Sedano, Francisco, 264
Lord of the Silver Miners, 98
Los Gallos Misticos, 159
Los Olmos Creek, 227
Los Tuxtlas Biosphere Reserve, 252
Loza y Pardavé, Pedro, 56, 77

M

Macumba, 223
Madre Santisima de la Luz, 47
Madrid, 31, 37, 61, 100
Madrigal de las Altas Torres, Spain, 168
Magno Exorcismo, 263
Mallorca, 153
Manila, Philippines, 37, 119, 120
Manso y Zúñiga, Francisco, 118
María Lionza, 220, 221, 222, 223, 224, 268
Marqués de Cerralvo, 118
matlazahuatl, 45
Mayo, 196, 199
Metepec, 41
Metropolitan Cathedral (Mexico City), 48, 114, 115, 177
Mexicali, 124
Mexican Revolution, 38, 126, 136, 158, 164, 203
Mexican War of Independence, 16
Mexican-Americans, 127
México (State of), 37, 41, 61, 72, 140, 153, 169
Mexico City, 1, 3, 4, 10, 31, 32, 34, 48, 65, 82, 114, 115, 118, 120, 122, 126, 137, 140, 141, 143, 144, 146, 153, 154, 155, 159, 163, 170, 171, 175, 189, 198, 202, 204, 208, 215, 220, 224, 244, 254, 264, 266
Mezquitic de la Magdalena, 75, 76, 78
Michael the Archangel, 238, 241
Michoacán, 13, 130, 137, 158, 160, 168, 171, 256
Mictecacehuatl, 188, 190
migrants, 124, 128
milagros (charms), 29, 234, 235, 267
Miracle of the Renewal, 27
Misión de la Purificación, 110
Mixton War, 15
Monastery of the Immaculate Conception, 181
Mono Blanco, 253
Monterey Bay, 155, 156
Monterey, California, 155, 156, 157
Monterrey, 19, 23, 24, 110, 267
Montúfar, Alonso de, 32
Morales, Francisco de, 32
More, Thomas, 170, 171
Morelia, 168, 203
Morelos, 42
Most Holy Mother of Light, 47
Museo de Arte Popular, 10
Muslims, 20, 100, 101

N

naborio, 93
Nagasaki, 121, 122
naguales, 253
Nahuatl, 3, 25, 45, 49, 54, 62, 71, 140, 147, 175, 249
Nanciyaga, 252
National Institute of Anthropology and History, 67, 106
Negro Felipe, 222
New Mexico, 180, 182, 183, 267
New Spain, 5
New Testament, 67

Nezahualcóyotl (city), 72
Niño Fidencio, 202, 203, 204, 205, 206, 207, 220, 268
Nogales, 199
Noriega Barceló, Sigifredo, 71
Nuestra Señora María Auxiliadora, 19
Nueva Galicia, 13, 14, 16, 25

O

Ocoroni, 196
Ocotelulco, 147
Ocotlán, 53, 54, 55, 57, 58
Oklahoma, 182
Olaguibel, 59
Olmos, José Gil, 252
Olvera Street (Los Angeles), 152
Oñate, Juan de, 25
Oran, Algeria, 169
Order of Saint Francis of Paola, 37
Order of Saint Jerome, 177
Ortiz y Rodríguez, José de Jesús, 56
Osaka, 120
Otancas, 54
Otatitlán, 59, 60, 61, 62, 63
Otomi, 147
Ouija Board, 265
Our Lady Help of Christians, 19, 21
Our Lady of Atocha, 100, 101
Our Lady of Good Events, 37
Our Lady of Good Success, 37
Our Lady of Mercy, 33, 35
Our Lady of Solitude, 43
Our Lady of Tonatico, 41
Our Lady of Tzocuilac, 45
Our Lord of Lightning, 106
Our Lord of Mercy, 55, 56
Our Lord of Wonders, 104
Oxtoteotl, 82

P

Pachita, 208, 209, 210, 211, 212, 213
Palma de Mallorca, 153
Pame, 153
Panita. See Zapata, Cipriana
Panoayàn, 174
Panteón Numero Uno, 214
Papaloapan River, 61, 64
papier-mâché, 85, 241
Parañaque, Philippines, 37

Paris, 163
Pátzcuaro, 13, 14, 26, 168
Pecos River, 182
Peralta, Gastón de (Marquis of Falces), 31
Perea, Esteban de, 183
Perea, Nicolás, 81
Pereyns, Simon, 31, 32, 33, 34, 35
Perin. See Simon Pereyns
Perro Aguayo, 74
petitionary devotion, 10
Philippines, 37, 104, 119, 120, 174, 209
Phillip II, 31, 43, 61
Phillip IV, 183
Picazo, Rafael, 132
Pinome, 147
pirates, 95
Pius X, 9
Pius XII, 38
plague, 15, 25, 28, 45, 46, 179, 238, 239, 241, 242
Plateros, 72, 98, 99, 100, 101, 102, 257
Plutarco Elias Calles Dam, 87, 88
Pobre, Juan de, 120
pochteca, 62
Pontifical Council for Culture of the Vatican, 260
Popocatépetl, 174
Porfiriato, 192
Portillo, Estevan de, 34
Portugal, 169, 177, 235
Primer Impacto (TV show), 53, 54
Prohibition, 215
Puctlancingo, 61, 64
Puebla, 39, 45, 48, 49, 90, 104, 106, 107, 148, 174, 178, 239, 241, 258, 267
Pueblo Mágico, 39, 90
Puente de Calderón, 89
Puharich, Andrija, 210
Purépecha, 7, 168, 230, See Tarascan Tribe

Q

Querétaro, 48, 144, 153, 243, 244, 247
Quiahuitzlan, 147
Quiroga. Vasco de, 168, 169, 170, 171
Quito, Ecuador, 61

R

Ramírez de Santillana, Isabel, 174
Ramírez de Santillana, Pedro, 174
Ravasi, Gianfranco, 260
Reform Laws, 106
retablos, 29, 84
Ribadeneira, Marcelo de, 122
Rio Grande, 181
roadside attraction, 90
Rodan, 74
Rodriguez, Abelardo, 215
Rodriguez, Lupe, 200
Roman Empire, 234
Rome, 21, 37, 94, 118, 122, 126, 130, 134, 137, 151, 160, 184
Romo Santino, Miguel, 90
Romo, Toribio, 124, 125, 126, 127, 268
Rubens, Peter Paul, 9
Rubio Félix, Pedro, 26
Ruiz y Flores, Leopoldo, 47
Russians, 155

S

Sacred peanuts, 79
Sahuayo, 130, 132
Saint Anthony, 258
Saint Christopher, 34
Saint James, 100
Salesian Order, 19
San Agustín de la Isleta, 180
San Angelo, Texas, 180, 184
San Bernabé de Capula, 238, 240, 241
San Blas, 155
San Carlos Borromeo Mission, 156
San Diego, 155, 156
San José de Gracia, 87, 88, 89, 90
San José, Juan de, 83
San Juan Bautista Mezquititlán, 7
San Juan de los Lagos, 20, 75, 76, 77, 125, 158
San Lazaro, Diego de, 238
San Luis Potosí, 71, 263
San Martín, Manuel de, 26
San Miguel del Milagro, 242, 266
San Miguel Nepantla, 174
San Pedro Tlaltizapan, 37
San Román, 93, 94, 95, 96
Sánchez del Río, José, 130, 132, 133
Sánchez, Ignacio, 133

Sandoval Íñiguez, Juan, 263
Santa Ana de Guadalupe, 124, 125, 127
Santa Clara del Cobre. *See* Villa Escalante
Santa Cruz, Manuel Fernández de, 178
Santa Muerte, 68, 188, 189, 190, 218, 220, 260, 261, 264, 266, 268
Santería, 223
Santiago Tepalcatlalpan, 65
Santiago Tianguistenco, 38
Santisima Muerte. *See* Santa Muerte
Santo Niño de Atocha, 100, 101, 256
Santo Niño de las Suertes, 66, 67, 68, 268
Santo Niño del Cacahuatito, 75, 77
Satan, 190, 253
séance, 265
Segovia, Antonio de, 13, 15
Señor de la Santa Escuelita, 113
Señor de Veneno, 114, 115
Serra, Junipero, 152, 153, 154, 157, 268
Shelter of the Sacred Heart, 163
Shikoku, 120
Siegal, Bugsy, 215
Sierra Gorda, 48, 153
silvas, 177
smallpox, 15, 37, 61
Sonora, 196, 199
Soria, Spain, 181
Sorte Mountain, 221, 223, 224
South America, 170, 222
Spanish Conquest, 1, 62, 172, 249
Spanish Inquisition, 32
Spanish Netherlands, 31

T

Tabacal Hill, 39
Tancoyol (mission), 48
Tarascan, 88, 168, 169, 172, 230
Tarascan Tribe, 171
Tarazona, 181
Tata Vasco. *See* Quiroga, Vasco de
Tatita Santo, 204
tatzingueni, 14, 17
Taviam Tribe, 152
Taxco, 41
Tehueco, 196
Tejada Olivares, Adalberto, 161
Tello, Feliciano, 46
Temple, Shirley, 20

Templo de la Epifania del Señor, 71
Tenache, María, 27
Teopintzintl, 14, 15
Tepehuanes, 54
Tepetícpac Texcallan, 146, 148
Tepeyac Hill, 3, 4
Teques Tribe, 222
teteuctin, 147, 148
Texas, 159, 180, 181, 183, 184, 200, 226, 227, 229, 267
Texuexes, 54
Tezcatlipoca, 81, 82, 83
Tijuana, 214, 215, 216, 217, 220
Tizatlán, 147
Tlacote, 243, 244, 245, 247, 248, 267
Tlalpan, 25, 65
Tlaxcala, 49, 146, 148, 238, 240
Tlaxcalan Martyrs, 146, 148, 151
Tokyo, 74
Toledo, Antonio Sebastián de, 175
Toledo, Spain, 31, 169
Tolentino, Sebastián de, 81
Tomochic, 198
Tonallan tlahtocayotl, 13
Tonatico, 41
Trece Brujos, 250
Tres Potencias, 222
Tres Reyes. *See* Epiphany
Turin, Italy, 20
typhus, 46
Tzocuilac, 45, 46

U

UNAM, 212
United States, 2, 68, 125, 126, 127, 132, 157, 184, 188, 192, 199, 206, 210, 214, 215, 218, 220, 226
Univisión, 53
Urrea, Teresa, 196, 197, 198, 199, 200
Utopia, 170, 171

V

Valle de las Cuevas, 202
Valles, Lino, 223
Venegas de la Torre, María Natividad, 166
Venezuela, 220, 221, 222, 223, 224, 268
Ventura, California, 201

Veracruz, 59, 61, 63, 94, 95, 98, 153, 155, 159, 161, 249, 253
Via Crucis, 106
Vikings, 223
Villa Escalante, 168
villancicos, 177
Villaseñor y Sánchez, José, 60
Virgen de Noche, 19
Virgen del Buen Suceso, 37
Virgin Mary, 3
Virgin of Dolores, 53
Virgin of Forgiveness, 32, 34
Virgin of Guadalupe, 3, 20, 22, 39, 75, 76, 82, 83, 107, 132, 140, 143, 146, 189, 194, 266
Virgin of San Juan de los Lagos, 7
Virgin of Talpa, 25, 26, 28
Virgin of the Immaculate Conception, 7, 49, 54, 58
Virgin of the Rosary, 25, 26, 27
Virgin of Zapopan, 13

W

Weeping Virgin of Monterrey, 19
Wernich, Teodoro von, 203, 204
Wichita Tribe, 182, 184

X

Xalapa, 161
Xicotepec de Juárez, 39
Ximénez, Juan Antonio, 55
Xiochténacti, 151
Xochipapalotzin, 150

Y

Yacatecuhtli, 62
Yaqui, 196, 199, 200
Yara. *See* María Lionza
Yermo Sisters, 163, 164
Yermo y Parres, José María de, 163, 164, 165
Yucatán, 13, 94, 95, 203

Z

Zacatecas, 71, 72, 73, 89, 90, 98, 124, 126, 137, 160, 257, 267, 268
Zamora, Michoacán, 158

Zapata, Cipriana, 206
Zapoltanejo, 166

Zóquite, 71, 72, 73, 74, 90
Zumárraga, Juan de, 3, 4, 5, 141, 170

Printed in Great Britain
by Amazon